A fascinating synthesis of religion and science, *Anatomy of the Soul* offers an illuminating journey through the Bible and the brain that has profoundly practical implications for how to live our lives more fully. Curt Thompson is a passionate student of both ways of knowing, bringing his unique perspective as a practicing psychiatrist and devout Christian to illuminate the overlap between the teachings of Jesus and the New Testament with my own field, interpersonal neurobiology. With an eloquent mastery of the interdisciplinary principles of the mind, the brain, and intimate relationships, our guide illustrates the healing power of integration at the heart of love, compassion, and well-being. Readers from religious and secular backgrounds alike will find this accessible and absorbing intersection of these two worlds to be deeply educational and inspiring.

> **DANIEL J. SIEGEL, M.D.,** author of *Mindsight: The New Science of Personal Transformation;* founding editor, Norton Series on Interpersonal Neurobiology; executive director, Mindsight Institute

As a bookseller who reads widely, I can say that it is not every day that a truly great book comes along by an exceptionally proficient psychiatrist who is also a good writer, a fabulous storyteller, and a mature Christian in love with the things of God, who yearns for the wholeness of God's Kingdom. It is also rare when the serious science of brain studies is explained in a way that is both interesting and immediately helpful, as well as rooted in a vital biblical perspective. For some of us, reading neurological lingo makes our brains go soft. Trust me on this, though: whether you are a person who wants to improve the stability and joy of your daily living, a follower of Jesus who wants to deepen your experience of spirituality, or a helping professional who wants to integrate comtemporary scientific theories with a distinctively Christian worldview, *Anatomy of the Soul* will be a thrill to read.

> **BYRON BORGER,** Hearts & Minds Bookstore, Dallastown, Pennsylvania

It has long been noted that God has two books: the book of special revelation (the Bible) and the book of nature. In *Anatomy of the Soul* psychiatrist Curt Thompson convincingly demonstrates that the book of nature, through recent neurological findings, can broaden and deepen our understandings of the Christian life. With rich insight and clarity, Thompson forges new paths in comprehending the marvels and mysteries of our Creator, who made us to live integrated lives centered in his designs and purposes.

> **DENNIS P. HOLLINGER, Ph.D.,** president and Colman M. Mockler Distinguished Professor of Christian Ethics, Gordon-Conwell Theological Seminary

Curt Thompson probes deeply into the truth of the self in its relational, emotional, and imaginative dimensions beneath the tight technological propensities of our society. He does so with remarkable agility as he moves between his special expertise in neuroscience and his firm grasp of theological verities. His title, a phrase from John Calvin, goes beyond "anatomy as metaphor" in Calvin to take "anatomy" seriously as a dimension in spiritual health. Thompson writes in an accessible way, his argument being illuminated by many specific narratives of persons enroute to deeper health that is grounded and wholistic. This will be, for many readers, a category-changing read.

WALTER BRUEGGEMANN, Columbia Theological Seminary

A must-read for those who desire to know and understand the spiritual journey.

DR. TIM CLINTON, president, American Association of Christian Counselors

Anatomy of the Soul is a very important book that beautifully integrates knowledge from the field of neuroscience with insight from the worlds of psychology and spirituality. Such integrative work needs to be done in order to have a holistic view of how people grow and transform—which is at the heart of the gospel message. Thompson's contribution is extremely valuable!

RUTH HALEY BARTON, president, Transforming Center; author of *Sacred Rhythms: Arranging Our Lives for Spiritual Transformation*

There are far too many books these days that insult either your intellect or your faith in God . . . or both. *Anatomy of the Soul* does just the opposite. In it, Curt Thompson weaves together the very new insights of brain scientists, the ageless wisdom of the Bible, and his own experiences as a therapist and follower of Jesus into a genuine volume of hope. There aren't many psychiatrists I know well enough to enthusiastically recommend, but Curt is certainly at the top of that list.

TONY CAMPOLO, professor emeritus, Eastern University; author of *Red Letter Christians*

Integrating psychology and Christianity is messy business. Critics come from many sides, quickly dismissing even the notion of a Christian approach to psychology. Dr. Thompson brings a unique message that challenges all of us to consider counseling, medicine, and a relationship with Christ. His heart for helping those who hurt, combined with his head for medicine and science, blend into an arguable case for rethinking this integration. Dr. Thompson has been my friend for years, and I'm thrilled for others to hear his wisdom and insight, and gain greater hope.

DR. MICHAEL EASLEY, former president, Moody Bible Institute; lead pastor, Fellowship Bible Church, Nashville, Tennessee

People of science should read this book for what it will teach them about faith, and people of faith should read it for what it will teach them about neuroscience. People who are hurting should read this book for what they can learn about mental, emotional, spiritual, and physical healing—one of the true meanings of the word *salvation*. The author is a practicing psychiatrist and a person of faith who understands both. In this book, he does a delicate dance between science and religion without missing a step, affirming Einstein's famous maxim, "Science without religion is lame; religion without science is blind."

WILLIAM J. CARL III, Ph.D., president, Pittsburgh Theological Seminary; author of *The Lord's Prayer for Today*

Anyone who cares a whit about emotional health, marital satisfaction, effective parenting, or hope for the future should carefully savor *Anatomy of the Soul*. Here, science affirms the great promise of Romans 12: that recalibrated minds produce transformed lives, and that such inner retooling can inoculate entire family systems from crippling emotional, relational, and spiritual legacies. Dr. Thompson's inspiring road map offers clarity and empowerment, not only for personal journeys and relationships, but also for ministries seeking to apply potent spiritual principles to the basic stuff of life.

BEVERLY HUBBLE TAUKE, LCSW, therapist and family counselor, Cornerstone Family Counseling, Fairfax, Virginia; author of *Healing Your Family Tree*

With wit and wisdom, illuminated by years of successful psychiatric practice and a profound engagement with Scripture, Curt Thompson leads us on a fascinating look at how recent discoveries in neuroscience can inform our understanding of ourselves and aid us in transforming our lives. Most strikingly, Dr. Thompson compellingly describes at the level of neurology what the Bible and religious experience have long testified to: the genuine possibility of renewing our minds! This book is hopeful and helpful, practical and potent. I recommend it to anyone who seeks to deepen their faithfulness and connection to God, their family and friends, and themselves.

DR. JEFFREY DUDIAK, associate professor of philosophy, The King's University College, Edmonton; author of *The Intrigue of Ethics*

This book is a *must-read* for those who are interested in spirituality and human transformation. Drawing from the latest scientific research on how people think, feel, perceive, and remember, as well as his own professional experience, Dr. Curt Thompson brings biblical insights to life in ways that not only make the Scriptures understandable but also illumine the life-changing experiences that biblical authors are writing about. If you've ever pondered what the apostle Paul means by inviting us to "be transformed by the renewing of your mind," you will find a good number of answers by simply reading this book. I enthusiastically recommend it!

PAUL N. ANDERSON, professor of biblical and Quaker studies, George Fox University, Newberg, Oregon

Very few understand the interplay of the brain and the soul as helpfully as Curt Thompson. Because he writes out of a rich experience of counseling hurting people, his awareness of our deepest pains is not simply clinical but personal as well. This is a hope-filled book that not only helps me understand fresh ways to minister to people who come to me in pain but also helps me understand myself better.

THE REV. DR. JOHN W. YATES II, author and speaker; rector of The Falls Church, Falls Church, Virginia

A few pages into *Anatomy of the Soul,* you will figure out that Curt Thompson has done lots of thinking about the ways people feel, and lots of feeling about the ways people think. Before long, you'll figure out that Curt has also helped lots of people figure out what their thinking and feeling brains have to do with their relationship with God and everyone else in their lives. By book's end, you'll think and feel differently yourself, and you'll realize a happy fact: he's helped you too.

BART CAMPOLO, speaker, writer, activist; The Walnut Hills Fellowship, Cincinnati, Ohio

Anatomy of the Soul is your one-stop resource for better understanding yourself. Dr. Curt Thompson has somehow managed to write a book that contains biology, psychology, theology, and a half dozen other "-ologies" that is, at the same time, incredibly easy to read and comprehend. The book has impacted me in a deeply personal way.

LISA WHELCHEL, actress, speaker, and author of *Creative Correction*

ANATOMY
OF THE
SOUL

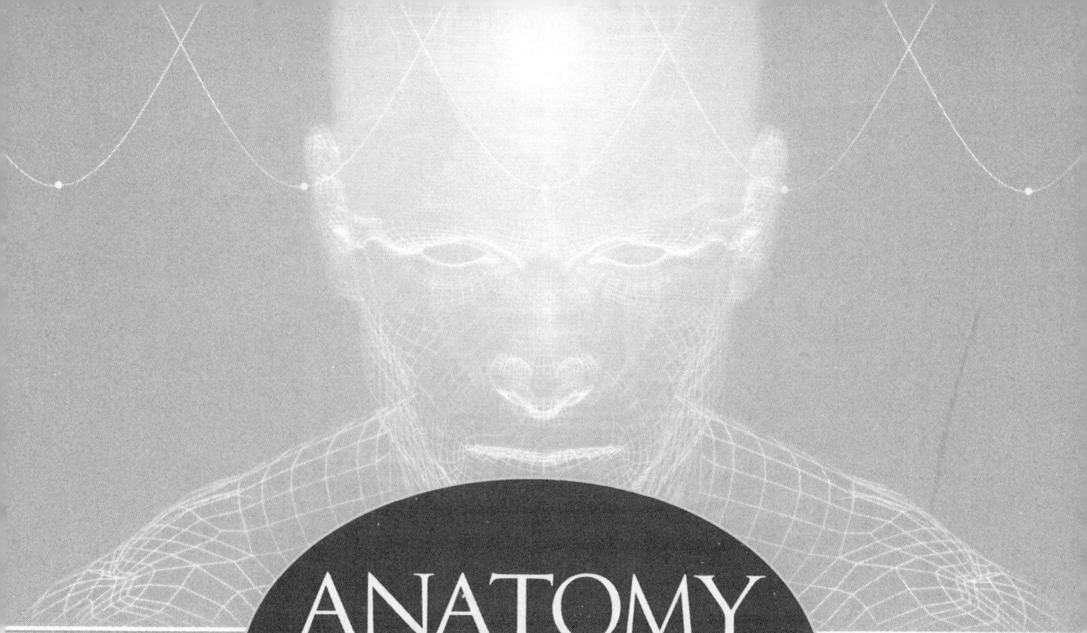

ANATOMY
OF THE
SOUL

Surprising connections between
neuroscience and spiritual practices
that can transform your life and relationships

CURT THOMPSON, M.D.

TYNDALE™
MOMENTUM

AN IMPRINT OF TYNDALE HOUSE PUBLISHERS, INC.

Visit Tyndale online at www.tyndale.com.

Visit Tyndale Momentum online at www.tyndalemomentum.com.

TYNDALE is a registered trademark of Tyndale House Publishers, Inc. *Tyndale Momentum* and the Tyndale Momentum logo are trademarks of Tyndale House Publishers, Inc. Tyndale Momentum is an imprint of Tyndale House Publishers, Inc.

Anatomy of the Soul: Surprising Connections between Neuroscience and Spiritual Practices That Can Transform Your Life and Relationships

Designed by Beth Sparkman

Published in association with the literary agency of Nunn Communications, Inc., 1612 Ginger Drive, Carrollton, TX 75007.

The examples in this book are fictional composites based on the author's clinical experience with hundreds of patients through the years. All names are invented, and any resemblance between these fictional characters and actual persons is coincidental.

Library of Congress Cataloging-in-Publication Data

Thompson, Curt, M.D.
  Anatomy of the soul : surprising connections between neuroscience and spiritual practices that can transform your life and relationships / Curt Thompson.
    p. cm.
  Includes bibliographical references (p.   ).
  ISBN 978-1-4143-3414-1 (hc) — ISBN 978-1-4143-3415-8 (sc)

  1. Brain—Religious aspects—Christianity. 2. Christianity—Psychology. I. Title.
BT702.T493 2010
261.5′15—dc22   2010002452

Printed in the United States of America

19 18 17 16 15
11 10 9   8   7

To Phyllis,
Rachel, and Nathan,
who have together given me the gift
of being known

CONTENTS

Introduction

The hospital room was bright but sterile. It was Mother's Day 2004, and I sat at the foot of the bed of the woman who had given birth to me. My eighty-six-year-old mother appeared drained and listless, moving little except her eyes. Her voice was weaker than usual, a reflection of her general physical deterioration.

While I was attending a medical conference the week before, my brother had called to tell me that our mother's health was quickly declining. What was most concerning, he said, was her resignation that life was over. She seemed to have no interest in surviving, let alone thriving.

In the days between my brother's phone call and this visit, my wife had remarked that my response to my mother's illness seemed to vacillate between distant, clinical indifference and unmitigated anger. I'd been terse in my replies to my wife's queries about my mother's condition and was certainly not forthcoming with my actual feelings. Here I was, an experienced, successful psychiatrist, a physician trained in the science and art of healing, yet I struggled to offer my mother support. I was a follower of Jesus, yet I was finding it virtually impossible to gather even a mustard seed's worth of compassion for her.

How dare my mother give up. How dare she be so passive, as she sometimes was, which reinforced the distressing emotional undercurrents that ran through our family. We were skilled at maintaining the illusion we were well when in fact we were, in some respects, rather ill.

My mother's apathy reactivated my sense of inadequacy and of being alone in the world. I could find little solace even in my spiritual experience. Not in prayer. Not in Scripture. Not in my deep and meaningful friendships. My mother was easing toward death and seemed not to care how I felt about it. She was fragile, but in my fear, aloneness, powerlessness, and anger, I didn't feel much compassion for her plight.

As I made the six-hour drive to the hospital that Sunday, I had time to reflect on my reaction and what was causing it. Along the way I remembered a workshop at the medical conference I'd just attended. It had been led by Dr. Daniel Siegel, a psychiatrist who explained how recent discoveries in neuroscience and attachment were truly helping people.

In particular, he said that an important part of how people change—not just their experiences, but also their brains—is through the process of telling their stories to an empathic listener. When a person tells her story and is truly heard and understood, both she and the listener undergo actual changes in their brain circuitry. They feel a greater sense of emotional and relational connection, decreased anxiety, and greater awareness of and compassion for others' suffering. Using the language of neuroscience, Dr. Siegel labeled the change "increased integration."

As I drove along that ribbon of Interstate 76 toward the hospital, it dawned on me that Siegel's work had something to say about my dilemma. I wondered if part of the answer to my own conflicts lay somehow in my mother's life story, which had begun with a series of losses. I realized I had listened to her tell it over the years only in a cursory way. I had never allowed it to truly touch me. I knew the facts without feeling any emotion. I decided it was time to wade into that sea of feelings and hoped that this excursion would somehow help save me.

And so now I sat with my mother in her hospital room. I prayed that I would be open to whatever God had in store for me—while quietly terrified of what that might be. I asked my mom to tell me the story I had heard a thousand times before but had never permitted entry into my soul.

The details were familiar—my mother had been orphaned at the age of three in the wake of her mother's untimely death and her father's inability to care for her. What was new, though, was my willingness to allow her story to move me. This time I heard it, not seeing an anxious, passive woman, but a frightened, sad orphan who had been abandoned and dismissed.

I'm not sure I even noticed when my weeping began. I couldn't see for the tears in my eyes. The grief was overwhelming, and soon I was swimming in a sea of emotion. I could no longer distinguish between my mother's feelings and my own. The disorientation I felt was palpable. Time simultaneously stood still and extended into eternity. Perhaps only a few minutes passed. It felt like hours.

One thing was certain. As my mother told her story, I was feeling my own narrative in a new way. The scared voice of the little girl my mother had been elicited feelings of compassion deep within me. As she revealed her history I experienced my own differently. For so long I had believed that my mother could easily have chosen to live a life of confidence and courage, but rather had chosen a path of passive dependence and fear—a path that enabled my own sense of inadequacy to take root. I had resented this but buried my indignation under garments of politeness and respect, perhaps hoping that my calm exterior would eventually create enough space for her to become the mother I needed.

My history—as I had understood it up to this Mother's Day—had been influenced by my being my mother's support. My father, as good a man as he was, was not always able to connect with my mother emotionally, especially when she was anxious. At those times, I tried to buffer her emotional distress. Actually (although I wasn't conscious of my motivation as a child), I comforted her to reduce my own anxiety; if she was okay, then I would be too. No matter how hard I tried, however, I couldn't do enough to enable her to comfort me. So in the end, I determined I could depend only on myself.

As I listened to my dying mother and felt compassion for her welling within me, my self-understanding was also changing. It wasn't just what I logically comprehended about the facts of my life, but what I felt while I sat there in the room. I could physically feel a change.

Not only did I see my mother with new eyes, I felt her life—and my own—differently. As if the proverbial scales had fallen from my eyes, I saw that she had not simply chosen to live her life the way she had. She had done the best she could without anyone to attend to her heart, to her emotional states, to her distresses and hopes. Her anxiety, fear, and passivity were not intentional; they were her coping strategy. Beginning at age four, she had developed strategies to ensure she didn't tick anyone off, and this eventually included God. It was the only way she knew to ward off the overwhelming feelings of desertion, and she had maintained this defensive posture into adulthood. She had not actively chosen this path but rather had reacted unconsciously. In other words, her timidity and caution became the default neurological firing pattern that shaped her mind.

I realized several important things in that hospital room. Perhaps there was nothing I could do to change my mother. More important, perhaps the difficulties I had experienced in my life were less her fault than I had believed. And more important still, perhaps my feelings of inadequacy were not so much my own fault as I had suspected. I had the distinct impression of God's voice telling me in those moments that I was no longer bound to my past.

As I began to understand my mother's story differently, I began the process of truly forgiving both her as well as myself. Right there in that hospital room I saw my own narrative differently. I began to see that I, too, had lived my life as well as I could. No longer was I so ready to condemn myself as being not quite enough. Not smart enough. Not funny enough. Not confident enough. Not tough enough. Just not enough.

Suddenly I was liberated from such thoughts of inadequacy and their accompanying feeling of shame. I saw myself as one who is loved as I am, with the expectancy of what I am becoming. I couldn't quite get my mind around my mind, so to speak, as all of this was happening. Yet when my mother died several weeks later, I felt free to move forward without regret.

In the years since this encounter with my mother, I have developed some terminology to capture and communicate what I experienced. I've come to call what I experienced *the process of being known*. This is a much deeper and richer experience than simply knowing the bare facts of my story. It reflects what neuroscience and related disciplines are teaching us about what it means to live an integrated life—both as an individual and as part of a community.

As a result of my experience, I became more excited than ever about new discoveries in neuroscience. I began to explain them to my patients and to train my patients to pay closer attention to various interactions within their minds. I witnessed their lives being transformed as they reflected on and implemented these same discoveries. Never before had I been so in step with those with whom I sat as an agent of healing. As each of my patients' grace-filled stories unfolded before me, I became more connected to parts of my own story. Their histories reenergized and challenged me to reconsider mine. Memories and feelings that I had left unattended were now awakening.

During this time, I realized that not since my psychiatric residency had my professional curiosity been so reinvigorated as it was by Dan Siegel's workshop. As I shared my discoveries with friends and colleagues, they encouraged me to consider collecting my reflections on neuroscience and Christian spirituality.

The journey that began in my mother's hospital room is more fully fleshed out in this book. My aim is to show you how your life, too, can be transformed by the renewal of your mind that can lead to the wholeness God intends for you. At your core—whether you live behind the facade of wealth, power, and pleasure or locked inside a prison of suffering, poverty, and hopelessness—you, like every other person, are desperate for joy, goodness, courage, generosity, kindness, and faithfulness. You long to manifest these qualities yourself and to see them in your children, your family, and your community.

New discoveries in neuroscience and related fields offer clues as to how you can develop these attributes. First you must become aware of how we are all shaped by the interactions within and between our minds. You then can become more intentional about your relationships.

If you, like so many others, have assumed that neuroscience deals strictly with the brain's physical structures and physiology, you may be surprised to learn how much it teaches us about the interconnection of our minds—both individually and within our larger community.

As you may know, your brain is made up of a left and a right hemisphere. While both sides of the brain are involved in just about every activity, the two hemispheres function differently. The left hemisphere processes in a logical and sequential manner; the right hemisphere processes in a more intuitive and holistic way. The two hemispheres function best, however, when they are integrated. In fact, neuroscience confirms much of what Scripture teaches us about the importance of living with undivided hearts and minds.

While it is true that we each have separate brains, our minds are inter-connected in many complex and mysterious ways. I believe our lives will be abundant, joyful, and peaceful only to the degree that we are engaged, known, and understood by one another. I also believe we cannot separate what we do with our brains and our relationships from what we do with God. God has designed our minds, part of his good creation, to invite us into a deeper, more secure, more courageous relationship with him and with one another.

So what relevance does this have to your life? That's what this book is all about. First, we'll explore fundamental aspects of the brain's structure and function to see how aspects of neuroscience point to God and affirm what believers have been living out as a community of faith for over four thousand years.

Once we've laid this groundwork, we'll consider how recent discoveries in neuroscience can provide answers to some of the questions being asked by many people today. You might be asking some of these questions yourself:

- In a world that is more connected than ever before, why do I so often feel so alone?

- Why do I find it so hard to change?
- Why can't I get past my past?
- Since my emotions often seem to get me in trouble, do they have any value?
- Why can't I just go it alone?
- Why do I so often "lose it" with other people?
- How does Jesus make a way for me to be freed from the grip of sin here and now—not just in the new heaven and earth?
- What does it really look like when we live in community as the body of Christ?

If you resonate with one or more of these questions, I invite you to join me on this amazing journey to better understand your mind and to find meaningful, sometimes surprising, and practical answers. This book includes some exercises (on the shaded pages) and discussion questions (beginning on page 273) to help you apply what you are learning.

We who desire to follow Jesus, who pant for God as a deer pants for water, have been given insights from God's own creation—the findings of neuroscience, attachment, and storytelling—that not only offer a different way to think about the mind but also create space for God to change us. These discoveries offer new language to reintroduce us to what God has been up to in Jesus from the beginning—another dialect with which God is calling, beckoning, and welcoming us to the dance of his new creation.

If this promise calls to you like the memory of a song you recognize but have never heard before, feel free to move in closer to the orchestra. You may find the music to be at once soothing, energizing, and disturbing. But don't be afraid. As Tolstoy proclaimed, we were created for joy, and this is the place I hope you find yourself as you read this book.

Chapter 1

NEUROSCIENCE: A WINDOW INTO THE MIND

Cara was in her early thirties when she came to see me. She sought help to ease the depression she had been battling since high school. She had friends, but much of what they had already achieved—marriage, professional advancement, and outward happiness—served only to remind her of what she had not.

Single, but longing to be in a committed relationship, Cara saw herself as less than desirable. She had already taken a year longer than most of her peers to finish the coursework for her doctorate in economics and was pessimistic about completing her dissertation within the next year. She wanted to teach in a university setting but hadn't pursued this possibility very aggressively.

Although she had run track in college and claimed that fitness was important to her, she rarely exercised. She ate poorly and occasionally drank too much alcohol to try to disconnect from her feelings of sadness and shame. The wine did little more than put her to sleep, and she would wake up to a dull drumming in her head the next morning.

Cara came to see me when the anxiety attacks began. They would waken her from sleep, and as her heart pounded and raced, she felt inexplicable fear coursing through her body and mind for what seemed an eternity. The wine clearly wasn't doing its job.

She said she wouldn't mind if she died in her sleep or got hit and killed by a bus, but she would never consider suicide. I asked her why. "I don't want to go to hell," she said, explaining how her life had changed in college when she began following Jesus. She had felt the first glimmer of optimism after becoming a Christian, but even her keen intellect and newfound faith could not keep the emotional wolves away from her.

She described her childhood years as a somber progression of grief. She believed her parents loved her, but she was frequently deeply sad without knowing why. Although conversations in her home were intellectually stimulating, they rarely, if ever, wandered into the realm of emotion or what members of her family were feeling.

When Cara was fourteen, her father died unexpectedly from a heart attack. Her mother responded by burying herself in her work as a physician. Her older brother responded by going off to college and never returning home. Cara responded by becoming an all-state athlete and honor student. Everyone she knew assumed that she was fine. But she wasn't fine. Not then, and certainly not now.

As Cara sat in my office, her mannerisms put her troubles in plain sight. Though obviously attractive, she slumped in her chair. She fidgeted with her hands. Her demeanor vacillated from nervous laughter to easily spilled tears, punctuated by moments of great effort to regain her composure—along with apologies for "being upset." It was as though she was holding back an entire reservoir of grief and had little remaining energy to keep it in check. Perhaps she feared that if the dam broke, she and everything she knew would be swept away into oblivion by a tidal wave of emotion.

Cara had tried psychotherapy. She had tried medication. She had prayed. She had read Scripture and devotional literature. She was part of a worshiping community and a small group of women who met regularly to deepen their spiritual lives. These helped, but nothing sustained any sense of stability or confidence. Most troubling to her, she could not understand why her relationship with Jesus did not seem to make a difference. Why was her psychological distress so unresponsive to prayer? Why was God so unresponsive to her plight?

Recent discoveries in neuroscience and related fields provide relevant answers to Cara's questions. Still, she was skeptical when I suggested these findings might give her direction and help her make sense of her life. It is for Cara, and others like her—you and me—that this book is written. Written to announce a new way of understanding and experiencing our life with

God, using the language of neuroscience and attachment—integral elements of God's good creation—as our guide.

Over many months of therapy, Cara began exploring the connection between her mind and her relationships with God and others. The following concepts—many of which are functions of the human brain—were the key to her healing, and one or more of them may be the key to your own. Since each concept builds on the next, they also serve as an outline of the coming chapters:

Being known. Our Western world has long emphasized knowledge—factual information and "proof"—over the process of being known by God and others. No wonder, then, that despite all our technological advancements and the proliferation of social media, we are more intra- and interpersonally isolated than ever. Yet it is only when we are known that we are positioned to become conduits of love. And it is love that transforms our minds, makes forgiveness possible, and weaves a community of disparate people into the tapestry of God's family.

Attention. What we pay attention to affects our lives. That may seem obvious, but what is often less apparent is exactly what we're focusing on—after all, so much of it occurs automatically or unconsciously. Furthermore, we often direct our attention primarily on what exists outside ourselves. Neuroscience has much to tell us about why it is so critical for each of us to pay attention to our own feelings, physical sensations, and thoughts.

Memory and emotion. Neuroscientific research reveals how profoundly both memory and emotion, much of it below our conscious awareness, influence all our relationships. Awareness of these functions of our minds leads to greater intimacy with God, friends, and enemies.

Attachment. In order to fully engage our relationship with God, it is most helpful to be fully aware of the patterns by which we have attached to our primary caregivers. The ways we have connected have important correlations with the structure and function of our brains.

An integrated mind. We'll explore how the mind, when left to its own volition, tends to disconnect. It often conspires to hide the truth (the depth of our emotion, memory, and relational patterns, as well as the reality of a God who loves us beyond belief) from ourselves and others. We then suffer the personal and communal consequences. And what does it mean to have the mind of Christ? I propose that it includes having a fully integrated mind—what the Bible calls "an undivided heart"—which draws us closer to and makes us more like Jesus. When we pay attention to disparate aspects of our minds that we sometimes (even often) ignore, we become more like him.

Sin and redemption. One way to comprehend the dynamic of sin is to see it as a matter of choosing to be mindless rather than mindful, which ultimately leads to our minds becoming dis-integrated. (I use the term *dis-integrated* throughout the book to refer, not to something that is decaying or falling apart, but to the opposite of integration, particularly between various parts of the brain.) In fact, the story of Eden shows how, like Adam and Eve, we are more interested in knowing right from wrong (a dominantly left-brain hemisphere function used to cope with fear and shame) than knowing God, which requires the integration of all parts of the brain. Through our redemption, this inclination can be reversed, making it possible for each of us to live with an integrated mind and play a larger role in God's redemptive plan. We can experience this as individuals and, more significantly, in the context of a community that is a living demonstration of God's love, mercy, and justice.

Community. In his first letter to the Corinthians, the apostle Paul lays out God's vision for community, one that is more achievable than we might ever have imagined. When we attend to the various functions of the mind, we can experience God's mercy and justice in the context of a community that is both differentiated and integrated. This is accomplished through giving and receiving love, which we experience most powerfully in the process of being known.

Like Cara, we live in a world that seems more desperate than ever before for healing, awakening, and transformation. While this is often most apparent in our internal struggles and interpersonal conflicts, it shows up elsewhere. For instance, as we become more technologically advanced, we invariably become more intra- and interpersonally isolated, and so push against the irrevocable principle that states flatly, "It is not good for man to be alone." Beyond that, global challenges such as terrorism, human trafficking, and global warming polarize nations, dividing us even further. As followers of Jesus, we believe that he is the answer to all forms of brokenness and division. New findings in the fields of neuroscience and attachment offer a fresh means by which we can understand and experience the abundant life to which Jesus has called us.

These new discoveries about how the brain and interpersonal relationships shape each other are a reflection of what has been passed down in the oral tradition; written in the stories, poetry, and instruction of the Scriptures; and experienced by the people of God for nearly four thousand years. In essence, God is using his creation as a signpost, supporting and sharpening our understanding of him, as well as pointing the way to Jesus. What we are learning is how part of God's good creation—neuroscience and attachment—speaks to us, serving as a counterpart language that affirms and enriches our faith dialect, which is comprised of Scripture and our spiritual experiences.

CREATION AND NEUROSCIENCE

The apostle Paul tells us that "since the creation of the world God's invisible qualities—his eternal power and divine nature—have been clearly seen, being understood from what has been made, so that people are without excuse" (Romans 1:20). The intricacies and complexities of everything from earthquakes to sea urchins to quarks to planetary orbits all point to God's power and God's nature.

Such is creation. And Paul suggests that when we pay attention to it, we discover things about God's power and his nature. Creation points to God. It of course does not define God completely—we do not fully understand God by fully understanding creation. The capriciousness of a tidal wave that kills hundreds of thousands of people is not an indication that God is volatile, nor should it be used as a measurement of his mercy. Rather, taken as a whole, creation points us in the direction of God's strength and personality.

One part of creation is humanity. And one very important element that makes us uniquely human is the brain/mind matrix. In the last ten years, research in various fields of scientific inquiry about the brain and interpersonal relationships has yielded exciting new data that helps us describe more fully than ever how they shape each other.

The fields of psychiatry, genetics, developmental and behavioral psychology, psychoanalysis, neurology and neuropsychology, developmental neurobiology, and structural and functional neuroimaging (creating visual images that represent the brain's anatomy and physiologic and electrical activity) add to our understanding of how we have come to be who we are and why we do what we do over time. Each of these distinctive fields, however, describes the human experience from its particular perspective, without integrating information from other areas of study.

The result can be summed up in the old story of several blind men feeling different parts of an elephant and describing the entire animal in terms of the particular part each man is touching. For one, the animal is smooth and hard, like a tusk. For another, it is leathery and tough, like the hide, and so forth. In the same way, knowledge from the many scientific fields has not been integrated into a single coherent body of knowledge that describes how the mind works.

In 1999 Daniel Siegel wrote a landmark book entitled *The Developing Mind*, in which he describes what it would be like to understand the mind through a more integrated approach. In other words, how would each of those blind men more fully understand the whole elephant if he were talking to the others, integrating data from each of their particular perspectives? It is likely that each would form a more accurate picture. Such is the model that Siegel proposes for understanding the mind. By connecting common findings from disparate fields of study, we will have a more complete picture, not only of how the mind works, but also of what changes will most effectively promote the health and healing of the mind—and subsequently everything else from relationships to communities to a bruised creation.

Siegel calls this integrated model for understanding the mind *interpersonal neurobiology*. This term expresses the reality that the mind is ultimately a dynamic, mysterious confluence of the brain and experience, with many aspects of it deeply connected (or potentially so) in ways that often go unnoticed. The interactions within interpersonal relationships deeply shape and influence the development of the brain; likewise, the brain and its development shape and influence those very same relationships. We will explore the details of how this mystery unfolds by considering several neuroscientific concepts that have great significance to the community of faith.

It is worth mentioning that these varied branches of study of human behavior have rarely considered spirituality in general, or Christian spiritual experience in particular. For decades, the perception among many behavioral scientists was that spiritual development is anathema to mental health. This led to a backlash of distrust and fear among people of many faiths against the organized scientific community of mental health researchers and providers, and the reaction was understandable.

Since the early 1990s, however, the place of spirituality in the evolution of mental health and the understanding of the mind has become more accepted.

The influential book *Handbook of Religion and Health*, written by Harold G. Koenig, Michael E. McCullough, and the late David B. Larson and published in 2001, brought this discussion into the mainstream. In fact, the importance of spiritual development is now acknowledged by many researchers and respected clinicians as one of the more important lenses through which we should view our lives.

In his articulation of interpersonal neurobiology, Siegel sheds further light on the significance of the intersection of neuroscience and mindful spirituality. Integrating our understanding of the mind and behavioral development, along with our spirituality, is now becoming a well-accepted, necessary paradigm for engaging our interpersonal and intercultural problems.

I mention intercultural problems for good reason. It is not difficult to imagine how a discussion of the brain might enhance your inner life. It might even affect how you interact with your spouse or children. But could it really have anything to do with peace in the Middle East? That may seem like a stretch. Yet consider Jesus' interaction with the Samaritan woman in chapter 4 of John's Gospel. Think how Jesus' self-awareness (albeit not as a neuroscientist) enabled him to bridge the deep cultural and gender chasm that separated them.

We will see how interpersonal neurobiology (part of God's creation) points us to justice and mercy, two fundamental themes to which Scripture calls us. And we are asked to extend that mercy and justice, especially where cultural brokenness and conflict reside. God's Kingdom is one of justice and mercy that he intends to proliferate to the uttermost parts of the earth, enveloping all aspects of life. He invites us to join him in creating that Kingdom, in ushering it in until it reaches its fullness in the appearance of Jesus. (We will address these issues of community, justice, and mercy in chapter 13.)

TO KEEP IN MIND (NO PUN INTENDED)

A matter of trust

As a psychiatrist, I see how difficult it can be for people to make sense of all the information, feelings, and impressions that hit them. My job is mostly to listen well, ask (hopefully) good questions, and wonder aloud about the discoveries that may lie waiting just outside the door of a patient's awareness.

I believe one common dynamic in my role as my patients' psychiatrist is that of engendering trust. Trust in me, yes, but ultimately trust in themselves. Trust in what they feel, understanding that those feelings stem from a cacophony of voices whose chorus speaks for their minds, communicating its desire to speak truly with them. Although the voices may sound confusing and raucous at times, it is largely their disorganization or the absolute dominance of some over others that causes the patient to trust none of them—or some of them to the exclusion of others. But those voices *do* speak from my patients' hearts and minds. And my patients must come to trust their ability to listen and discern what the voices are trying to say.

I look at the creation of this book in a similar way. In it, I present a synthesis of a great deal of information that has been rumbling about in my head for several years—but it is really the outgrowth of dozens if not hundreds of encounters with other people. Most of it, in fact, is the harvest reaped from seeds sown by others.

Take again the work of Dan Siegel, whose workshop had such an impact on me. Five years ago, this book would not have been possible. Dan's efforts paved the way for the integration of the disparate dimensions of the fields of mental health and Christian spirituality that are examined in this book. I have also been so deeply influenced by many other loving, challenging, and hopeful people, both personally and in their writings, that I could not begin to imagine where their thoughts end and mine begin.

Citing each point of data that contributes to an overarching idea in a book's text can be very helpful, especially for researchers who weigh their own investigations against such data. But for the purposes of a book such as this, which challenges the reader to integrate rational thought with other forms of awareness, these citations could eventually become more cumbersome than useful and serve merely as an exercise in organizing other people's thoughts. I am not suggesting that scientific writing is merely that. Hardly, and in fact it is the standard for most texts presenting objective data.

But this book is not primarily about presenting data. That form of engagement is overshadowed by a left-brain mode of mental operation that encounters the world in a logical, linear fashion. This manner of processing is absolutely necessary and good, but it has crescendoed over the last four hundred years to dominate our cultural way of thinking to the extent that other equally important ways of perceiving the world, namely those related to the right brain, are relatively underappreciated. Research is important and helpful, but it is not to be worshiped.

Left-brain mental processing disregards the right-brain emotional elements of trust that are necessary for life to thrive. When I know that I know something because I can logically prove it, I step away from trust. When I no longer trust, I am no longer open to being known, to relationship, to love. This book invites you to trust while reading the text, and in so doing to move from trust to hope, even in the very way you encounter the text itself.

At the same time, I do not want you to swallow my words uncritically or trust them simply because you may have the sense that they make sense (although I hope they do). For that reason, I have chosen to provide the scientific data behind my ideas in a bibliography of books that have influenced me, which you will find at the end of this book. If you desire to tackle any aspect of the subject matter presented here more deeply, I believe they will help you, too.

Language of the mind

Throughout this book the terms *brain* and *mind* will be used often. As I will describe shortly, these words do not refer to identical concepts, although they are, not surprisingly, closely enough related to seem interchangeable. However, when speaking of either, it is important to be aware that the mind (or brain) is fluid and always changing, if often only in imperceptible ways. In this manner, the mind is never static, and we will do well to engage it with the same humility with which we approach the God who has created it and fashioned it to reflect his very nature.

Not only do our minds change, but scientists' understanding of how the human brain works is also developing. That means anytime you read "the brain does this" or "the mind does that," what I am saying is more akin to "This is how we currently believe the brain behaves."

Language of faith

Finally, it is important to stress that this is *not* an apologetic work. I am in no way attempting to *prove* the reality of spiritual dimensions of life or a particular theological or philosophical position by examining the brain. Nor did I write this book to verify the existence of God or confirm that followers of Jesus are right and everyone else is wrong.

When you get to the end of this book you won't be able to say to your friend, "Now I *know* there's a God because this book identified God's spiritual chip in the temporal lobe of my brain." If you seek a deeper relationship with Jesus, I believe this book will be helpful. If living a life of goodness, patience, mercy, kindness, and courage is your heart's desire, then don't put this down. But empirical proof, I'm afraid, is not what you will find here. Although the material validates the Christian spiritual experience, this book does not seek

ANATOMY OF THE SOUL

to neurologically underpin Christianity or to invalidate other religious experience. (For some, this may be somewhat disappointing.)

As neuroscience has become a hot commodity, several prominent scholars, such as Steven Pinker and Daniel Dennett, have in fact attempted to use it to *disprove* the reality of God and the validity of religious experience. It seems to me that one way to express their perspective is to say that if we can reduce our experience (in this case, of God) to that which we can measure (our genes and our neurons), we can eliminate the necessity of the God we thought existed.

This statement oversimplifies their positions, but my point is this: I think it is fair to say that at our core (though perhaps not at our surface) most of us either want to believe in and have a relationship with God or we don't. Either way, we'll find ways for our left hemispheres to "prove" what our right hemispheres are longing for—or are too terrified to desire. This book, then, won't prove anything. But if you hunger and thirst for God, and if you somehow sense that in Jesus you will be closer to having your hunger satisfied and your thirst quenched, then feel free to plunge right in. I hope you enjoy what you discover.

Chapter 2

AS WE ARE KNOWN

Jeremy was tired.

Bright and articulate, he came to my office with a common complaint: he had been to see several therapists to treat depression, without success. He had had several bouts of depression over his lifetime, beginning when he was in college. Each time it had left him listless. Irritable. Demotivated, but fearful and unable to pull the plug on his rat-race life. He was always striving to get to what life might have waiting for him tomorrow, worried that it wouldn't deliver. When Jeremy wasn't anxiously considering his future, he was stuck in the past, mulling over the choices he'd made. As a result, his mind often wasn't really present in the here and now.

Jeremy was a well-educated man in his midthirties. He and his wife had two young children. Despite the speed with which he was advancing in his career as an attorney, he described great dissatisfaction with his work and said he felt largely unappreciated by his boss and invisible to his colleagues. He took little joy in his occupation despite his financial success. When asked what he dreamed of doing with his life, he demonstrated little awareness or imagination for what this might be, despite his apparent capacity for creative thinking.

He was also struggling in his marriage. He and his wife, Catherine, had tried unsuccessfully for several years to have children before eventually conceiving. This had taxed their relationship emotionally, as she had often felt responsible and guilty, and he, chronically disappointed. Once their children were born, however, he had found that their presence did not alleviate the underlying marital tensions that had been present years before they had begun trying to have children. He described his wife as hardworking at home with their young daughters but knew she longed to pursue her own career as well. Although Jeremy believed that Catherine loved him, he felt she neither really understood him nor had much interest in understanding him more fully. He thought she was selfish, although he felt guilty admitting this aloud.

Sex was a chore. Jeremy continued to find Catherine physically attractive but was tired of her frequent resistance and excuses to avoid even overtures of physical intimacy. This perceived rejection fed his growing listlessness and lack of motivation in the workplace. He felt unable to communicate with Catherine effectively and sensed that the stereotypical roles of male and female had been reversed in their relationship. He wanted to talk about feelings, but she was resistant. She became irritable whenever he initiated a conversation about a conflict they needed to address. He would sulk and withdraw, which of course did little to improve their communication. Without deep friendships with other males, Jeremy had no other outlets in which he could talk about his life and feel understood and connected.

I asked Jeremy about his spiritual life. He told me he had become a Christian in college and experienced communion with God and fellow believers then. But that seemed a lifetime ago. Years of the day-to-day grind had left him in a place that felt far removed from his undergraduate days. Spiritual vitality was a distant memory and not something he had much time to think about. He was too busy just trying to survive. Every now and then he thought about his relationship with God—but that relationship seemed to be making little impact on his life. He and Catherine attended a local church fellowship, and he prayed occasionally; he even made it a point to pray with his daughters at bedtime when he wasn't too worn out. Loving God was important, but it was like an idea circling the airport of his consciousness, waiting for life's more urgent matters to get off the ground so there would be room for Jesus to land.

He told me he was intrigued, however, that I would even ask him questions about his spiritual life. Then he acknowledged that one reason he had come to see me was that he had been told I was a believer. How that would make a difference in his treatment he had no idea. But one thing was certain. Jeremy wanted to change. He made this clear, and in the course of the very first interview he was awakened to the idea that he wanted his relationship with God to change as much as he wanted anything else. His problem was that he had no idea how to change anything. His depression. His marriage. His job. His spirituality. As I said, Jeremy was tired.

I told him I believed that not only was change possible, it was likely. I also mused that his life was one in which he was not known well—that he had little practice in the experience of being known by others. I mentioned that notable among those "others" was God, but that this was perhaps merely an extension of his encounters with people in general, beginning with his family of origin and continuing into his relationships with his wife, daughters, colleagues, and friends. One way he could begin to change that, I suggested, was to learn and then to incorporate into his thoughts and actions some of the discoveries made through research in the fields of neuroscience and attachment. His initial reaction was one of curiosity but slight confusion and incredulity as well. He did not yet understand the difference between knowing and being known.

⬦

We live in a world that values knowing things. From an early age, Jeremy had excelled at that, ultimately earning a law degree from a prestigious university. As a professional, he was respected for his grasp of intricate details of legal theory and strategy.

Knowing, as Jeremy discovered, brings power and influence. It is an activity that involves a primary subject (or person) thinking, feeling, or acting while separated from the idea, object, or person toward which his or her thoughts, feelings, or actions are directed. This type of knowing is not so bad for facts. Not so good for people.

Knowledge—often understood in terms of factual information that translates into a relational power gradient between persons—does not guarantee goodness or courage or love. It certainly can support the emergence of those qualities, but in and of itself it does not produce them. Ultimately, then, knowledge alone does not satisfy. What does satisfy is being known.

The process of being known is the vessel in which our lives are kneaded and molded, lanced and sutured, confronted and comforted, bringing God's new creation closer to its fullness in preparation for the return of the King. It is the communal container in which the information about the mind and relationships that we will explore in this book takes its shape and gives birth to the graces of love, joy, peace, patience, kindness, goodness, faithfulness, gentleness, and self-control.

We long to experience and develop these attributes—what Christians call the fruit of the Spirit—in ourselves, our children, and our communities. We want these qualities to come as naturally as breathing. We believe they are the natural by-products of hungering and thirsting for righteousness. Those of us who are followers of Jesus believe that he is the way to our becoming filled with these things and that developing them is a means of colaboring with him to usher in the Kingdom of God. As we work for justice. As we treat our parents and children with grace and dignity. As we (ideally) love friends as well as enemies, whether they are our employers, our neighbors, or our spouses. But often these attributes feel unattainable. We do not always easily inhale and exhale them in an effortless, rhythmic motion of breathing. Instead, all too often it is as if we are suffocating in their absence.

This was Jeremy's experience. His behaviors, thoughts, and feelings did not reflect these qualities. His memories painfully reminded him of being something other than peaceful, patient, and wise. He had become discouraged and weary with how difficult it was to inculcate them into his being, how long it took for him to change.

Jeremy *knew* things. But he hadn't *been known* by anyone in such a way that he felt understood, forgiven, or encouraged. Not by people nor by God. And to the degree that he was not known, the one thing he could not *know* was his own heart. This, in turn, limited the development of the characteristics of God's Kingdom in his life.

If, as a Christian, you admit your frustration over the lack of growth in your life to another believer, he or she is likely to reassure you that Jesus, or God, or the Holy Spirit will accomplish the change you long for. Often this encouragement is accompanied by a Scripture such as "he who began a good work in you will carry it on to completion until the day of Christ Jesus" (Philippians 1:6). This is all well and good. Yet these words don't seem to help much when your supposedly Christ-centered marriage is coming apart at the seams. Or when you can't effectively communicate with your teenage son who smokes pot; when you can't get your alcohol consumption under control; or when your adult daughter continues to move in and out of abusive relationships and you feel helpless to save her. Sometimes your struggles aren't even personal. You may be deeply conflicted over corporate and community issues such as the church's position on sexual standards or how to faithfully engage in politics without fostering a spirit of condescension and division. I think you get the picture.

Jeremy got the picture. Despite *knowing* about God's mercy and compassion, he longed to display goodness, kindness, and discipline, both as an individual and in a family and community that reflected them too. Yes, he could truthfully assert that God would bring this about, but he felt unable to participate in that action—and so he was moving through life fearful of admitting that he had no more tricks in his bag.

In other words, though he couldn't have articulated it, Jeremy had smacked against the limits of knowledge. Like him, all of us at some point discover that our theology, even if it is neatly packaged, doesn't on its own keep us from losing our tempers with our children or becoming rigid and self-righteous during the conflicts we have with our spouses, our coworkers, or our children's teachers.

Many of us hold steadfastly to our theological and scriptural mandates. We may find that what we are told to believe does not match our intuitive experience and often lacks relevance in our daily lives. Our Christian faith seems to be mostly a cognitive assent to a series of rational beliefs that don't seem to help us resolve our family conflicts, our struggles with sexuality, our sense of isolation, or our ongoing burden of shame and guilt. For instance, we may pretend we have a reasonably strong marriage while occasionally (albeit feeling guilty and disappointed) devouring a graphic scene in a romance novel or mentally undressing a female coworker.

We keep hoping for God's magic wand to sweep over and transform us— but his incantation never seems to arrive. We sometimes begin to give up the possibility that we will become what we want to become, our hope disappearing like a life preserver floating out of our reach and sight line as we move over the crest of another wave in the unforgiving sea of life.

Likewise, many of us hope that spirituality can be a deep and meaningful pathway for substantive change in the world at large. We long for justice, for things to be "put to rights," as it were, in the Middle East, our neighborhoods, and our homes. So often, though, things seem to get worse, not better.

While some believers cling to a well-defined theology, others are comfortable with a well-intended but lifeless spirituality that is not much more than a loosely cobbled-together matrix of convictions casually accepted from someone in authority, usually from parents, but often from pastors, teachers, or lay leaders. These believers mechanically go through the motions of church, wondering all the while what in the world they're doing. They recognize that the deepest part of themselves is empty and spent. They don't understand why they repeatedly do what they don't want to do, both to themselves and to other people, not unlike the apostle Paul in Romans 7:21-25.

As followers of Jesus, we all believe that the fruit of the Spirit is worthy of our pursuit and try to act in accordance with those cognitive assertions we call faith. But sooner or later we discover that these character qualities seem out of reach in the relationships that matter most to us. We swear that we will never become our fathers or mothers while we stamp their fingerprints on our children. Like the apostle Peter before Jesus' crucifixion, we declare with exhaustive conviction our allegiance to the Messiah but are overwhelmed by our inner fears and blindness. We find ourselves weeping bitterly in the wake of our betrayal of others and ourselves. We, like Jeremy, are tired. We want change, but we don't know how to make it happen.

BEING KNOWN BY GOD

Despite the interest in spirituality in much of the West, and North America in particular, our overall experience of God's power and life-giving vitality is often limited—especially when it comes to growth and reconciliation in our relationships. We often see life in Jesus as being more about survival in this life until we "die and go to heaven" than about grace, adventure, and genuine, concrete, life-giving change.

This is partly due to the way we encounter the process of knowing and being known. We tend to place a great deal of emphasis on the ways and the degree to which we *know* God (or know things *about* God) rather than to the degree we are *being known by* God. Yet in his first letter to the church at Corinth, the apostle Paul emphasizes the connection between our love for God and our actively perceived, sensed, and felt experience of God's feelings, sensations, and thoughts about us:

> Knowledge puffs up while love builds up. Those who think they know something do not yet know as they ought to know. But whoever loves God is known by God. (1 CORINTHIANS 8:1-3)

Pause for a moment and ponder the following. When you consider the state of your own or someone else's spiritual health, how often do you ask, *What is my experience of being known by God?* Or, *Does she demonstrate that she is being known by God, and if so, in what ways?* If you are like me, you often inquire or reflect on what or how much you *know* or *know about* God. This is to be expected in the world in which we live.

The same can be said about how we encounter each other. When evaluating our friendships, we frequently consider them in terms of how well we know our friends or how well they know us, not so much in terms of how we experience being known by them. This distinction is important.

From the emergence of the Enlightenment in the seventeenth century through the mid-twentieth century, "knowing things" became prized above all else. But not just any way of knowing. We have most valued knowing facts, knowing the "truth," and knowing that we are right. Right about the way things work, the way to behave, and the way to think about issues of faith. Research that is "valid and reliable," as conducted by "experts," has become the standard by which we judge the trustworthiness of any idea. We even subject our experience of faith to research scrutiny in order to give it more weight apologetically.

Let me be clear. I am not saying that research or knowing empirical truth is unimportant, but I am emphasizing how much our lives revolve around knowing in a manner that assures us we are "right." We have failed to see that this need to be right, to be rationally orderly and correct, subtly but effectively prevents us from the experience of being known, of loving and being loved, which is the highest call of humanity.

At the same time I recognize that over the last fifty years our society has begun to operate as if this way of knowing—comprehending facts, knowing what is true, and being right—is no longer a valid way of engaging the world. We no longer believe that we can know something outside of ourselves with certainty because everything has been deconstructed to our subjective experience. However, even though our society now insists that we cannot make objective truth claims for others ("I can't claim that what I believe is true for you, let alone the whole world"), we in fact all live as if objective truth does exist. We still live as if we believe cold-blooded murder, for example, is wrong. Knowing things is still important to get us through everyday life. We need to know that our cars will start. That gravity works as we have come to expect. That our friends will pick us up at the airport when they say they will. Knowing that we are absolutely right about a lot of things is very important to our survival and sense of well-being. That includes knowing, or knowing things, about people. And about God.

It is not hard to see why we are infatuated with knowing things in this way. It gives us the illusion that we are secure and in charge. We are no longer vulnerable. We believe we are safe, protected, and happy. We delude ourselves into thinking that we know God, but God as we believe him to be—in control and invulnerable—not God as Scripture describes him to be: risk-taking and able to be hurt badly. We no longer have to trust since we've got him all figured out. Knowing things and being right is very important to us, but when overemphasized it comes with a price, as Julie's story illustrates.

Julie's assurance that she was certain of what she believed about herself and the world, and especially about her spiritual life, provided the foundation of her mind's inner workings. Not that she had reflected on this consciously. She hadn't. It wasn't until this assurance of certainty, this practice of knowing, was cracking that she had to acknowledge that this way of being was her lifeline. She had just broken off a relationship with a young man who loved her deeply and wanted to marry her. She loved him in return but told me, "I couldn't put my finger on it, but there was just something about him that bothered me, and I knew God was telling me that this was not the right relationship."

However, after the breakup, not only did she not feel relief, she was overcome with intense anxiety that caused her to worry incessantly about the relationship and everything else in her life. On her first visit to my office, she said that her main problem was anxiety. If she could get that to stop, she told me, she was sure she would be okay.

Julie was a domestic policy adviser to a U.S. congressman. She was smart and ambitious—her colleagues saw her as a rising star. She knew she belonged in politics and saw her future unfolding on Capitol Hill. She was sure of her political positions as well as her religious ones.

But the breakup changed all that. It unsteadied her in ways she would not have predicted. Now she was unsure whether she wanted to stay in Washington or even continue shaping public policy. As her doubts grew, her concentration became less acute, and she was less motivated to engage in her work. But this wasn't the only thing that bothered her.

Julie had been a follower of Jesus for so long she couldn't remember a time when she wasn't. Like many people I see, she had been reared in a Christian home. When I asked what she meant by that, she said her parents had seen to it that she and her two younger sisters and brother attended church regularly. Her father was an elder in the church; her mother held a Bible study in their home; and conversations about theology were commonly held around the family dinner table. She described her conversion when she was in sixth grade and how important her high school youth group and involvement in Young Life had been to her. In college, she had started a ministry to address the needs of the homeless around the urban campus of her university. This was where she had developed her keen sensitivity for the plight of the poor and the call for justice, leading to her interest in public policy.

But Julie noticed that just as her certainty about her vocational calling was eroding, so too was her assurance of what she "knew" about her relationship with Jesus. Despite her sense that God was telling her to break up with her boyfriend, the rending of that relationship had led to unrest and anxiety regarding her relationship with God. Where once she had known without question the nature of God and what he wanted her to do with her life, now everything about her experience was in doubt. She had so many questions that she could not answer. What if what she sensed God telling her about her boyfriend wasn't God at all? What if she was wrong? How could she know if she'd been right? Why was she now so anxious if she had done what she thought God wanted her to do? What if her relationship with Jesus had never *really* been real, never *really* been what she thought it was? Why couldn't she *know* the way she had always known? Why couldn't she just stop obsessing about all these questions?

What had begun as a sense that something wasn't right about her relationship with her boyfriend had evolved into a crisis of faith. Yet she didn't see the connection between the anxiety that kept her awake at night and her conclusion that she no longer knew what she thought she once knew, especially about God. As one who has had my fair share of doubt and uncertainty, not the least being about my relationship with God, I was empathic to her real experience of inner turmoil. In fact, for her it was now beyond what she would describe as turmoil and had developed into what could easily be called suffering. Her anxiety built as she realized none of her well-practiced coping strategies—prayer, Bible reading, conversations with fellow believers, or the study of classic apologetic works—were shoring up her faith. The standard answers were not touching her questions.

In an attempt to help her see the root of her anxiety, I began the task of knowing her. Not just knowing facts about her, but knowing *her*. Actually, the better way to say this is that I began to invite her into an experience of being known. As I asked her about her life story, beginning with her experience of growing up in her family, I noticed subtle but important aspects of this young woman's physical reactions. Her face was often slightly strained, her jaw tightly clenched. She sat, not relaxed, but forward and almost on the edge of the couch. Her nervous laughter and forced smile seemed like defenses for the wall of fear and uncertainty just behind her eyes. She fought off tears on more than one occasion, tears that represented a salty flood of overwhelming emotion that terrified her. When I mentioned what I had noticed, she seemed even more distressed. She fought harder to keep the anxiety, the fear, and her unbridled weeping in check.

It was clear I was moving in too closely, too quickly for her comfort. She was experiencing being known in a way that was catching her off guard in an unpleasant way. Because of this, I shifted the conversation in another direction and asked her about the role emotion had played in her family as she grew up.

She looked both relieved (that I was no longer pointing out her physical responses) and puzzled, as if she saw no point in talking about this. She described her father as seemingly trustworthy but distant. She respected him—given his position as an elder in the church and the ease with which he could articulate the language and practice of faith—but admitted she had had limited interaction with him on an emotional level. She felt it quite important to please her father but had never voiced this aloud to anyone, including him. She worried she would not live up to his expectations but did not permit herself to reflect on this much since it was an anxiety-provoking distraction from getting ahead in life.

I asked if anyone in her family spent much time asking about what she felt—not what she *thought*—about what was important to her. Did anyone seek to know what her emotional sense of her life was?

"No," she said flatly. "I don't think anyone in my family would think to ask those kinds of questions."

It soon became clear that, despite Julie's many achievements, her inner life was largely unexplored terrain. It was important in her family to get good grades, to behave admirably and with aplomb, to do the next right thing. It was especially important that she believe the right things about God, theology, and her faith experience.

When she went off to college, she began to explore new ways of seeing the world. Anytime she wanted to discuss these new viewpoints with her parents (especially her father), she would be corrected or dismissed if the questions she raised were contrary to what they believed. Neither her father nor her mother sought to more fully understand Julie's emotional responses to what she was learning at school. This upset her, but even her emotional distress was something she did not feel the freedom to mention to them.

I suggested that her problem was more complex than anxiety. I invited her to attend a workshop I regularly conduct for new patients that helps them look beyond their outward symptoms. In this meeting, I provide an overview of how aspects of brain function (including memory, emotion, and neuron synapses or connections) and relationships shape one another. In this setting, Julie could begin considering how her own brain functions and history of relationships were shaping one another. This information would provide her with more tools as she sought to change the way she was living and relating to other people and to God.

I told her I thought that after she completed the workshop, she would benefit from a trial of psychotherapy with a therapist who could help her better integrate this information over time. I suggested that the therapy work would enable her to explore her world of emotions, memory, and attachment patterns. Ultimately this would reduce her anxiety, though mostly as a by-product of other more significant changes taking place. Finally, while I did not believe she required anxiety-reducing medication then, I told her we might also want to consider it in the future.

I told her I was confident that she would find help and healing for those things that were most troubling for her, but that along the way she would likely discover things about herself that might be surprising and at times frightening. Also, I told her that what she learned about the brain and interpersonal connections would point to important aspects of how God operated in her life. As she paid more attention to her brain's functions and how they intertwined with her human relationships, her relationship with God would open to new vistas that would bring freedom and adventure.

Her reaction to my recommendations was swift and surprising. She curtly stated that she was here to get help. More specifically, to get answers. And she wanted those answers today. She was not interested in some long, drawn-out process that would involve a lot of psychobabble. She wanted to be fixed, and she wanted it done quickly. In short, she wanted to know what her problem was and the simplest solution to fix it. She told me that she had expected me to give her a few easy suggestions that would stop her anxiety and end her constant obsessions about God and her former boyfriend.

Furthermore, she dismissed any possibility of using medication, which seemed to her to be a clear indication of weakness. She wanted no "assistance" from something that would make her feel even more vulnerable. Her physical demeanor reflected the terse words coming out of her mouth. She moved closer to the edge of her seat, crossing her arms and legs and holding herself tensely. Her jaw was set. Once again, she was working to keep tears at bay. She told me she did not have time for what I was recommending—she had to get back to work. She simply wanted things to "be the way they were before—before I was this anxious."

I gently suggested that going back to the way things were before would, in fact, be one of the worst things she could do. For "the way things were before" was largely the reason she found herself where she was now. The idea of being known, of sitting with someone and allowing him or her to enter into her soul in a way no one else had was terrifying—even if it would heal her anxiety. And her fear expressed itself in her reluctance to begin psychotherapy.

Julie's story is an example of how desperately we want to know things at the cost of having little experience in being known. More to the point, our desire to be in control at times will lead to the development of clinical symptoms of anxiety, depression, or substance abuse. But often our "symptoms" are subtler. Consider the upwardly mobile couple whose marriage is fraught with resentment. The high school student who, despite being bright and affable, is failing his courses and bewilders his worried parents by telling them there is no point to what his teachers ask of him in class. The grandfather who struggles with how his own father's neglect of him makes it seemingly impossible for him to contend with his irresponsible son and the way his grandson is now being raised. The office manager who remains in a job for several years despite having a boss who is overbearing, demanding, and unkind. Families that are fractured. Churches that split. Countries that go to war. You may wonder what being known has to say to these things. It has a lot to say, but for many of us, the prospect of being known is just as terrifying as it was for Julie.

We unknowingly live out this resistance to being known in much of our lives, not the least of which is in our religious practice, as demonstrated by our obsession with knowing and believing the right things about God, about Jesus, about our theology, and about "right behavior." This imbalanced way of being is often a defense against our feelings of insecurity and shame.

THE RISKS AND REWARDS OF BEING KNOWN

The problem arises when you, like Julie, are afraid—and I use the term *afraid* deliberately—that you are wrong. Of course, given that you may pay so little attention to what you are feeling, you may hardly notice your fear and defend against it by finding more ways to support your belief that you "know that you know what you know."

When you keep your relationship with God exclusively fact-based and rational, it's easy to make judgments about others and yourself. Such judgments reduce your anxiety and increase your sense of safety and protection. However, this way of being also has the curious effect of increasing the isolation you feel, both from others and within your own mind.

If you allow yourself to be known by God, you invite a different and frankly more terrifying experience. You are now in a position of vulnerability. If you permit others to know you, they can make their own assessment of your worth. They can react to you. You give them power to be affected by you and in so doing to affect you. You grant them the option to love you or to reject you. In essence, you must—must—trust another with yourself.

However, I will argue that it is only through this process of being known that you come to know yourself and learn how to know others. There is no other way. To be known is to be pursued, examined, and shaken. To be known is to be loved and to have hopes and even demands placed on you. It is to risk, not only the furniture in your home being rearranged, but your floor plans being rewritten, your walls being demolished and reconstructed. To be known means that you allow your shame and guilt to be exposed—in order for them to be healed.

To be known is one of God's passions. While he desires for us to have the experience of being known by him, just as important is his desire to experience being known by us. This is not simply for our benefit, as if he is not affected by us. *He desires to be known by us as much for what it does for him as for what it does for us.* And that is why the need to be right about God often gets us into trouble. As a friend of mine once told me, "Christianity is not about being right. It's about being loved."

At this point some might begin to worry that I am saying that God needs us in the way that we need him. I am not. But I am saying that you and I *affect* God as significantly as he affects us. Not in terms of ultimate power, but rather in terms of the emotional valence, or level of intensity with which he feels. I believe he allows himself to be deeply affected by our attitude toward him, though often we don't grasp this aspect of his character. After all, it is not easy for us to imagine that we have this much significance in God's life. Our incredulity only emphasizes the shortcomings not only in *what* but also in *how* we have come to know things *about* God through our experiences in our families. More to the point, it emphasizes what our experience of being known has been like.

You cannot know God if you do not experience being known by him. The degree to which you know God is directly reflected in your experience of being known by him. And the degree that you are known by him will be reflected in the way in which you are known by other people. In other words, your relationship with God is a direct reflection of the depth of your relationship with others.

Perhaps you have not experienced what it means to be truly known; consequently, you have limited experience in opening yourself up to God in this way. You may have grown up in a family in which your emotional life was either unattended to or overwhelmed by caregivers who were themselves burdened with the weight of their own emotional conflicts—their own lack of "being known," as it were. This form of generational sin inserts itself perniciously throughout the very fibers of your being, and as we will see in later chapters, even in the very way your nervous system wires itself.

This was Julie's experience. The unwillingness of her parents to discuss or even acknowledge Julie's emotions and questions as she was growing up had lifelong consequences. She simply did not know how to recognize or learn from her emotional states; instead, she had learned to zealously guard the door to her feelings. This made it difficult for her to know and be known by others, including God.

The path of being known may at times feel too difficult to travel. Julie decided it wasn't worth the risk and after just a few sessions decided to look for another therapist who would promise to fix her anxiety fast. Jeremy, however, decided to open himself up to the process of being known.

Early on, when I asked him when he had decided to become a lawyer, he told me his dad and grandfather had both been attorneys. So I inquired if he had always wanted to be a lawyer too.

A shadow seemed to cross Jeremy's face. No, he admitted. During a service project before his senior year of high school, he'd helped tutor kids in an inner-city summer school program. He had reveled in the challenges and been proud of the progress made by the young boys, who had all looked up to him. On the final day of the program, the school principal shook Jeremy's hand and said, "You're as natural a teacher as I've ever seen, Jeremy. Go get your teaching degree; then come see me. I'll have a classroom waiting for you." When he got home that night, Jeremy told his parents he wanted to become a teacher.

"They didn't even respond to that," Jeremy said. Instead, they reminded him that he'd been awarded a scholarship from his father's firm on the under-standing that he major in pre-law.

"Wow, what was that like for you? Were you disappointed when your parents failed to affirm or even acknowledge your obvious gifts in the class-room?" I asked.

Jeremy shrugged. "It's water under the bridge now," he said.

"Yes, but to have your parents dismiss your dream that way. You must have wondered if all the hours you'd devoted to that summer school program even mattered."

Through this conversation and others like it, Jeremy slowly began to understand what it meant to be known, to have another person validate and accept his feelings, preferences, and dreams. For the first time, he understood what it meant to be accepted for who he was rather than what he knew or what he did.

It didn't happen overnight, but eventually he began seeking to know Cath-erine too. Rather than withdrawing when she snapped at him after a long day at home with the girls, he learned how to draw her out. Previously she had wanted to avoid discussing any conflict between them, certain that he would use logic to "win" the argument. Now, though, she realized Jeremy would really listen when she admitted her own fears and longings. He encouraged her as she began to consider how she might resume her work as a graphic artist from home; she expressed her sadness when he told her about his unfulfilled and long-buried passion for teaching underprivileged kids.

Perhaps most meaningful to Jeremy, though, is his renewed spiritual life. No longer is he afraid to express his doubts, fears, and disappointments to God. His Scripture reading has come alive as he has begun to pay attention to the way God has always sought to connect and restore those who seek him. And he is earnestly praying for career direction: should he leave the law pro-fession to pursue his passion to teach?

Jeremy and Julie took different paths to address the issues that brought them to my office. Yet they had started in the same place—outwardly suc-cessful yet inwardly defeated. Your story may feel overwhelming too. Or you may have little idea what any of this means or how it applies to you because your story is missing so many pieces that the experience of being known feels irrelevant. You feel comfortable enough simply knowing; being known would just get in the way of getting on with getting things done. But perhaps, like Neo in the movie *The Matrix*, you sense that something is wrong, something is incomplete, something is disturbing you "like a splinter in your mind."

What if you had a set of tools, drawn from recent discoveries about the brain, our relationships, and how they shape one another, to assist you in the way of being known? What if the Holy Spirit were wielding these tools as a means to invite you into a life of grace and adventure? The best place to begin exploring the answers to these questions, I believe, is within the mind itself.

Chapter 3

LOVE THE LORD
YOUR GOD WITH
ALL YOUR . . . MIND

I think I'm losing my mind."

No, I didn't hear this from a psychotic. Instead, I heard it from George, a patient of mine who'd had to pick up his intoxicated seventeen-year-old daughter from an underage drinking party the weekend before. His daughter, Kristin, had done this once before, and it had embarrassed him terribly. And now she'd done it again, drinking herself into unconsciousness so that he'd had to carry her into their home.

As he sat in my office, George had the appearance of a ragged, beaten pauper, not the dot-com multimillionare that he was. He was an expert in the latest technology—and he was all about being wireless. But the wiring of his daughter's brain? He knew nothing. And he was ignorant of the role he played in shaping her mind. He said he was a man of faith, but at the moment, God seemed rather impotent when it came to his daughter's life. George's anxiety was growing like a tsunami, and for all his economic clout, he felt powerless to stop the tide.

Even if you've not been in such an extreme situation yourself, you, like everyone else, have probably thought or said, "I'm losing my mind" sometime. Maybe when your checkbook wouldn't balance. Perhaps when you couldn't remember where you put your keys or seemed unable to stop your critical, shaming thoughts about someone. Or on those Sundays when you yelled at your spouse and kids on the drive to church, only to paste on a smile and begin the perfect family act as soon as you pulled into a parking space. (I think all church services should begin with confession. Right at the door as you enter. That way God could take care of all the yelling between family members that preceded the worship service.) What exactly are we talking about, though, when we talk about losing our minds? What exactly do we think we're losing?

In this book, I want to help you understand how God can work through your mind to transform you. Before we go too far, however, it's important that you understand this marvelous tool that he created and now works through. For centuries people have been intrigued with the notion of the mind, and various cultures have had different ideas as to what it means. The Hebrews spoke of the soul. The Greeks spoke of the psyche. Today we also use words like *consciousness* (or our ability to be aware that we are aware of things); *intellect* (our capacity to reason); and *spirit* (a deeper subjective force that somehow seems greater than just the part of me that "thinks").

Jesus also speaks of our minds—perhaps most notably he tells us to "love the Lord your God with all your heart and with all your soul and with all your mind" (Matthew 22:37).

Scripture speaks of the mind in a number of other places as well:

We have the mind of Christ. (1 CORINTHIANS 2:16)

The mind controlled by the sinful nature is death, but the mind controlled by the Spirit is life and peace. (ROMANS 8:6)

Do not conform to the pattern of this world, but be transformed by the renewing of your mind. (ROMANS 12:2)

We long for our minds to grow into and to be what God envisions for them to be. What does it mean for us to love the Lord our God with all our minds? Or to be transformed by the renewing of our minds? Though I'm not sure anyone has that completely figured out, I believe if we indeed love God this way, or allow him to transform our minds in this way, our lives are more likely to demonstrate the fruit of God's spirit: love, joy, peace, patience, kindness, goodness, faithfulness, gentleness, and self-control (Galatians 5:22-23).

THE MIND DEFINED

While God doesn't spell out for us exactly how the mind works, scientific research provides intriguing clues of some of the processes he may work through. As we begin to consider the various functions of the mind in this chapter, I invite you to consider Daniel Siegel's definition:

> The mind is an embodied and relational process, emerging from within and between brains, that regulates the flow of energy and information.

He uses this to summarize the mind's function in his books *The Developing Mind, Parenting from the Inside Out,* and *The Mindful Brain.* Let's examine this idea in more detail.

1. *The mind is embodied, which means it is housed in your physical self and depends on your body to function.* Of course, the mind includes the brain, but other parts of the body play a role in the flow of energy and information. For instance, you become aware that you are anxious in part because you can sense your pulse rate increasing and feel your heart pounding in your chest.

   One question I ask a patient who is attempting to describe what he or she feels is, "*Where* do you feel [sad/angry/embarrassed]?" Though the patient may not be used to contemplating these sensations, it usually takes only a moment or two for the person to identify how his or her body is experiencing a particular emotion.

   As Christians, we sometimes dismiss our physical experience as inferior to the abstract, ethereal part of our consciousness where we "imagine" or "think about" spiritual matters. Yet Paul describes our bodies as the temples of the Holy Spirit, so clearly they're involved in our deepest spiritual experiences. In fact, in order to love God with your mind, you must love him with your body. If you are not paying attention to what your body (or "gut") is telling you, it will be difficult to love God with your mind because you will be disconnected from it. It is true that many experiences feel as if they don't necessarily require the presence of your physical self (e.g., the "feeling" of sadness and the imagery in your mind that accompanies it), but if you don't have a brain, or by extension, a body that it senses, you don't have an experience.

2. *Not only is the mind embodied, it is also relational.* Your sense of your mind is dependent on and shaped by your interactions with other people. In fact, you, like all babies came out of the womb looking for interaction with your caretaker. From the moment you entered the world, your mind has been powerfully shaped by your environment, and no part of that environment is more important than the interactions you have with other minds.

   Much more than a toy or blanket, a parent's facial expression, tone of voice, or scolding glance will actively impact the way the mind of the child—in this case the brain/body portion of it—will function. From the beginning of life, no one's mind functions completely independently from the minds of others. There is no such thing as a self-made man or woman. Think about it for a moment. Even when we are not interacting with other people, a great deal of what we daydream about includes our imagined interactions with others. In this way, even what we consider to be the privacy of our own thoughts involves the activity of relationships.

3. *The mind is a process that regulates, or helps shape, the flow of energy and information.* The mind is *flowing*, not static. How many times have you asked your spouse or child, "So what are you thinking?" only to hear, "Nothing." As *if.* Don't you just love that? We may not be aware of what we are thinking, feeling, or doing in our minds, but the mind is ever active. Even when we are asleep, our minds are at work generating dreams.

   Energy refers to the electrochemical changes that take place in the brain. Whenever we have a thought or a feeling, there is a corresponding firing pattern of these electrochemical charges along the neurons, or brain cells, as they communicate with each other and send signals to the rest of the body. We do not experience anything without there being a corresponding neuron firing pattern that represents that experience. And that "experience" is what we mean by *information.*

   Today various neuroimaging technologies, including positron-emission tomography (PET), functional magnetic resonance imaging (fMRI), and single photon emission computed tomography (SPECT) allow researchers to compare the intensity and location of metabolic activity in various regions of the brain across different circumstances, such as when a person is praying or meditating, looking at pictures of faces with different emotional expressions, or imagining particular images or words. Different feelings or thoughts can produce different images.

In other words, our experiences are inextricably woven together with our neural firing patterns, and therefore, we cannot separate the two.

As we'll see, we cannot speak of the mind loving God or being transformed without speaking of the body. To love God, we have to use our brains, and for our minds to be transformed, our brains must be equally changed. We cannot experience being known without knowing the body. In order for us to be fully human—in this age or the age to come—bodies are required. Again, I must emphasize: the Gnostics are wrong in their belief that we must strive to transcend our bodies because matter is evil. No body, no mind. No mind, no anything, at least for us as humans. As we consider the mind's makeup in more detail, let's begin at an obvious starting point: the brain.

THE BRAIN

Over the last several years, I have noticed how much patients benefit when they have a better working understanding of the structures and function of the brain. It seems to help them see the connection between the activity within their bodies and their thoughts, feelings, and behaviors. It also gives them a greater appreciation of what makes them uniquely human. Finally, it enables them to pay more attention to the various aspects of their minds through which God is speaking. Out of this emerges a deeper connection with God. For in order for us to encounter the God who claims to have taken up residence in our temple-bodies, we need to be as familiar with these temples as possible.

The human brain is composed of approximately 100 billion neurons, or brain cells. These cells come in different forms and serve different purposes, but their general way of functioning is similar. They communicate with each other biochemically at points of connection called synapses. Actually, a synapse is not a point of literal contact, but rather the very narrow space (called the synaptic cleft) between the neurons themselves. It is across the synaptic cleft (each only about 20 nanometers—20 millionths of a millimeter—in width) that each neuron signals its neighbor through biochemical messengers. Each cell has the capacity to synapse with up to approximately 10,000 other cells. For you math whizzes, that means that the total number of possible connecting patterns between all these neurons is virtually infinite. Not literally so, but almost. (Men, you now know how it's possible for your wives or girlfriends to have all those mood changes. They are simply taking advantage

THE HUMAN BRAIN

Looking from the outside toward the lateral portion of the left side of the brain:

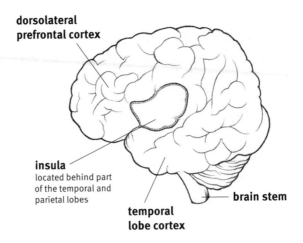

dorsolateral prefrontal cortex

insula
located behind part of the temporal and parietal lobes

temporal lobe cortex

brain stem

Looking from the middle to the right side of the brain:

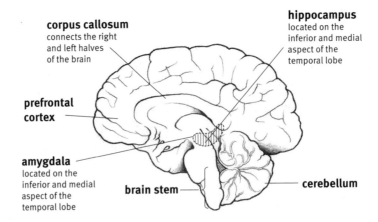

corpus callosum
connects the right and left halves of the brain

hippocampus
located on the inferior and medial aspect of the temporal lobe

prefrontal cortex

amygdala
located on the inferior and medial aspect of the temporal lobe

brain stem

cerebellum

of all that neural payload. And you women now understand why the men in your lives seem to have so few mood changes. We are still trying to *find* our neural payload, let alone use it.)

Scientists use two primary models when describing how the brain develops and functions. One is a right/left model; the other, a top/down system. Both offer valuable insights as we consider the role of the mind in being known.

Right and left model

The brain is divided into two halves, or hemispheres, the right and the left. They are connected by a strip of tissue known as the corpus callosum. It is through this tissue that the two hemispheres have the opportunity to "talk" with each other through the neurons synapsing with each other. (For a complete overview of the brain and its structures, see the diagram on page 32.)

Each of these hemispheres carries out different duties:

RIGHT BRAIN/RIGHT MODE

From birth (some experts believe even sooner) through the first eighteen to twenty-four months of life, the right hemisphere tends to create more interconnections between neurons than does the left hemisphere, which means that the functions of the right hemisphere develop more rapidly during this period. The right side of the brain helps babies develop the following functions:

An integrated map of the body. As infants grow, they gain a subjective awareness of their bodies in time and space. This goes beyond sensing pain or touch. Rather they must learn that they actually *have* arms and legs whose movements they can control; that they have stomachs that have hunger pangs; and that they can sense when they are wet and need a diaper change. This awareness is not fully mature at birth. It must develop neurologically, and that development is dominantly linked to the right hemisphere by way of millions of synapsing neurons.

Visuospatial orientation. Infants also develop a sense of three dimensions—where they and objects are in space in relation to each other. They begin to sense their own personal space and location as they move through space and time. This helps them develop coordination and focus attention on spatial objects. They learn to sense space, not only during an event, but also later when they remember that experience or when they visualize objects.

Nonverbal communication. Between 60 and 90 percent of all communication between humans is nonverbal, expressed through eye contact, facial expression, tone of voice, body language, gestures, and the timing and intensity of physical responses. The neurons of the right hemisphere generate nonverbal cues that are sent to other people and also interpret all the nonverbal signals received from others. Much is communicated to growing infants through these nonverbal cues. Long before they can speak, babies are taking in and encoding in their neurons all that is going on around them—if and how they are touched; the tenor of the voices they hear; and others' responsiveness to their nonverbally expressed needs.

Holistic sense of experience. At birth, humans can see a myriad of details but cannot extrapolate the overall mood or environment of their setting. The ability to grasp this holistic sense, however, begins to develop early. As an adult, you use this ability all the time. When you walk into a room, you may instantly sense what the room feels like based on the lighting, how the furniture is arranged, or the color of the walls and carpet. If you walk into that same room when it is crowded with people, you may instantly feel either discomfort at being in the midst of strangers or excited as you recognize the friendly faces gathered for your surprise birthday party. That holistic, take-everything-in-at-once moment is correlated with the neural activity of the right hemisphere.

Social and emotional context. Humans are not born with the ability to determine the social or emotional context that they're in. Generally, young children are beginning to develop this skill—though some people master it better than others. Have you ever been in a conversation with someone who goes on and on without noticing how she is monopolizing the conversation? Or have you had to endure lame attempts at humor by someone who thinks he's funny but is not? Such folks have trouble sensing the social context of the moment, which helps guide the flow of conversations and other interactions. Most people intuitively navigate these moment-to-moment social interactions by taking in the numerous cues around them. This capacity, too, is a function of the right hemisphere.

LEFT BRAIN/LEFT MODE
The connections between the neurons in the left hemisphere begin to increase at a faster pace at about eighteen to twenty-four months of age. The dominant functions of the left hemisphere are language, linear, logical, and literal

processing—the four Ls. The development of language is an expressed version of the linear flow of thought processing. We *speak* what we *think*. Although neuroscientists are not certain that all thoughts and language are formed in the same way, the fact that a child begins to speak is one of the first indications that she is beginning to process her world in a linear fashion.

One of the more common questions young children begin to ask is *why*. Such questions imply a growing need for order and for things to "make sense" in logical, linear ways. This need includes social and relational situations and is related to our need for stories to proceed logically. We want events early in a story to connect meaningfully with those that follow later. When they don't, we tend to create connections in our minds to help us make sense of the details. We do not like to remain confused, since this increases our anxiety. The left brain tries to resolve any such confusion.

For example, if a child feels ashamed when his father uses an overly harsh and demeaning tone of voice with him, the child's left hemisphere will try to make sense of why he feels so bad. If his father does not repair that emotional injury by apologizing and owning responsibility for his own actions, the boy will likely conclude that he did something to provoke his father. He will not likely figure out that his father is responsible for creating the shame he feels. The child will probably feel responsible and will try not to upset his father so that he won't experience the same feelings of shame again.

Even as adults, we sometimes jump to conclusions about God when our experiences don't make sense because they are confusing or painful. God may not lay out for us why our good friend developed cancer or our son lost control of his car and hit a pedestrian. In such situations, our left brain drives us to try to make sense of God's place in the situation. We may conclude that we're not on his radar and thus must not be very important to him; that he is not loving after all; or that he is disappointed in us. These assertions largely develop from the neural networks within the left hemisphere.

Another important sign that the brain's left-mode operation is developing is literal processing. For example, when some family friends were visiting us over their kids' spring break, I asked the five-year-old daughter if she enjoyed kindergarten. She promptly replied, "I'm not in kindergarten." Since she was on spring break, in her mind she was *not* in kindergarten—literally, at that time. While her reasoning will become more nuanced as she grows, this type of response may predominate in children whose parents' relational style encourages them to overdepend on left-mode processing in order to cope with emotional distress. Compared to other people, these children are more inclined to pay attention to literal mental operations as they interact with others. They may grow into adults who have a need to prove they are *right* by referencing what someone *literally said*, having missed the nonverbal cues that contextualized the meaning of the person's words.

Part of the logical, linear, and literal left-brain processing includes "right versus wrong" thinking. Recently I stood with my friend at the crosswalk of a quiet street with no traffic in either direction. But he waited hesitantly for the Don't Walk sign to turn to Walk before venturing into the crosswalk. This rule was important for him to keep.

While perhaps extreme, his reaction reflects our belief that there is a right way to do things, a right way to think about God and theology, a right way to understand the interpretation and role of Scripture, or a right way to behave. Rules do serve the greater good by supporting personal and social structure. Yet we must take care against being so caught up with being "right" that we lose focus on what it means to be loving. It can be easy to mistakenly equate the two. For example, some parents believe that doing something their way— the "right" way—is so important that they will stop at nothing to ensure that that is what their teenage son does. This can be anything from how consistently and well he does his homework to how many (if any) and what type of body piercings he sports to what he believes about Jesus. Such a tendency becomes dangerous when being right outpaces their capacity to be flexible and open to truly knowing their child.

WE AND I: TOGETHER BUT SEPARATE
Although the left and right hemispheres have separate functions, their integration is crucial. The right hemisphere's contribution is to imagine it as the part of the brain that enables us to be enraptured in the present moment. Its holistic processing enables us to feel connected to everything around us through the multiple sensory modalities of our bodies and minds. It provides no distinct sense of a separate "I" but rather a deep awareness of the sensation of "we," a sense of connection. This hemisphere drives us to feel at one with the universe, with no concept of past or future. In the right-hemisphere neural regions, time as such does not exist, which means we are unencumbered by our awareness of the painful memories of our past or our anxieties of the future.

As appealing as that may sound, the right hemisphere won't help you change your flat tire when you're alone on the side of the interstate. For that you need the left hemisphere. Since the left hemisphere is governed by a linear mode of operation, its networks are committed to logically solving problems like a flat tire. It progressively enables you to find the jack in the trunk of the car, take off the lug nuts, and replace the flat tire. It likes order and for things to "make sense."

The left hemisphere is all about the past and the future. It tends to systematically take in all the data that the right hemisphere is transponding to it through the corpus callosum and linearly, logically compare that to what is stored in its neurobiological history. Its focus is on "me" as distinct from the rest of creation. The left hemisphere, through its ability to analyze, enables each of us to distinguish ourselves from one another in order to know who "I" am and what "I" want. We enjoy the idea of having a sense of individuality, of being a separate "me"—that is, until we begin to collect all of our emotional baggage that is uniquely "mine" and feel the separation of loneliness and isolation.

The left hemisphere, then, tends to be more dominant in situations in which we seek to "know" things. It separates us from the objects we wish to examine and analyze, which is critical if we are to interpret what we are experiencing. When such analysis is the dominant mode by which we encounter other people or God, however, joy becomes merely a defined concept. Love is something we know about but do not know. However, the right mode of operation enables us to open ourselves to be touched by God and known *by* him in such a way as to become living expressions of love. The integration of the left and right systems is required to experience being known by someone else.

LATERALITY AND SPECIALIZATION

Laterality refers to the tendency of different functions of the brain to be separated and disproportionately associated with one of its two different sides. As we have already seen, the left and right hemispheres contain neural networks that accomplish distinct and separate tasks. The brain is not a homogeneous group of cells that all do the same thing.

This lateralization enables the brain to work more efficiently. Certain functions are enhanced when the neural networks dedicated to them are repeatedly fired in a concentrated fashion. These specialized areas work most helpfully, however, when they are brought together in an integrated way in which different domains communicate with each other. (We will explore this further when we examine the role of the prefrontal cortex in chapter 9.)

In this sense, the brain operates much like a company made up of many departments, each of which works hard to do what it does best. The company can work most efficiently when its sales, marketing, research and development, and accounting divisions are well trained in their respective areas of expertise and communicate efficiently with each other. If, however, the marketing department fails to communicate with the other departments, the entire company will suffer.

But what happens if a region dedicated to one function, such as speech or sight, is damaged? New evidence suggests that the brain has the capacity to recruit healthy neurons to assist in or take over the work of neurons that have been damaged by injury or disease. This indicates that the brain is more flexible than we thought even twenty-five years ago.

Top-down model: The triune brain

In the mid-1960s, the neuroscientist Paul MacLean offered another model for thinking about the brain. He termed the model the triune brain, based on his observation that the human brain seemed to function as three interwoven brains in one. In MacLean's model, the brain consists of the reptilian complex, the limbic circuitry, and the neocortex.

The most primitive, and earliest to develop, portion of our brains is the reptilian complex, or reptilian brain. This includes the brain stem and the cerebellum. The brain stem, which is positioned at the top of the spinal cord, is responsible for life-sustaining functions such as breathing, heart rate, and blood pressure. The cerebellum is largely responsible for our sense of physical balance. (Incidentally, some of the more recent research suggests that these older, more primitive areas hold keys to a great deal more of our humanity than has previously been believed, especially regarding the cerebellum's involvement in the regulation of emotion.)

These regions are highly responsive to even the slightest environmental shifts that spell danger, and respond quickly to these changes for the purpose of self-preservation. Many researchers believe that the neurons in this location initiate fight-flight response (though some would suggest that this likely emerges from parts of the limbic circuitry, which is introduced below). In the face of threat, this part of the central nervous system acts automatically without input from parts of the brain responsible for conscious, reflective thinking. That explains why your body swerves to avoid an oncoming car without any conscious reflection.

The second part of the triune brain to develop consists of the limbic circuitry, also known as the paleomammalian brain. Located above the brain stem, this constellation of interconnected neuron tracts and clusters of neuron cell bodies lies on the inner, deeper border of the cerebrum. The limbic circuitry is largely responsible for recognition and memory of fear, attention

TRIUNE BRAIN

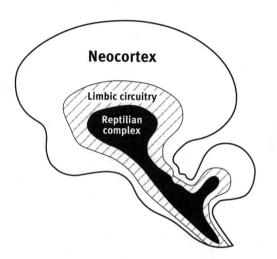

to salient internal or external environmental stimuli, and pleasure. This area of the brain relates to the generation and modulation of emotion. It is the wellspring of primal neural activity that eventually emerges, once processed in the cortex, in the form of fear, joy, disgust, anger, hurt, disappointment, relief, and dozens of other emotions. It is highly connected by nerves to the other two parts of the brain to assist in the modulation of both the higher (cortex) and lower (brainstem) activities of the brain.

The neurons of the brain stem and limbic circuitry do not involve conscious mental activity. They generate sensations and activity that do not translate directly into thoughts or feelings that we "know that we know." Instead they both monitor and create electrical impulses that are directed to many other regions of the brain, most notably the cortex, which does register consciousness that we are sensing "something" and triggers some action, whether mental or physical.

The third, and last to develop, part of the brain, the neocortex or neomammalian brain, is the spongelike, wrinkled layer of the central nervous system that is involved with our higher complex social, cognitive/linguistic, abstract, creative, sensory, and motor abilities. The region of the neocortex that uniquely sets us apart as humans is the anterior, or front part of the brain, known as the prefrontal cortex, or PFC (see page 32); this is positioned just ahead of the strip of neurons that control motor behavior. In the PFC, the energy of the mind interacts with information of the mind to enable us to demonstrate love (especially of the agape nature), learn algebra, appreciate Rembrandt's art, harness the power of restraint, and discern and make decisions, among other higher-level activities.

When we think about what "makes us human" biologically, therefore, we think of the PFC. (Chapter 9 explores this portion of the brain in greater detail.) However, contrary to what we might assume, the PFC does not generate most of our daily activity. In fact, the brain stem and the limbic circuitry (the parts we have in common with alligators and cats) are responsible for most of the neural activity of our moment-to-moment functions, which means most activity occurs apart from conscious awareness. (If Beethoven had needed to pay attention to make sure that he kept breathing or that his heart kept beating, we wouldn't have his First Symphony, let alone his Ninth.)

In other words, we are constantly influenced by the lower layers of our brain system, which we frequently do not pay much attention to. Vital life-preserving signals as well as memory and emotional states that are not automatically wired for conscious awareness are generated and translated through these systems before being transmitted to parts of the neocortex, especially the right hemisphere. We sense something in our "gut" or intuit a reality that is beyond rational awareness, leading us to action without clear, logical cognition. For instance, if you unexpectedly see your former boss—the one you think fired you unfairly—while shopping in the produce section of the supermarket, your heart rate and breathing rate may increase. You may also feel your face flush as you quickly move to the next aisle, all without your being aware of any of your physiologic or behavioral responses.

However, other portions of the neocortex in which networks *are* correlated with consciousness enable us to override some of these actions. Imagine that you're walking through the woods and see a long, thin, dark object lying across your path. Your visual sensory neurons will send a signal to your visual cortex that almost instantaneously gets to your brain stem, which triggers an increase in your breathing and heart rate so your musculoskeletal system can move quickly away from this object. This happens before you're consciously aware that you might have spotted a snake. You'll react a bit differently, however, if you're with your young son. You won't bolt in the opposite direction. Instead, aware of your son's presence, you'll slow down your reactions long enough to observe the object more closely—only to discover that it is a stick rather than a snake on the ground. This is a simple example of a top/down override that serves you well.

At other times, this top/down tendency works to your disadvantage. For instance, if your lower brain indicates that you are experiencing certain sensations or feelings that you find unpleasant, you may choose to ignore them. This may cause you to dismiss emotional states to which you really should attend or ignore what your deepest inner self is trying to tell you. In fact, when you dis-integrate in this way, you may be ignoring what God is trying to tell you, running from parts of you that he wants to heal and parts of him that he longs to have known by you.

Neuroscience research has discovered that people with a reasonable balance and level of helpful integrated communication between the different areas of their brains tend to have reduced anxiety and a greater sense of well-being. In other words, they have put themselves in the position to be available for the Holy Spirit to create those very characteristics that we so long to take root in us: love, joy, peace, patience, kindness, goodness, faithfulness, gentleness, and self-control.

By the way, you have probably noticed that the reptilian cortex reflects the highest level of processing within some members of the animal kingdom—namely, the reptiles. The limbic circuitry, also known as the paleomammalian brain, is the highest level of neurological development in animals like cats and dogs that display emotion (although your dog doesn't smile at you, no matter what you think). These similarities between humans and animals remind us that we are deeply connected to the rest of creation.

WORKING THE SYSTEM

Not only can we learn a lot about what makes us human by studying the anatomy of the brain, we acquire additional insights from considering its various *systems*. Systems cut across regions and involve multiple levels of the brain, often within both the right and left hemispheres. These include sensory, motor, and affect regulation (emotion management) systems. Additional systems regulate fear, stress, and our level of engagement in social situations, depending on their perceived danger or comfort.

The foremost examples are the sympathetic and parasympathetic nervous systems. The sympathetic system activates the body's readiness for defensive action, functioning like an accelerator. When put into motion it raises blood pressure, increases pulse and breathing rates, and tenses muscles. It is what we term the fight-flight mechanism of the body. By contrast, the parasympathetic system acts as the brakes, slowing and calming the body by decreasing blood pressure, slowing heart and breathing rates, and relaxing the body muscles.

These bioinfrastructures are not restricted to brain cells or networks of cells. They also include hormones that circulate throughout the body to chemically regulate and connect disparate areas of the body. Some of the better known include gamma-aminobutyric acid, or GABA (the chief inhibitory neurotransmitter); serotonin; norepinephrine; dopamine (neurotransmitters that affect mood); and the stress hormones, including cortisol (a hormone that biochemically regulates the human stress response).

Each of these systems has a specific neural circuitry or biochemical route that connects different parts of the brain and body. One system of particular interest to researchers in the last ten years is that of mirror neurons, which leads to mimicry. Virtually all intentional human behavior is ultimately mimicked. When we learn how to hold a fork or express a look of surprise, mimicry is involved. The mirror neurons fire when we witness another human undertake a behavior that has distinct intention. This system prepares the identical motor neurons in our brains to fire. For instance, if I see someone pick up a cup to drink from it, my mirror neurons will fire, preparing the "mirrored" neurons responsible for picking up and drinking from a cup to fire.

This has important implications for actions such as empathy. Empathy can be described as an action rather than merely a feeling alone because we *demonstrate* empathy through nonverbal and verbal cues or actions that project the *intent* of connecting with another's state of mind. When a child is the subject of another's empathy, he or she will likely undergo the activation of his or her mirror neuron system related to empathy. In other words, children learn how to be empathic with others by seeing it demonstrated toward them. This mirror neuron system is one of many that are vital in regulating how we interact both within our own minds and in relationship with others.

The more we understand the role of such systems, the more actively we can regulate them. For example, if I am aware that my fear is deeply connected to my breathing and heart rate, I can reduce my fear simply by consciously breathing deeply and slowly whenever I sense myself becoming fearful.

THE EXTENDED BRAIN

The central nervous system includes the brain and spinal cord, yet neuro-scientists also speak of the extended brain. This refers to the brain's connections, via cranial and peripheral nerves, to other organs, most notably the viscera (the heart, lungs, and the digestive tract).

These nerve tracts transport sensory information to and from those organs and the brain—a quiver in our stomachs or a heaviness in our chests. These sensations influence our moment-to-moment choices, often apart from our awareness. The ancient Hebrews, who often referenced the area of the bowel when speaking of the "soul," were not so far off.

PREMATURE AT BIRTH

We are all born prematurely. I am not referring to the gestational time frame of pregnancy but to the length of time required for a human being, once born, to reach comprehensive independence. Human beings require more time than any other mammal, relative to their life span, to reach adulthood. A foal is up and running in a matter of minutes. A blue whale may live for up to eight decades, but after birth is ready to leave its mother within one to two years and is ready to reproduce within five to eight years.

Remember this difference the next time you wonder whether your child will ever grow up. Can you imagine your newborn son getting up to run around within minutes of his birth? He would be into everything before the nurses could catch him, and you'd be too exhausted to do anything about it. Human infants (thankfully) simply don't do that. We couldn't take it if they did.

Of course, humans reach more sophisticated endpoints in our development than any of our zoological relatives. We think, perceive, construct bridges, and write plays and symphonies. With our more sophisticated brains, we depend less on what we might call "instinct"—automatic lower brain impulses that drive the behavior of lower animals. We are more dependent on higher brain functions that include but are not limited to thoughts, feelings, sensations, and the awareness that we are aware. This eventually leads not only to abstract and creative mind activity and behavior, but perhaps even more important, to the ability to consciously be aware of what other people are thinking, feeling, and intending to do. That leads us to consciously choose actions that fly in the face of our "instinctual" impulses. We say please and thank you. We share our cookies. We open and hold doors for other people.

This degree of sophistication takes time to develop. The brain's neurons and synapses require lengthy periods to integrate in ways that provide for the multiple functions they will eventually carry out. Adult humans protect their children from life-threatening forces so their brains have time to develop these special abilities and slough off those networks that aren't needed. We don't have very highly developed olfactory networks, for example, as they're not critical for our survival (as opposed to a gazelle or a wolf). Parents who provide for their children's physical and emotional security free the brains of their infants, toddlers, and adolescents to wander off in the direction of Tinkertoys, baseball, and Tchaikovsky.

This long period of time also offers the chance for adult caretakers to make new brain connections, albeit ones that are quite different from children's. Anyone who has parented (or even babysat) knows how little you know in the beginning and how much you have to learn in order to do your job. That takes time. Time to develop patience and resilience in the face of nighttime feedings. Time to develop wisdom and patience when you need to offer choices to your toddlers. And time to learn how to thoughtfully initiate conversations with your teenager.

Rarely do you see bad parenting among animals, which are neurologically less sophisticated. The more complex we are, the more we can do, which unfortunately means the more suffering we can create. So not only is there an extended period of development of the brain after birth, there is an unfolding drama between child and parent, with no guaranteed outcome, that both shapes and is shaped by those very neural network interactions. Again, this process points us to God. After all, his active work of creation and redemption is being worked out over a long period of time. Our history of becoming and being human as a race is recapitulated in each individual's movement from birth to adulthood. From the biblical narrative, we know that God has loved us—travailing, celebrating, wooing, suffering, dying, and being raised again— over time, using various methods and tactics. But his ultimate intent, to bring us from birth to adulthood as a human race, much as we do with our own children, has never changed. If you feel overwhelmed with how long it seems to be taking your child to mature, God knows exactly how you feel.

MIND CHANGERS

Growth spurts

If you are a parent or can remember being a teenager, you won't be surprised by what I'm about to tell you. Not only during children's youngest years, but also during adolescence, the brain undergoes great transformation and sculpting that lead to all kinds of new and rearranged neural connections.

We describe the brain as having a great deal of plasticity. This refers to its capacity, at a cellular connection level, to make new synapses and to prune away those synapses that don't get much firing action. It also refers to the actual growth in size and maturity of certain neurons. In both infancy and adolescence, neural networks are forming and re-forming almost daily.

In infants, this translates to new insights and behaviors that occur as they learn about their bodies and their environments. Despite our possible impression that infants don't "do" much of anything, if we could observe the activity of their brains, we would see that they are constantly attempting to make connections in their minds. As infants grow into toddlers, they become more verbal and mobile, two more signs of the bewildering pace of neuron growth and connection.

While this idea of plasticity may be easy to accept in small children, its effects on teenagers can be more baffling. After all, adolescents are old enough to understand algebra, so why can't their rooms be as neat and tidy as their math problems? Why is it that one minute life is "the bomb" and the next that "bomb" has exploded? And what makes our teenagers certain that someone else (usually one of their parents) is responsible for the detonation? The changing moods of teens can be attributed in no small part to this neuroplasticity in the context of a surging sea of sex and growth hormones that leaves them feeling confused and disoriented. (Of course my daughter, who is a gifted writer, would very much like to have written this section. She would, no doubt, explain that it was actually her parents' brains that underwent a mysterious change when she reached adolescence.)

Adults are often impatient with the effects of all that plasticity. What was God thinking? (We conclude, perhaps, that he wasn't.) In those moments of exasperation, remember that your children (or students, athletes, or youth group members) are not out to get you. They are simply doing the best they can to cope with having a much more fluid collection of neural connections than they had when they were ten. Life can seem to have lost clarity and be full of existential crises: *Am I good-looking enough? What dialect, exactly, do girls speak? Will my friends still like me if I hang out with this other group of people? What if I don't get into the college of my choice?*

As you look back on your own adolescence, you may wonder, *Why did I get so worked up about that?* Part of the answer is, your brain was on the move. The fact that you would feel one thing one minute and something categorically different the next is as much about your neurons as it is about your friends or your parents. If you did not have parents who understood this, you may recall how difficult it was to get along with them. When parents are aware and accepting of these changes, they are better able to navigate these times with flexibility and patience.

Nurture or nature?

How much influence do your genes have on your brain? If one of your parents had depression and you suffer from depression, will your children be more vulnerable to becoming depressed? Is it a "simple" issue of genetic inheritance, in the same way your eye color is?

What is both complex and amazing about the mind is how it emerges under the influence of what neuroscientists call epigenetics. Simply put, this means that gene expression is influenced—turned on and off, accelerated and slowed—by experience. For example, some people may have a genetic predisposition for being more anxious than other people. But if their parents are deeply attuned to their emotional temperaments, the genes that turn on their children's anxiety response will tend to be quieted, and they're more likely to develop a sanguine approach to life. On the other hand, if their parents behave anxiously, they may activate the genes that encourage anxiety to emerge, even in the most benign circumstances.

Intentional change

When I was in medical school more than twenty years ago, I was taught that the brain had the capacity to grow and change only through childhood and adolescence. The adult brain did not change and develop. This was not good news for everyone. Just ask my wife, who had to live with *me* back when neuroscientists thought that was true. More than anyone, she is grateful that the new data strongly suggests that the brain *can* continue to develop new connections and networks of neurons, especially in those areas that correlate with the experience of memory and emotion.

This neuroplasticity can be enhanced and facilitated by our intentional behavior. Dan Siegel provides the helpful acronym SNAG to refer to the process by which we "stimulate neuronal activation and growth." Neuroscience research has identified what I call a neuroplastic triad, three activities that will enhance the likelihood of this growth and activation:

- *Aerobic activity.* Engaging in this form of exercise for at least forty-five minutes per day, at least five days per week, is good for the heart and the mind. When your body feels good as a result of exercise, your mind also functions better.
- *Focused attention exercises.* Practicing certain activities, such as centering prayer, can help you learn to purposely focus your attention where needed. This is important when you want to do some mental rewiring. We'll explore focused attention exercises in chapter 9.
- *Novel learning experiences.* Any learning that expands your meaningful level of creativity, such as learning a foreign language, to play an instrument, or to build furniture, encourages neuroplasticity. Memorizing the first ten pages of the phone book does not qualify—unless you have a very creative way for using that memorized list of numbers.

This is not to imply that plasticity is equally available to us across the lifespan. It is not. There are periods in childhood and adolescence in which the brain is more flexible than later on. That is why it is generally easier for young people to learn to play an instrument or speak a foreign language than it is for adults. It also helps explain why we can predict that teenagers who begin to drink are at greater risk for becoming alcoholics than those people who begin to drink after age twenty-four.

LOST AND FOUND

As we end this extensive look at the human brain, I hope you have renewed hope. No matter how fixed your thinking or behavior is, research tells us that you can make significant changes in the way you remember your past; the way you experience the way your parents treated you; or for that matter, the way you treated your own adult children when they were young. In other words, even though you cannot change the events of your story, you can change the way you *experience* your story.

Have you ever wondered if, when people begin to follow Jesus, they really experience the change he promised? And if so, how does it happen and what role, if any, does the individual play? Does this sound like a distant rumbling of what you have heard echoed before, that God is a God who *changes* us?

Of course we have stock theological answers like, "It's through the power of the Holy Spirit." Or, "He does it by grace, and that's a mystery." Great.

While there certainly is truth in those statements, giving a theological answer to someone's agony over his or her failed attempts to overcome a pornography addiction or to forgive an abusive parent usually produces only guilt. People's anxiety over their finances or their singleness doesn't respond easily to Paul's admonition to "not be anxious about anything, but in every situation . . . present your requests to God" (Philippians 4:6). When we hear that, most of us become even more anxious because we're not very good at not being anxious.

But what happens when we begin to consider that we can change the way our brains are wired? Perhaps it can point us to what God is up to when he invites us to love him and give us hope that the tools he's built inside each one of us can help us move toward lasting change.

Remember George, who told me he felt as if he were losing his mind as he wrestled with his teenage daughter's second bout of drunkenness? When he came to see me a few days after the incident with his daughter, he felt helpless, angry, and desperately worried.

We talked about a number of things over the next several sessions, including the different elements of the mind that we've just explored. As he began to better understand how the mind works and how it is related to a person's experiences, he was positioned to become more closely connected to himself, his wife, his daughter, and Jesus. Not only did he find his mind, but he found his daughter and his God in the process.

In the next chapter, we'll explore the first step George took. He had to turn the ignition key of his mind. He had to begin to pay attention. First, though, we'll consider the story of another man who changed history by doing the same thing.

Chapter 4

ARE YOU PAYING ATTENTION?

H e was minding his own business, or so he thought. It had been a hard day, beginning with an early-morning rescue operation to locate several of the flock that had wandered off. Unfortunately, one of the missing sheep had fallen into a ravine, requiring a slaughter he hadn't counted on. Late in the afternoon, a driving dust storm had threatened to scatter all the animals again. As he led them around to the north side of the mountain to more plentiful grazing areas, he had to pause often to count the sheep.

It happened just after the chaos of the storm. At first he thought it might have been because of his hunger or thirst. Maybe it was due to the sweltering heat. Perhaps it was the result of fatigue and the monotony of his job. But the man could swear he was seeing something he'd never seen before. Something you just don't see every day in the desert. And he had been in the desert a long time. He knew others who had seen things that weren't really there when they had become too thirsty. Was that what he was experiencing? There was only one way to find out. He would move in closer to investigate.

He walked a few paces and blinked his eyes. His impression didn't change. It was still there. Flame billowed all around and through the dark, treelike shrub. Yet the bush itself was not burning, even though at this time of year it was exceptionally dry. If set ablaze, it would be consumed in minutes—which was why he now was fully aware of the strangeness of what he was witnessing.

49

This shepherd had seen plenty of brush fires in his day, usually caused by lightning. This was something different. The small shrubbery refused to give in to the heat. It didn't char, and there was no smoke. He was puzzled and fixated; drawn and captivated.

It was the voice that undid him. Seeing things was one thing. Hearing a voice coming from the flame he wasn't certain was really there was too much. But it was the simple act of paying attention to something, something unusual in an otherwise bland landscape, that would change the life of Moses forever.

You may be familiar with this biblical story from Exodus 3. It is an intriguing account of a man who had been on the run from the world in which he grew up, on the run from Pharaoh, and on the run from himself. Only on the far side of the desert was his attention awakened to things within and without him. There at the edge of the world he paid attention to the Voice that spoke to him in a dialect like none he had ever heard. His life likely would have remained the same had he not paid attention; had he not paid attention, he would have missed the opportunity to "go over and see this strange sight" (Exodus 3:3).

Stories abound in Scripture of people whose first step toward growth came as they paid attention to God's calling. Adam. Eve. Cain. Noah. Abraham. Sarah. Moses. Gideon. Deborah. Samuel. David. Mary. Joseph. Wise astronomers. Jesus. Paul. From Genesis through Acts, the Bible weaves a rich tapestry of narratives describing people's response to God's initiative. Furthermore, the way the biblical characters chose to pay attention had significant, sometimes life-threatening consequences.

But what were they paying attention to that convinced them they were hearing from God? How did they know the words weren't just the product of indigestion, a fight with their parents or spouses, or just wishful thinking? (I know I'd be a lot more open to the thought that God had told me to pack up my wife and children and move to Colorado if my extended family was getting on my nerves and I really liked the mountains.) *What they paid attention to affected their lives.* Or even more likely, in the spirit of the new neurospirituality articulated by Andrew Newberg (*How God Changes Your Brain*) and George Vaillant (*Spiritual Evolution*), some would interpret these experiences as mere reflections of particular neuron firing patterns, unrelated to any *real agent* outside themselves.

It's easy for us in our modern and postmodern ways of thinking to simply assume that these folks connected with God in a special way that is unavailable to us. Some people casually dismiss these stories outright, reducing "the word of the Lord" to imaginative, primitive thinking on the part of ancient writers who, though well-intended, really didn't know that much about the way the world works.

If you haven't read the accounts of some of these heroes of the faith lately, it would be good to review them. Consider how and to what they paid attention. In Moses' case, we are not surprised that he paid attention. Who wouldn't have? It was a burning bush, for crying out loud. But the biblical account reveals that Moses actually *regarded* the bush. After he had attended to this natural phenomenon, he pondered his response. His action was not automatic, it was considered.

God speaks with Moses *after* he sees that Moses is willing to pay attention to him: "When the LORD saw that he had gone over to look, God called to him from within the bush, 'Moses! Moses!'" (Exodus 3:4).

I suspect that God really enjoys the attention that he gets from us. The degree to which we pay attention to him affects not only us. It affects *him*. God was pleased enough that Moses was paying attention to him that he went further than lighting a botanical candle. He decided to talk with him. When God talks and we attentively listen, wonderful, beautiful, terrifying things happen.

From the viewpoint of neuroscience, what does it mean for us to pay attention? And how does paying attention affect all of our relationships, not least the one we have with Jesus?

NOW THAT I HAVE YOUR ATTENTION

Whenever we act on our world, whether intentionally or automatically, we employ the function of the mind called attention. Attention can be considered the ignition key of the mind. A vast array of our mental and physical actions follow what we attend to.

We frequently pay attention *voluntarily*. For instance, you are intentionally reading this sentence; on the golf course, you mark out the slight slope in the putting green to judge the likely path of the golf ball in order to sink it in the cup (or in my case, I carefully watch exactly how far off the fairway the ball lands in the woods so that I can find it); or you try—you swear you are trying, despite her protests to the contrary—to pay attention to your wife's emotional story about her conversation with her controlling mother. And, of course, we have all had experiences in which someone tells us to "pay attention!" leading us to focus on the task at hand.

At other times we activate our attention *automatically and unconsciously.* For example, the sensation of pain in your finger as you're chopping onions causes you to look down at the cut on that finger; you're awakened in the night by the high-pitched cry of an infant; or you steel yourself for the sudden onset of a panic attack as the heart palpitations and shortness of breath begin.

We intuitively know the difference between choosing to focus our attention on something, such as setting the alarm on the clock radio, and having our attention captured involuntarily by a stimulus that we perceive physically or emotionally, such as the sound of that alarm clock. Furthermore, we recognize that there tends to be a continuum between our voluntary and involuntary ways of attending to things. Imagine you suddenly happen upon a beautiful vista as you are hiking. You feel captivated by the beauty that has caught you by surprise. But almost immediately you begin the seamless transition to purposefully looking at that same vista because of the pleasure it brings. The boundary between instinctive and intended attention seems to blur to the point of being indistinguishable.

Many experiments have been done to identify the part of the brain that most often correlates with the activation of attention. It is the dorsolateral prefrontal cortex (DLPFC), a part of the frontal lobe of the brain (see diagram on page 32) that is generally considered to be the anatomical location of the neurons responsible for our voluntary focusing mechanism. When you select the target of your focus, this part of the brain begins to act like a spotlight, making synaptic connections with other layers of neuronal tissue that correspond to the various aspects of what you are concentrating on. It "shines a light," so to speak, on the multitude of different elements of the brain that are coming together to help form what you are focusing on. For instance, if you are remembering the argument you had this morning with your coworker, your DLPFC will act to recruit other neural networks from disparate parts of the brain that represent visual, linguistic, and emotional perception that all come together to create the image you have in your mind.

The brain is constantly filtering dozens of stimuli, enabling us to focus on some things while eliminating others from the mind's view. For instance, right now as you read this sentence, other incoming sensations are competing for your attention. The sound of music coming from your son's room. Objects in your peripheral vision. The aroma of your coffee. To what will you lend your most focused attention?

When our attention is captured involuntarily, alternative parts of the brain often initiate the process. It is common for sensory input from visual, auditory, or tactile areas of the body to send signals to the brain stem, initially bypassing the cortex. Remember that the brain stem is the site of neurons that control fight-or-flight responses that are so important when we face life-threatening situations. Sudden shifts in sensory input that link to the brain stem trigger automatic physical responses appropriate to the situation. These reactions, as I described earlier, are taking place before the part of the brain that is responsible for conscious awareness (the cortex) is engaged. These processes occur in nano- to microseconds. The signals sent from the brain stem to the heart, lungs, and muscles are also sent to other parts of the brain that eventually, via the limbic circuitry, make their way to the cortex and our conscious attention. When that seamless transition happens we have engaged the DLPFC. The importance of the connections between the DLPFC, the limbic circuitry, and the brain stem, *and how we pay attention to these connections* will become clear shortly.

All well and good, you may be thinking. *No surprise so far.* It only makes sense that our lives are affected by what we pay attention to, and if we don't pay attention, we are likely to have problems. If you don't pay attention to the pedestrian in the crosswalk, you may run him over. Simple enough. But despite the fact that we believe that paying attention is important, the truth is we live much of our lives inattentively.

I tell my patients that one of the most important questions they can reflect on is the following: *How well am I paying attention to what I am paying attention to?* This is a question we will return to over and over. [It is one thing to pay attention to something. It is quite another to pay attention to what we're paying attention to, especially the activity of the mind itself. It requires a deeper activation of the mind to select and attend to those things that we are not practiced at attending to, *especially the very activity of the mind itself.*] For the way we attend to elements of our experience wires our brains in certain patterns—and the way we attend to others' minds (particularly our children's) influences the wiring of their brains as well. Beyond this, the way we attend to various elements of our mind's activity also greatly influences our relationship with God. On the surface this may not be hard to accept; what is difficult to contemplate is just how much we are not paying attention to, especially spiritually.

LIKE FATHER, LIKE DAUGHTER

And so we return to the story of George and his seventeen-year-old daughter Kristin, whom we met in the last chapter. Naturally, George was worried.

Kristin, a junior in high school, had been drinking since she was fifteen. Her mother had originally brought Kristin to see me, not because of the alcohol, but because she was having panic attacks. They would occur unexpectedly before she played her varsity basketball games or whenever she traveled away from home to stay with relatives or vacation with friends. During each attack, she developed sudden overwhelming fear and heart palpitations, and she often vomited. Beneath the spikes of panic ran an undercurrent of subtle anxiety that she felt much of every day. At first the alcohol calmed her anxiety. But then she began to use it to blunt the distressing feelings she had but didn't understand very well.

When I first began to see Kristin, we talked about her alcohol use as well as her anxiety. She said that alcohol addiction was not what she wanted for her life, but she didn't know how to stop. She was afraid that if she stopped drinking, the panic would return. She agreed to a trial of medication that reduced her panic, and she entered a local alcohol recovery program for teenagers.

Next we began to explore her awareness of what made her anxious. With little hesitation she said, "My dad." She detailed how he had been "shocked" when he discovered her alcohol problem. She also said, "He's always on me about my basketball performance and my grades. He wants me to get a scholarship to play ball, and if I don't, he thinks my grades aren't going to be good enough to get into the college I want to attend. I don't get it. I mean, it's not like he doesn't have enough money to send me to school."

Kristin was, in fact, an above-average student at a high school that had rigorous academic standards. She rather enjoyed her learning experience and took great pleasure in her extracurricular activities. To her way of thinking, her father's level of concern did not fit the effort she was putting into making something of her life.

As we spent several months working together in psychotherapy, a new vitality in Kristin's spiritual life began to emerge. She described how her prayer life had become quite meaningful and how the friends she had made through Young Life and her church youth group helped make following Jesus something real, something beyond mere platitudes. To meet a school requirement, she started working at a soup kitchen once a month and could already see how the gospel made sense only when you were somehow serving those less fortunate than yourself. This from a seventeen-year-old. Very cool.

But George was still worried—even though Kristin's panic was gone and she had stopped drinking. Even after her grades went up and her spiritual life was clearly maturing. Though she was my patient, he seemed to be the one who needed help.

On occasion, I would meet with Kristin's parents to give them updates of my impression of their daughter's progress. Even as she improved, George relentlessly expressed his concern that she was not studying hard enough and that she might start drinking again. His recollection of transporting her intoxicated body into the house was never far from his mind.

Finally I asked him to tell me about *his* anxiety, about the feelings and thoughts of *his* life. He could talk only about his daughter. He had a difficult time turning the focus of his attention to his own emotions. It took great effort on his part (and mine) before he could shift his attention to himself and reflect on what he was feeling.

With Kristin's permission, I told George that one of her greatest distresses was the way he worried about her. Though he was often gone from home due to his work commitments, when he was there, most of his interactions with her revolved around her performance in just about all areas of her life. The nonverbal as well as verbal message was clear: "You can (and need) to do better." All his hovering, even from a distance, had clearly fed Kristin's anxiety.

I told him plainly that I thought that one reason Kristin was so much less anxious now was because she had found in our psychotherapy relationship (as well as in her recovery group and her youth group) a place where she could process her feelings about her life—and especially about him—and make sense of why she was so anxious. I emphasized that before Kristin had begun therapy, she had spent much of her "anxious" time pondering his behavior toward her. She had been focusing her attention on something outside of her own mind. Through the course of therapy, however, she began to pay more attention to what *she* was sensing *within* herself. Her reflections turned to her own feelings, physical sensations, and thoughts, *not simply what she was thinking about outside of herself.*

I suggested to George that perhaps he would also benefit from beginning to pay attention to what he was experiencing within himself—besides his thoughts about Kristin. By doing this, I told him, I thought he could more effectively reduce the rather constant drumming of apprehension that he was convinced was due to his daughter's choices. Clearly George was not paying attention to what he was paying attention to. He certainly was paying attention to his perceptions about his daughter's life, but he was paying little attention to other, more powerful forces within his own mind. These were really the crux of his troubles, and to some degree, the source of Kristin's troubles as well. In other words, Kristin was not his problem; he was his problem.

George was inattentive to how his role as a technology executive was taking him away from life at home and, as a result, how deeply sad he was over missing many events in his daughter's life. Although he knew this to be a fact, he would not permit himself to sense that sadness for long because it led to additional feelings of guilt. And these emotions so frightened and overwhelmed him that he just kept them locked away in some distant mental storage trunk, safely protected from his conscious awareness.

Neither did he pay much attention to the nonverbal messages he sent to Kristin when he spoke with her. When the three of us met together, it was not hard to see how his tone of voice and facial expression reflected the strain of his own feelings. I noted to George that Kristin was not the only one receiving the nonverbal cues that his brain/body sent. *His own body and brain received those same messages.* Through these nonverbal cues, *he* was making himself afraid. I wondered aloud how exhausting it must be to carry that much anxiety with him day in and day out. He admitted that it would be a relief if he could release this burden. But then he slipped back to his mental hand-wringing over images of Kristin's troubles.

Since I knew that being a follower of Jesus was important to him, I asked how God fit into this story. What did God feel or think about these circumstances, and how did that affect him? Was George aware of how God was affected by him? (Notice that with this question I was not asking how George was affected by God, but rather the other way around; we often don't reflect on how we actually affect God, but more on this in chapter 6.)

George's answers were instructive. It was clear that when he considered what God thought of him, none of it was very good. Guilt was the dominant theme, reflected in the fleeting images, sensations, and thoughts of God's displeasure and disappointment with him. "I know I'm not meeting his standards—but I really want to," George told me.

I wondered aloud to him what it must be like to pay so much attention—to take and bask in—the converging images, thoughts, and feelings of God's disappointment. I pointed out that these impressions didn't leave much room in his mind for the image of a God who loved him. And the likelihood of that changing was not very great if George wasn't even aware that this perceived disappointment was what he was paying attention to.

Then I asked what it was like growing up in his family of origin. No surprise there. His own father was demanding and emotionally distant. His mother lived to do his father's bidding. In their family, having a relationship with God meant following a set of rules and regulations set down by the church. George had no idea that the way he had developed emotionally in his family continued to influence his experience of God.

He recalled that when he was about fifteen (incidentally, around the same age when Kristin began to drink), he decided he was going to "check out" of his family. After enduring years of criticism and harshness from his dad, he decided that academics and sports would become his life. He received plenty of accolades from his teachers and coaches, so he didn't need his family again for much of anything, including emotional support. I asked when he had last reflected on his life growing up. His answer was revealing: "I never do. There's nothing there to think about."

Like George, we can be inattentive to a great many things: our thoughts and feelings, the nonverbal signals we send and receive from others and ourselves, the memories from our developmental years. George was oblivious to the many things that were influencing his experience of God and life. He was missing the undercurrent feelings of sadness and guilt, how his facial expressions and tone of voice revealed his impatience and irritability, and his own mildly increased heart and breathing rates whenever he spoke with his daughter or about his daughter's problems. He was not aware of the activity of his brain stem and limbic circuitry or their influence on his behavior. Nor did he realize how they were shaping the development of his daughter's brain. Moreover, *ignoring these aspects of his brain's function resulted in his missing ways that God was attempting to capture his attention. Ignoring his brain was the equivalent of ignoring God.*

Because George never dealt with the anger and hurt his own father's criticism had caused, when Kristin became a teenager, George was unable to relate to her or understand how his own criticism was affecting her. Without that point of connection, the only way he could evaluate her was by her behavior—which, admittedly, did not always look good.

SAINTS WITH CLAY FEET

Just as for Moses there was a bush and for others in Scripture there were dreams, voices, angels, family dynamics, and other impressions, so God speaks to us using signposts (perhaps minus the flame) mediated by the activity of our brains. If we are not paying attention to these functions of the brain, we will not be able to attend to what God is trying to tell us.

Perhaps you already pay attention to many of these things. You sense God's promptings and respond to them. You read the subtle body language of your teenager communicating her exasperation. You try to listen with empathy to your brother's complaint about your father. But we all have areas of our lives in which we could pay better attention in order to be more aware of what we are aware of.

Consider David. Israel's second king was a man after God's own heart, but he was also a man after another man's wife. He failed to discipline his children as well. Both shortcomings ultimately contributed to the corruption and downfall of the kingdom. Yes, his psalms reveal the heart of a sensitive poet, but where was the delight and meditation on God's law (Psalm 1:2) when he was having sex with Bathsheba, the wife of Uriah the Hittite? To what was he not paying attention?

Another example of a hero with clay feet is Gideon. He paid attention to God at a time in Israel's history when practically no one else did. (And by the way, if someone told us today that an angel had called him "mighty warrior," we would probably assume he had been hallucinating—it's quite easy for us to dismiss the voice of God.) It took a great deal of courage for Gideon to act on what he sensed, heard, and saw. Paying attention ultimately led to an Israelite military victory over the Midianites, even though the Hebrews were vastly outnumbered.

But not long after this victory, Gideon created a religious sculpture for his own pleasure, making it from the gold offered to him by his countrymen as payment for his leadership. He then put it on display in his hometown. His friends and neighbors began to worship the statue, creating problems for Gideon and his family (read Gideon's complete story in Judges 6–8). What was *that* about? Somehow Gideon had not anticipated how his actions would affect other people.

And what of Samuel, one of Israel's greatest judges? The man who as a young boy heard and attended to God's voice eventually had great difficulty cultivating the same sensitivity in the ears of his own children (see 1 Samuel 8:1-5). Certainly in some very important ways he was paying attention to God, but how was it that in other ways he was not, especially when it came to important shortcomings in his sons' character? Once again, his failure to pay attention had lasting effects on the entire nation. The Hebrews pointed at Samuel's sons and their unjust behavior when they asked Samuel for a king. The degree to which we pay attention will have implications, literally, on the generations that follow us.

The point is that we all have areas of our lives that we don't attend to. Don't get me wrong. We desire to do so. Most of us even believe that we do pay attention to our children, our spouses, our parents, and our God. We would never choose *not* to pay attention to them. (Okay, that's not totally true. I'm sure there are times when my wife believes I am choosing not to pay attention to her. She could be right.) Unfortunately, we are often not aware of the ways we are not aware. And the lives of even heroes of the faith attest to this.

I suggest that many elements of our mind/body matrix are means by which God is trying to get our attention, but we have not had much practice reflecting on them. We, like George, often don't focus on our feelings, memories, what our bodies are telling us, or the depth and meaning of our narratives. The more we pay attention to these things—what our brains are telling us— the more we are ultimately paying attention to God.

In 1 Corinthians 6:19 Paul writes, "Do you not know that your bodies are temples of the Holy Spirit, who is in you, whom you have received from God?" This statement—that the body is the *temple*—would have great significance to a first-century Jew, since the Temple was the centerpiece of his or her life, both socially and politically. This was where God lived, and it was in this place that one met God, spoke with God, and heard God's voice.

For Paul to say that God now lives through the presence of the Holy Spirit in a person's *body*, as opposed to the physical, centrally located Temple, represented a sea change in how his readers would understand the way to experience intimacy with God. Paul was not saying that God *is* the body but that in order for us to attend to God, we have to attend to the place where he lives. Our brains assist us in doing this. By paying attention to our mind/body experience, we are paying attention to what the Holy Spirit is telling us.

The more George paid attention to the functions of his brain, the more he began to hear God in ways he had never heard him before. I gave him an exercise to practice that would enhance his capacity to focus, along with a meditation exercise that helped him be more aware of what he was feeling in his body. (Both exercises are explained in chapter 9.) I explained to him that as he practiced them, he was actually changing the neural networks and circuitry in his brain.

George's relationship with God began to take on new meaning as he realized that paying attention to God was literally creating a new mind within him. And that newness was related to the new mind that Paul writes about in Romans 12:2: "Do not conform to the pattern of this world, but be transformed by the renewing of your mind. Then you will be able to test and approve what God's will is—his good, pleasing and perfect will."

In other words, God built in us the ability to pay attention to what we pay attention to, which creates space for us to hear him; and out of this flows abundant life—testing and approving God's good, pleasing, and whole will. Goodness, pleasure, wholeness—they all begin with paying attention to what we are paying attention to.

In addition to the changes in his life with God, George became more aware of everything around and within him: his feelings, his memories, the importance of his narrative, and the effect these things were having on those around him. Notably, *he became more aware of what his daughter Kristin was really experiencing.* As he sought to increase his attention to his own multi-layered experience, the nature of his relationship with Kristin changed. We talked about how paying attention creates space for God to do what he promised Moses: "If you listen carefully to the LORD your God and do what is right in his eyes, if you *pay attention* to his commands and keep all his decrees, I will not bring on you any of the diseases I brought on the Egyptians, *for I am the LORD, who heals you*" (Exodus 15:26, italics mine). By engaging his attention, therefore, and especially attending to what he was attending to, George initiated a process that led to healing.

Learning to become intentional about what George was paying attention to was not the final step for him; in fact, it was really the beginning. In the remainder of this book, we will explore various functions of the mind that are affected by the degree to which we are paying attention. These include memory, emotion, and the relational process of attachment. Each of these also affects our walk with God and can contribute to life and peace.

HOW TO PAY ATTENTION TO WHAT YOU'RE PAYING ATTENTION TO

For the last 3,500 years or more, people who have truly walked with God and been known by him have nurtured that relationship through the spiritual disciplines. We will explore several of these, along with the ways they promote greater integration within and between human brains, in more detail later. For now, it is enough to focus on three major streams that provide structure and support for those disciplines.

In his book *Reaching Out*, Henri Nouwen proposes that a healthy spiritual life includes three significant features—three legs of a stool upon which everything else rests. They include study of (especially, but not limited to) the Bible; prayer; and community. I encourage you to reflect seriously on the depth of your activity in each of these three vital areas of living life with God. These are not requirements you must fill to make sure God is happy. Nor are they the eleventh commandment. Simply put, these three dimensions of living facilitate vital changes in the stories of those people who hunger and thirst for righteousness. This can include you. Among other things, they will strengthen your ability to pay attention to what you are intending to do.

Nouwen rightly points out that if any one of the three legs is missing, the stool will not long stand. Consequently, as we progress, I invite you to consider the place each of these holds for you. If you sense that any of them seems to be absent or has fallen by the wayside, do not judge or condemn yourself. Simply begin where you are and consider taking a small step to reengage yourself with that area.

Chapter 5

REMEMBERING
THE FUTURE

Do you remember where you were when you first heard about the terrorist attacks of September 11, 2001?

What is three times four?

Do you recall your first day of school?

When did you learn how to ride a bicycle—can you visualize that time and place?

Do you get the sense that Jesus vividly remembers the angry tirade you directed at your six-year-old yesterday?

How are the questions above alike? Obviously, each assesses how well you recall a particular fact or experience. How are they different? Did you notice that remembering three times four is twelve "feels" different than thinking back to your first day of school? That's because these questions require you to use different neural pathways within your brain. (That also helps explain why you can remember specific details of the annual review your boss gave you eight months ago but can't recall the particulars of the conversation you had with your spouse last night.)

In chapter 4, we considered the vital function of attention—the ignition key of our minds. In this chapter, we explore memory, another critical operation. Memory is continually at work from the time our central nervous systems develop this ability. While we don't know precisely when that is, some researchers believe it begins before birth. In this chapter, we'll consider how memory connects us to—or disconnects us from—God and our neighbors, often in unconscious ways. We'll also explore how becoming familiar with memory's role in our lives can help us produce the fruit of the Spirit.

Acknowledging the importance of memory in everyday life does not require much of a stretch. Common sense tells us that if we don't remember to change the oil in our cars, call our fathers on their birthdays, or recall the conversation we had with our spouses last night, we will have problems. However, we are often unaware of the depth to which memory contours our lives. It is important enough that some researchers dedicate their entire careers to exploring its role. But its relevance was also apparent to some of the first people to keep written records of their journeys with the Creator. Their stories and words suggest that forging a deep connection to God and others largely depends on the effectiveness with which we remember:

> I will remember my covenant between me and you and all living creatures of every kind. (GENESIS 9:15)

> I will remember my covenant with Jacob and my covenant with Isaac and my covenant with Abraham, and I will remember the land. For the land will be deserted by them and will enjoy its sabbaths while it lies desolate without them. (LEVITICUS 26:42-43)

> Remember that you were slaves in Egypt and the LORD your God redeemed you. (DEUTERONOMY 15:15)

> Remember, LORD, your great mercy and love, for they are from of old. (PSALM 25:6)

> Remember these things, Jacob,
>   for you, Israel, are my servant.
> I have made you, you are my servant;
>   Israel, I will not forget you. (ISAIAH 44:21)

> And he took bread, gave thanks and broke it, and gave it to them, saying, "This is my body given for you; do this in remembrance of me." (LUKE 22:19)

I thank God, whom I serve, as my ancestors did, with a clear conscience, as night and day I constantly remember you in my prayers. (2 TIMOTHY 1:3)

These texts are but a small sampling of Scriptures that illustrate the weight and consequence of memory. Long before memory became an important field of scientific inquiry, the ancients knew that what we remember profoundly affects our relationships with every *thing* around us—not only with living creatures, but with the physical universe as well (see the Leviticus passage above).

So much of the life each of us lives, in fact, is one that is remembered. In this sense, part of "working out" your salvation (see Philippians 2:12) includes paying attention to how the act of remembering the past simultaneously creates the future in your mind.

MEMORY AND THE BRAIN

As we begin our exploration of memory, let us once again look to the brain. Chapter 3 explains that each experience we have correlates to a particular pattern of neuron networks firing—the seamless fusion of energy and information. This pattern develops the first time we do anything. Whenever we repeat an activity, we fire that same set of neural networks. In 1949 Donald Hebb, a Canadian psychologist, published the highly influential work *The Organisation of Behaviour: A Neuropsychological Theory.* Out of his research on learning and memory grew a concept known as Hebb's axiom: neurons that fire together wire together. In other words, neurons that repeatedly activate in a particular pattern are statistically more likely to fire in that same pattern the more they are activated. Once the initial neurons in a network fire, there is a very high probability that the related neurons will also activate and move along the same bioelectrical pathway to the end of that network without veering off to some other set of neurons.

Think of it like this. If you had to make your way through a dense jungle forest that no one had traveled before you, you might make your first path with a machete. It's possible that someone who came along later would be unable to trace your steps, given the thickness of the foliage. However, if a series of people followed directly behind you, they would increasingly wear down the path, making it easier to recognize your trail. The more frequently people traversed this route, the more likely future travelers would use the established path rather than create a new course through the forest. Also, once travelers began this course, they would be unlikely to decide, partway through the jungle, to wander off; in fact, the probability is very high that they would follow your trail to the end.

This image helps illustrate what neuroscientists mean by memory. When we "remember" something, we are firing neurons that have been fired before—to a greater or lesser degree of frequency. The more frequently those patterns have been fired, the more easily they will fire in that same pattern in the future. That's why you may immediately recall the ingredients and steps to preparing spaghetti, which you make every week, but need to consult the cookbook when preparing a holiday dish you haven't made for a few years.

The more we activate the neurons that correlate with a particular experience, the more likely we will be to "recall" or enact that same experience. This is the general way the brain works to create memory. In a sense, life becomes a living memory, because so much of what we do is the repetition of what we have done in the past. We are grateful for this complex neurological mapping system when we remember our anniversaries. But what if our wiring "remembers" to respond to someone's feelings of anger or disappointment by sulking or yelling at that person? This reality shapes our life with Jesus no less than our life with our friend or our teenager.

Just as particular anatomical regions of the brain correlate with the mind's system of attention, so different areas of the brain are associated with various forms of memory. Your mind contains multiple memory schemata—essentially the mental codification of your experiences. These schemata use different neural networks that exist throughout the brain. These networks are involved in several distinct forms of learning and memory, and they mature at different rates and stages of development.

Examples of these schemata include immediate, short-term, and long-term recall. Each of these terms refers to the time interval between the encoding of a memory and its retrieval. Most people are capable, for instance, of immediately recalling a sequence of up to seven random digits, but often not more than that (thus, seven digits in a phone number). With practice we can remember more, but that practice requires time and multiple firings of the neural network that represents a greater number of numbers.

Another system of the brain, mostly involving the right hemisphere, encodes forms of memory that include subjective impressions, feelings, and sensations of experience. A separate system encodes factual data, such as the number of days in the month of September. This, in turn, differs from the system that is responsible for recognizing the faces of people you know. When you see your spouse walk into the room, you don't have the sense that you are "remembering" him or her, yet that is precisely what your mind is doing.

Often, different systems work together to produce a particular remembrance, such as when you are asked to identify someone you have not seen in many years in a photograph. As you look at the picture, you may immediately perceive that you know who that person is, but you may be unable to bring to mind his or her name or the context in which you remember that person. Your mind begins to splice together different layers of memory, considering an infinite array of contextualizing data until something clicks. At that moment you are flooded, not only with the name of the person in the photo, but with many other details about who you are in relationship to each other.

These systems are vast in their detail. However, each seems to follow the Hebbian principle: neurons that fire together wire together. From a neuroscience standpoint, therefore, remembering is essentially the process by which neurons increase their probability of firing together. Keep this in mind as we consider how changing our memories can rewire our futures—essentially, this is what Scripture points to when it speaks of "the renewing of your mind" (Romans 12:2).

For our purposes, we will focus on two of the most general classifications of memory—*implicit* and *explicit* memory—and discuss their relevance to our lives.

IMPLICIT MEMORY

Researchers believe that *implicit memory* is the first form of recall that emerges in the human mind. In fact, it is present at birth, and some evidence suggests it begins to operate in the third trimester of pregnancy. Implicit memory is often equated with unconscious learning and recall. From an anatomical perspective, it involves lower, more primitively developed (although not necessarily less sophisticated) regions of the brain. This includes, but is not limited to, the limbic circuitry, the amygdala, and the brain stem, along with other regions of the right hemisphere.

Conscious attention or mental activity is not required for implicit memories to be encoded or retrieved; in other words, you don't have to pay attention to something in order for your mind to remember it. Implicit memories quite frequently occur in everyday experiences such as walking across the room or riding a bicycle. Every time you do these things, your body automatically "remembers" how to do them. You typically don't have to think about how to proceed, nor do you have the sensation that you are remembering the action. The brain has encoded and is now expressing, through Hebbian wiring, behaviors that are enacted using neural networks that bypass circuitry usually activated for conscious, intentional mental activity. While you can think about the action of riding your bike if you want to, as you begin to pedal you do not experience an awareness of engaging in something you've done in the past.

In addition to activities like walking that we engage in without conscious awareness, implicit memory comes in the form of perceptions, behaviors, emotions, and bodily experiences. The right hemisphere, as you may recall, is more involved in developing a comprehensive map of the body and the neural integration of nonverbal elements of communication. For this reason, implicit memory is often revealed through nonverbal communication and body language.

Implicit memory also uses what neuroscientists commonly call mental models. The implicit memory models that we form early in life tend to emerge automatically in response to certain internal and external stimuli. For instance, perhaps when you were a child, your parent's furrowed brow was consistently followed by an angry outburst. If, when you are a young adult, your girlfriend also furrows her brow, you're likely to feel threatened every time you see her frown. The problem, of course, is that she may not be angry, merely puzzled. But the mental model dismisses cues that indicate you are in a different setting from the one in which you grew up. (As a result, your puzzled girlfriend will be very interested in your working on a new model. Or she will work on finding a new boyfriend.)

Implicit memory is active throughout the life span, which means people can experience a great deal over time and "remember" those experiences without actually being aware that they are experiencing something connected to their past. When I had been married for only a few years, my wife made an interesting observation about my behavior whenever we visited my family. "You know, Curt," she said, "every time we go there, this guy shows up. He looks like you, sounds like you, and even has your name. But I'm not really sure who he is, because he doesn't behave like the man I married."

This transformation seemed to happen rather magically. When I would return home, I would begin to behave more tentatively and anxiously. In short, I related to my family more as I had when I was growing up—more like a young boy than an adult. And it took my wife pointing this out before I was even aware of it. Obviously, this behavior negatively affected our relationship.

She thought she had married an adult, not an insecure teenager. (Fortunately, since she revealed this to me, I am now more likely to behave as if I'm nineteen rather than thirteen. I've grown a lot in the last twenty years.)

Implicit memory may also dominate during extremely traumatic situations. For example, consider the experience of a woman who is sexually assaulted on the running trail near her home. During the assault, her body and mind may be so traumatized that her conscious attention turns away from what is happening. In order to protect her mind from the acute emotional devastation she is undergoing, her brain may cease to encode explicitly what is happening to her (as you will see later in this chapter, explicit memory requires conscious attention). She may, in fact, dissociate, her mind's attention drifting to something less painful than what she is undergoing at the moment.

A few hours after the violent incident, she might "wake up" in her apartment, having only a vague recollection of how much time has passed or why her clothing is so dirty or her arms and legs are bruised. Later that week, however, she might walk near the running path, only to be overcome by sudden, overwhelming fear; an inability to breathe; a sense of disorientation; and a painful sensation in her abdomen and pelvis. She still has no clear recall of the actual rape, only the accompanying implicit memories that present themselves emotionally and physically. In fact, she might never be able to completely recall the details surrounding this harrowing event.

Her story—and my story of the way I automatically regressed when I was with my parents—illustrates how complicated life can become if we are unable to connect certain elements of an implicit memory with the explicit memories of the same event. If we are not aware of how our implicit memories are connected to the real-life events that fostered them, we will have problems.

And Brad had problems. For several weeks, he and his wife had been deadlocked after a fight they'd had one evening. The argument began when Brad admitted he had failed to call his mother-in-law that day to wish her a happy birthday. Since he had promised his wife he would make the call, his wife told him how disappointed she was. In fact, she was obviously angry, since this was not the first time he had failed to follow through on something important to her.

It wasn't the couple's fight that was so unique. It was Brad's reaction to his wife's anger. He left the house, got in his car, and took off. He drove around his neighborhood, ignoring his wife's calls to his cell phone and returning only several hours later.

What intrigued me was Brad's lack of concern about his own behavior.

"I'm telling you, you should have heard her," he said. "I mean, I felt bad about not calling her mother. But I don't know what to do when she gets mad like that. There's no dealing with her." I asked how she had spoken to him and whether she had become physically hostile. He said she was "extremely harsh" but there was no physical altercation between them—this time or during any other argument. He added that he was compelled to leave the house because "I didn't want to say something I might regret."

Had he considered other options, I asked, such as taking a time-out from the conversation? He said that thought had never occurred to him. I also wondered aloud how his decisions, not only to leave the house, but to ignore his wife's frantic phone calls, struck him now. He seemed slightly perplexed, as if questioning his behavior was stranger than the behavior itself. No, he said, it was clear to him that if he hadn't driven around that night, he might have done something to escalate the conflict (as if leaving the house had somehow made things easier).

I asked Brad to reflect on how he typically handled situations in which people were angry with him. After some pondering, he said, "I avoid those situations whenever I can." We began to talk about what it was like growing up in his childhood home. His father was an alcoholic who became sober around the time Brad was ten. He could recall his age because that was about the time when his father started to become angry. Yes, he had stopped drinking, but he had done little to work on the emotional and behavioral sources of his alcoholism. Consequently, when Brad's dad came home after work, the entire family had to walk on eggshells, hoping to get through the evening without his anger flaring up.

Brad recalled that at some point after his father stopped drinking, he would find himself riding his bicycle before dinner as to avoid being at home when his father arrived. At other times, when his father would unexpectedly explode, he would use his two-wheeled escape pod as a way to keep the terror of his father from wrapping itself around his mind like a python. He recalled that when he finally obtained a driver's license, his car became a small haven of solace for him, a rolling tabernacle of music that enabled him to ignore his feelings, which were so overwhelming. He reflected that as he grew into older adolescence, he no longer feared his father's anger as much. What he feared more was the impulse to physically hurt his father during one of his tirades. And so he drove.

As Brad finished his story, his facial muscles began to relax. Soon after came the tears. For the first time, he connected his defense against his father's anger to his decision to drive around after the fight with his wife. Brad had had no idea he was experiencing an implicit memory the night he sought to protect himself from his wife's anger. Essentially his behavior toward his wife stemmed from a constellation of mental models—from the way he sensed and subjectively interpreted his wife's nonverbal cues, to what he felt in his own body, to his impulse to get in his car and drive away. Without his awareness, Brad's mind was recalling dozens of experiences from the past, leading him to employ the strategy that had worked in the home in which he grew up but was destructive in his current household. However, until our discussion, he had had no idea that he was "remembering" anything the night he and his wife quarreled. To him, the problem began with the fight with his wife.

Brad made important connections between these implicit memories and the painful events of his younger years. As he *paid attention* to the reactions that he had formerly displayed mindlessly and automatically, he was able to put them in their proper context, recognizing that his wife was not their primary source. He no longer needed to withdraw from her anger, which had left her feeling abandoned and had damaged their relationship. With practice, whenever he experienced conflict, he was able to consider that his feelings and the impulse to run away were originating from another time and place.

Brad also developed concrete ways to change how he reacted to his wife when she became angry with him. He worked to consciously pay attention to his physical and mental reactions, altering them over time. (These changes were largely made as he learned about emotion, which we will explore in more detail in the next chapter.) Doing so gave him more space to determine when he could do something about his anxiety without feeling overwhelmed. As a result, his reactions made more sense to him, as well as to his wife. He could continue to talk with her when she was angry, and his wife now felt understood rather than abandoned. Hot-rodding around the neighborhood was no longer necessary.

Making sense of your own implicit memories

It's not hard to apply the implications of this vignette to your own life. Think back to a conversation you may recently have had with your child, the one in which you lost your temper. Or the e-mail from your boss that seemed to confirm your suspicion that she is "out to get you." Imagine the dozens of interactions you have had with your friends, spouse, or parents in which you responded based on implicit memories without being aware of their connections to past experiences.

Research in marriage and family therapy suggests that approximately 80 percent of the emotional conflict between couples is rooted in events that pre-date the couple knowing each other. That's why one of the questions I commonly ask in marriage counseling is how much of each spouse's reaction to the other is his or her "80 percent." In other words, how much of the conflict is not so much a direct outgrowth of a current event as something that flows from parts of their minds that are remembering?

As you contemplate the recurring conflicts in your own life, I encourage you to consider how often you automatically react to other people's words, actions, or body language in ways that seem to harm, rather than restore, your relationships. Honestly evaluating your reactions enables you to redirect the focus of your search for a solution to a problem back to yourself. At first glance this may not seem all that pleasant—you have enough problems; why do you need to take on more? But there is great freedom in this discovery. Though a somewhat trite expression, it remains true that the only thing you can truly change is your own behavior.

I want to emphasize that I am not suggesting that your problems are unrelated to outside forces or that other people don't create real, objective difficulties for you (Brad's alcoholic father certainly did). Nor am I implying that your suffering is imagined or a product of unconscious memory. No, I am only pointing out that in order for your experiences to change, you must first change what you are doing. From a memory standpoint, that means that you must be aware of how your own recollections, particularly your implicit ones, create problems that you may attribute solely to others' behaviors and attitudes. Another important reason to expose and address these unconscious memories is to relieve the existential pressure that builds up around current circumstances that evoke the implicit memory.

As you plunge your own hands into the soil of the story from which your implicit memory germinated, took root, and flowered, you may want to share these discoveries with the person with whom you are in conflict, assuming there is a mutual desire for growth in the relationship. Often the one listening to your story will be more compassionate as he or she sees that you're attempting to make sense of your response. As Brad worked through this part of his life, his wife was able to be more patient with him, even early on when he struggled to remain present with her when she became angry.

It is not hard to imagine the almost infinite ways that your implicit memory may be creating your future simply by firing the same wiring repeatedly, usually in an unconscious haze. Even if you are a follower of Jesus, you may not understand why you repeatedly behave in ways that get you and others close to you into trouble.

The good news is that you do not have to remain in the morass of your implicit memory, straitjacketed by things you don't know you don't know. Despite the fact that you cannot turn back the clock and change the actual events of your life, *you can change your experience of what you remember and so change your memory*. As you pay more attention to this possibility, you will become aware of what Jesus is doing in real time and space to facilitate healing and renew your mind.

EXPLICIT MEMORY

When we speak of remembering something, we are usually referring to our explicit memory. It is comprised of two subgroups: factual (sometimes called semantic) and autobiographical memory. You draw on factual or semantic memory when asked to name the city where you were born, the date of the signing of the Declaration of Independence, or the day of the week that garbage is collected on your street.

Autobiographical recall occurs when you activate conscious awareness of something you experienced in the past, such as what you ate for breakfast this morning, the trip you took to the Grand Canyon last summer, or the fact that you have now asked your son to clean up his room three times. With autobiographical memory, you have a distinct awareness of the passage of time. You can distinguish the difference between five minutes ago, yesterday, and last week. The flow between factual and autobiographical memory is often subtle, but the two types of explicit memory are distinct, and they involve somewhat different parts of the brain.

Explicit memory usually begins to develop between the age of eighteen and twenty-four months when the hippocampus, a dense circuit of neurons below the cortex, fully integrates into the matrix of the brain. One reason we have no recollection of learning certain actions as young children, such as eating with a spoon, is because we learned these activities before the hippocampus was fully involved in our mental processing.

With the emergence of the hippocampus, the mind is able to unite separate aspects of implicit memory experience, gathered from distinct areas of the brain that provide data in the form of sensations, feelings, bodily awareness, and perceptions. In this way the hippocampus acts as an integrating cartographer, creating a contextualized mind map that can recall facts and that connects implicit with explicit memory. Only with the development of this part of the brain can children begin to know and remember—and be aware that they are remembering—facts about everyday life. They will be able to identify their elbow or recognize the letter *A*. These are examples of semantic memory.

The activation of explicit memory—both encoding and retrieving recollections—requires conscious attention. When you access an explicit memory, you have the clear sense that you are recalling something. This "feeling of remembering" enables you to tie moments together into a streaming progression that becomes the story of your life. Humans' ability to tell stories, which distinguishes us from all other living creatures, is a crucial part of how our minds connect us to God and others. Memory is the cornerstone of this undertaking.

In other words, we must pay attention in order to remember our narratives. This may seem patently self-evident, yet despite multiple exhortations from Moses, Joshua, and the prophets, the ancient Hebrews somehow found it easy to disregard their narrative, suffering the consequences of their forgetfulness. We, of course, often do the same thing.

With the growth and neural integration of the prefrontal cortex with the hippocampus, each of us begins to develop a sense of self across time. This mental time travel, the mind's multisensory awareness of the person's past and present, along with the subsequent projection into an anticipated future, is termed autobiographical memory.

You can distinguish exactly when and where you told your husband what you would like for your birthday. You're sure it was last month. You were sitting in the family room. You were drinking tea while he was reading the paper. Now, he tells you he's sure you told someone else what you wanted, which is why he bought you something else. (This proves, first of all, that we don't always remember events in the same way. It also illustrates that reading the paper has the distinct capacity—though only in men—to turn off the few hippocampal neurons that are dedicated to remembering what their wives tell them. Further research obviously is required in this area.)

Moving further into your past, you see yourself as a third grader. You visualize and smell the pancakes that your mom used to make you for breakfast before school. Or you shudder as you remember the faces of the classmates who bullied you during recess, or the way your dad shamed you for not defending yourself. The truth is, some memories are much more distressing than others; a few are so painful that you may actually attempt to turn your attention away from them, sometimes even as they are forming (as the rape victim described earlier).

Note that such autobiographical memories are deeply experiential; in other words, they're recalled as *a clearly engrained part of an event that occurred in a particular place at a particular time.* Perhaps you may be thinking, *Well, of course. That's obvious. I can see myself in my third-grade classroom and the corner I stood in for putting gum in Sally Bruchmeister's hair. What's so special about that?* The truth is, there are a couple of situations when such recall is very challenging.

First, preschool children are not able to recall or differentiate time segments as easily as adults. Three- and four-year-olds may have a hard time accurately remembering what they had for breakfast yesterday, let alone what they were doing last week. This is generally considered to be normal childhood amnesia. As you recall, the brain is exploding with growth and pruning in the first three to five years of life. It takes time for all of the neural circuits to fire repeatedly enough to create more lasting wiring patterns. (It is important that parents of younger children understand this so we don't assume our children should remember something just because we told them once or twice. This also helps explain why our kids need countless reminders to say please and thank you. Their forgetfulness usually stems, not from a willful refusal to comply with our requests, but from brains that have not yet fully matured.)

This form of memory does not come very easily for many adults either. For instance, a bright, articulate college student may not recall anything of his life story before about age thirteen. He makes straight A's at a highly esteemed university, but he can't remember being in the sixth grade. He is able to recall *as a fact* that Mr. Hancock was his sixth-grade teacher, but he cannot picture himself being in that class or "see" any events from that period of his life. He barely remembers the house he lived in before his family moved when he was sixteen, although he knows that he lived in Memphis.

Perhaps you relate to this student's story. If so, you may have great difficulty comprehending the trajectory of your life from beginning to end. This phenomenon will be explored in more detail in chapter 7, when we examine the role of attachment.

MEMORY IN THE BANK?

We sometimes think of memory as the mind's safe-deposit box, a place where we deposit valuables in the form of remembered experiences. Just as we might head to the bank to open the locked metal container where we store our grandfather's solid gold watch, so we might think that when we want to remember an event, we simply go to our brain's safe-deposit box to retrieve the event we want to examine. When we do, we assume it will be there, unchanged from when we last thought of it.

But memory is in fact *not* like that locked metal box. Every time we remember something, the memory itself changes, for the neural networks that are associated with that mental image are either reinforced to fire in a similar but slightly different fashion, or they are shaped and altered to fire differently. A simple example might help. If a young man who was just married yesterday is now recalling his wedding while sitting on a jet, the way he recalls his special day will be influenced by a particular set of feelings, images, and sensations as he waits for the plane to take off.

His current mental processes will influence the picture he already has in his mind of what happened the day before. In other words, the context in which he is remembering—both the setting and his feelings about it—will shape the very memory he is having. If he and his bride are departing for their honeymoon, his mental state will be of one sort. However, if he has just boarded a military transport plane that will touch down near an active military combat zone several hours from now, very different layers of his brain's networks will be actively interweaving their influence upon his hippocampus, synapsing with the neurons that represent the "unchangeable facts" of yesterday's ceremony. As this example illustrates, our memories are not static things that sit inertly in the safe-deposit box of our minds. They are changed by the very circumstantial information in which we both encode and recall the events in question.

The concept that there is no safe-deposit box, that memory is always changing, is related to the suggestion from neuroscience that as far as the brain is concerned, there is in fact no such thing as the past or the future. This does not mean that no real events have taken place in the past or that we cannot accurately anticipate the future. It does not imply that your sister's ill treatment of you or your coach's inappropriate sexual advances did not happen or that they're all in your head. Rather, it means that your brain, whether it is remembering the past or anticipating the future, is simply activating a particular set of neural networks. When fired, these networks create the awareness of a past event or images of the anticipated future. Your brain activity, however, is taking place only in the present moment. There is no "past" as such inherent in this activity.

This is important, given how much weight many people give to what they perceive as the past, as if it were an objective reality apart from what their brains are constructing in the present moment. So while you may have viewed the events of your life story as if they were irrevocably chiseled in granite, you have more power than you thought. You can begin to respond to this "objective reality" quite differently if you embrace the deeper reality that in some respects your past as you have viewed it doesn't even exist.

This has several advantages: first, it frees you to be more attentive to the present moment, the only time you will ever really have. Being in the present moment also reduces the body's anxiety markers (heart rate, blood pressure, breathing rate, cortisol output, etc.). Finally, when you are less anxious, you are more open to creativity in how you visualize and assemble your narrative. If you believe your past is fixed and there is nothing you can do to change it, you tend to respond in one of two ways. Given that the past cannot be changed, you simply "forget" it and move on. Or if incidents from your past are so overwhelming that you are constantly flooded by traumatic thoughts and memories, you may feel hopeless and unable to move forward. Either way, you will actually be stuck because your narrative will always be colored by the incidents you long to put behind you.

MEMORY AND THE CONSTRUCTION OF NARRATIVES

The hippocampus and prefrontal cortex, which must develop and become integrated before a person is capable of explicit memory, begin to mature at about the same time that the neural processing centers for language are being integrated. Your expanding factual and autobiographical memories, therefore, are tightly intertwined with words, which soon flow into rivers of thought, concepts, and ideas. But they do so in concert with the influence of implicit memory. The ongoing sequencing of your streaming mental images (including both implicit and explicit memories) is understood through the vehicles of thought and language. This becomes your history, your narrative.

You construct your understanding of the world and your place in it through the lens of your own story. And the manner and context in which you reflect on your story (in your mind) or tell your story (to others) become part of the fabric of the narrative itself. In other words, the process of reflecting on and telling others your story, and the way you experience others hearing it, actually shapes the story *and the very neural correlates, or networks, it represents.*

Additionally, we weave together our individual stories into the fabric that becomes the larger, more inclusive story of our community.

Perhaps when you were a young girl, your mom reacted with sympathy and warmth whenever you were sad after coming home from school or playing with friends. Each time she responded to you that way, a constellation of neurons was activated, and that network was reinforced and strengthened. You came to expect that your mom would validate you, even when you were unhappy.

If, on the other hand, every time you told your mom you were sad, she looked at you with derision, you felt ashamed as well as sad. Each time the two of you repeated this dance, your memory was strengthened and the association between shame and sadness became stronger.

Even as an adult, then, you are likely to avoid the conscious awareness of sadness at all costs, so that you may avoid the accompanying feeling of shame. This won't be good for your friendships, marriage, or parenting, as it will be difficult for you to be empathic with others' sadness. If, however, you encounter a therapist or a good friend who, when you feel sad, responds with empathy and comfort, your memory of the feeling of sadness will change, even if ever so little at first.

You will not have changed the facts of your past, but you will change your memory of it. You will also change your future because now that you have experienced a different reaction to your sadness, you can anticipate a different response. If you purposely recall the moment in which you felt empathy from your friend, you will continue to strengthen that memory and your future response to sadness.

How can a therapist's or friend's response have such a powerful effect on a long-held association between sadness and shame? Simply put, your right brain, with its nonverbal awareness, can be "surprised" by an encounter with another person's right brain. If, when you feel sad, you see a look of compassion rather than impatience or disgust, your right brain will register that response as something novel and likely respond with a different output of its own. Such a dramatic shift in your right-brain processing is necessary for such an association to change, and it is possible only when your right brain encounters another right brain. That is why cultivating deep, emotionally intimate friendships; engaging in psychotherapy; or meeting with a spiritual director can be so beneficial.

Writing Your Autobiography

Once you've journaled your answers to the questions on pages 274–275, consider handwriting your autobiography. Writing out your life story on a piece of paper requires focused attention and enables you to think more slowly and deliberately than you would if you were typing. This helps activate your right hemisphere, which is correlated with nonverbal and implicit memory—feelings, sensations, images, and perceptions—that is connected to the memory you are writing about. Inevitably, memories that you have not thought about for some time may surface as a result.

Of course, as you write by hand, you will also activate the left hemisphere, which processes information in a logical, linear fashion. This process of combining language (left mode) with visuospatial, nonverbal, implicit experience (right mode) causes neurons from the right and left hemispheres to synapse more robustly with each other. In other words, you foster the integration of your brain.

Start by thinking of your earliest memory. After you have recorded that memory, continue writing as much as you can remember about the first decade of your life in as much detail as you can. Do not become overwhelmed by trying to write about later events. Also, do not be concerned about keeping everything in strict chronological order. Simply record what comes to your mind, paying close attention to describe sensations, feelings, images, colors, and the like—not just factual events. Then continue with your second and third decade, and so forth.

After you have written for a while, choose a trusted friend, pastor, priest, spiritual director, or counselor to whom you would be willing to read your story and who would be equally willing to ask you questions about what you think and feel about your narrative. Ask yourself, *How did this experience of reading my narrative to a person I trust change what and how I remember and what I feel?*

You may sense that this could be somewhat intimidating, exposing the most intimate details of your life to another, especially if you have never done this before. Essentially, you are entering into what Paul reflects in 1 Corinthians 13:12. You are making possible the experience of being known. As you construct your narrative, you're likely to discover that your implicit and explicit memories are being woven together in a way that makes more sense, especially as you experience someone else listening to you in an empathic manner. You will begin to connect implicit memory with the events that produced them. That, in turn, will lead to greater awareness of the true source of your deepest feelings. As Brad discovered, his desire to avoid conflict had almost nothing to do with his wife and almost everything to do with his dad. This discovery enabled him to begin to alter his responses to those around him, and it can do the same for you today.

Once you have read your narrative to a confidant, go back and reread what you have written, paying close attention to what you feel as you read. If other memories begin to surface, feel free to add them. Over time, as you believe you have exhausted what you remember from one decade, proceed on to the next. You will soon see the tapestry of your life weaving together in colors and textures you were unaware of.

If you do not remember many details from your early childhood, do not despair. As you begin this process of remembering, reflecting, and telling your story to others, you will activate neural networks that have been dormant, perhaps for many years. This process of remembering will begin to wake them up. This does not guarantee that you will eventually remember every detail. However, you are likely to become consciously aware of many more memories, which will enhance and change your memory of your past and so shift your anticipation of your future.

One final reminder before we move into the area of emotion in chapter 6. God's Word is a written record that affirms the importance of paying attention to memory—and not simply to facts and not in a way that allows our implicit memory free rein over our behavior. As the psalmist writes,

> Praise the LORD, my soul;
>   all my inmost being, praise his holy name.
> Praise the LORD, my soul,
>   and forget not all his benefits—
> who forgives all your sins
>   and heals all your diseases,
> who redeems your life from the pit
>   and crowns you with love and compassion,
> who satisfies your desires with good things
>   so that your youth is renewed like the eagle's. (PSALM 103:1-5)

Even now, as modern science learns more about memory, Scripture reminds us that over three thousand years ago our ancestors were sure of what neuroscience is now confirming. For when we *remember* all of the benefits of the Lord—his forgiveness, healing, redeeming, crowning, satisfying, and renewing—in the fullness of our regenerated memories, our future, and the future of our children and of others with whom we are in relationship, will be changed.

THE BIBLE AS AUTOBIOGRAPHY

One reason many people find Scripture to be so regenerative is that, fundamentally, it is a story—one told by many different voices. All of its authors were confronted by a Person. And in the course of that encounter, whether it lasted a moment or over a lifetime, each storyteller was changed by that other Voice. He or she was transformed by a God who would not be limited by left-brain, logical, linear theology; reconstructed by a God who in the beginning got his hands dirty in the soil of creation and later got them bloodied in the agony and beauty of redemption.

God knows that unless our right brains are transformed and our neural networks are integrated from left to right and from bottom to top, we will remain in the narrow, constricting, well-hewn grooves of the networks we have formed over our lifetimes and that we so often help create in our children.

Notice how, in the Scripture passages listed at the beginning of this chapter (pages 64–65), the speakers aren't simply inviting the original audience (or us) to conjure up facts about God or history. Rather, they and we are called to greater connection and intimacy with God, our neighbors, and the earth. Remembering, therefore, is not simply a function of the mind. It is an embodied expression of our lives as we recall the concrete, earthbound actions of God and people. It is an invitation to grace and adventure that involves all God's people. It is not just the past in our heads. It is the present in our doing.

That is why I believe that faithfully telling and listening to our stories is one of the single most important things we can do as followers of Jesus. Storytelling inevitably engages our memories—both the speakers' and the hearers'—and so opens the door to a different future. The Bible is so powerful in part because it contains the *story* of creation, rebellion, redemption, and recreation, all of which are told in the rich, messy, beautiful, tragic, hopeful tapestry of the lives of God's ancient people.

In Deuteronomy 6, Moses admonishes the people of Israel to remember that the Lord is the one and only God and to love him with "all [their] heart and with all [their] soul and with all [their] strength" (v. 5). But he does not stop there. Instead, he goes on to give a detailed description of how the people are to remember God:

> These commandments that I give you today are to be on your hearts.
> Impress them on your children. Talk about them when you sit at
> home and when you walk along the road, when you lie down and

when you get up. Tie them as symbols on your hands and bind them on your foreheads. Write them on the doorframes of your houses and on your gates. (vv. 6-9)

In these verses Moses offers various everyday settings in which the Israelites can construct memories. These activities are not intended just to get them to recall facts about the past. They are intended to integrate all of the right and left hemispheres of the people.

In verse 10 Moses transitions to the future, indicating that remembering and telling their story would affect the Hebrews' experience as a community in the coming months and years:

When the Lord your God brings you into the land he swore to your fathers, to Abraham, Isaac and Jacob, to give you—a land with large, flourishing cities you did not build, houses filled with all kinds of good things you did not provide, wells you did not dig, and vineyards and olive groves you did not plant—then when you eat and are satisfied, *be careful that you do not forget the LORD, who brought you out of Egypt, out of the land of slavery.* (vv. 10-12, ITALICS MINE)

Moses reminds the Hebrews that they are to engage their collective memory about how God, a real Person who appeared to them in the form of a pillar of fire by night and a cloud by day, accomplished tangible, earthbound deeds for them. God did not intend the law of the Ten Commandments to substitute for a relationship with him. He did not simply issue a systematic list of logical, linear, literal dictates intended to speak only to the Hebrews' left brains.

In other words, Moses is not simply asking the Hebrews to remember facts about the past, which would involve only their hippocampi. Instead, they are to engage in actions that integrate their right and left hemispheres. As they recount the story of the Exodus again and again, the Israelites will express so many things:

- the agony of grieving mothers at the hand of a frightened despot
- the humiliation of slavery and powerlessness
- the mixture of hope and worry in the face of strange and sometimes devastating forces of nature
- the odor of lamb's blood everywhere

- the screams following the sudden death of the Egyptians' firstborn sons and daughters
- the chaos of a million or more refugees, suddenly on the move to literally God knows where
- the surreal drainage of a sea that a moment before had appeared to be a death sentence
- foaming, flaming-eyed horses drowning under the weight of greed
- unfathomable exhaustion and relief

Picture a Hebrew family gathered comfortably around a table decades later. They are eating good food and listening to an elderly family member recount the story of their people's deliverance. The entire drama of the Exodus shared over bread and boiled lamb shank will be seen, smelled, and felt by the listeners. The family members will take in the speaker's nonverbal cues, and that mealtime will become part of the larger landscape of the people's story. The storyteller himself will recognize the amazement in the eyes of his listeners and his original memory will be revitalized—and expanded—in his own mind. He will come away from the telling with an even deeper awareness of his relationship with God and more confident of God's ultimate protection. His family's present and future will be shaped by the *telling* of the story—not just the facts of the story.

To love God with all of our mind is to engage our entire memory, not limited parts of it. To love God means not being limited to logical sequences of systematic theology. Loving God is autobiographical. It is about remembering our past and anticipating our future. It is about a God who will not be kept at a distance but uses each of our stories to confront, terrify, comfort, convict, and woo us.

REMEMBERING GOD

Patients often tell me that even though they don't trust others, at least they trust God. That simply isn't true.

They may believe that God is more trustworthy than other people; however, that doesn't mean they truly trust him. The truth, thanks to our neural networks, is that we all tend to do with God exactly what we do with the people in our lives.

Your memory creates your future. That's because you imagine the future through the neural networks created by your past. It was true for the Hebrews, and it is true for you today. The experiences that will drive your responses in the future are embedded within your memory. No wonder, then, that we often struggle to release ourselves to God. We may have no template in our brains to facilitate that process.

The way you understand and try to make sense of Jesus will be filtered through your memory and your story. That's because God generally works through the system that he created and called good, our mind/brain matrix. He uses our implicit and explicit memory functions, not only to draw us closer to him, but also to heal, renew, and vitalize those very functions. And this doesn't happen only metaphorically.

I think we are often surprised at the ways we don't trust Jesus, simply because he frequently contends with those shards of ourselves that are either too wounded or too asleep to trust him. He wants to heal and awaken those dimensions, but we are often just as loathe to trust *him* with those parts as we are to trust others with them. That is why the Incarnation is such a beautiful idea. God, in Jesus, came to touch our minds—and that includes our brains. The question is whether we will encounter Jesus as he is rather than the way our implicit and explicit memories filter him to be. (Of course, since all our thoughts, feelings, senses, and understanding of God are filtered through our humanity, no one has a completely accurate understanding of deity. Some experiences of Jesus, though, are closer than others.)

But what if you have few experiences—and thus few neural correlates— to help you understand how it feels to be truly loved, forgiven, or comforted? What if most of your experiences have taught you that you need to keep your emotional distance from others? Or what if you tend to become impulsively and wholly absorbed by relationships, only to find that you have no sense of yourself or what you want?

You won't necessarily feel Jesus' compassion and forgiveness just because someone tells you about them. While they might make logical sense, and you might even occasionally experience what it means to forgive or be forgiven, your experiences may have been so infrequent that they aren't easily transferred to other situations requiring forgiveness. Likewise, you probably believe in patience, kindness, and forgiveness, yet you may find them hard to embody.

For forgiveness to be established within you so that it flows as effortlessly as your breathing, you need to have some mental model of what forgiveness *feels like in your memory*. Otherwise, your life will feel dry as dust even if your theology is razor sharp. Despite what you assent to ideologically, you will still lose your patience when your twelve-year-old spills his drink all over the keyboard, even though you've told him over and over not to eat or drink near the computer. When he apologizes for destroying the keyboard, forgiveness will not be your default response. If forgiveness hasn't been modeled for you, it will also be quite difficult for you to anticipate a future in which you will readily forgive.

THE FORGETFUL PROPHET

Fortunately, Scripture is replete with stories that provide ample imagery of the God who comes to find us despite our memory lapses. Consider the prophet Elijah. First Kings 18–19 records his deadly confrontation with the priests who represented the cultic worship of Ba'al. In answer to Elijah's prayer, fire fell from heaven, supremely demonstrating Yahweh's power and authority, after which the prophet and his allies slaughtered the pagan priests. In so doing, Elijah directly challenged not only the religious system but also the political establishment led by King Ahab, a passive, frightened ruler nagged by his angry, browbeating wife Jezebel. God put on a spectacular show— unforgettable, in fact. Or was it?

After the consuming inferno, Ahab, behaving more like a young and immature boy than an adult, quickly ran to his queen to report on the events. The power-mongering Jezebel then sent the prophet a threatening message: by this time tomorrow, you're a dead man.

Though fearless in the face of the impotent Ahab, Elijah was terrified by the domineering Jezebel. He wasted no time fleeing to another country at least eighty miles away. That was a lot of sandal tread. He burrowed deep into the desert, expecting to die in the wilderness. The day before, he was telling the king what to do. This day, he was done. Finished. What was *that* about? Within hours of facing down nearly one thousand religious leaders (who were now dead at his behest), he was turning tail in the face of this angry woman and her henchmen. How is it that Elijah, who seemed to act with fearless-ness before the false prophets, shifted so quickly to a position of resigned hopelessness?

The real answer, of course, is I don't know. Elijah had just experienced God taking action in real time and space, answering him at his personal request— but suddenly seemed to be having trouble remembering that. Yes, he could recall as facts what had happened, but those facts seemed to be, at the moment he headed for the hills, simply facts. He lacked the dynamism and vitality to enable him to confront the queen in the way he had the king.

Obviously, we don't have CNN's Anderson Cooper interview to provide us

Elijah's inner machinations on the subject. Based on the account in 1 Kings, Jezebel appears to have been the real power behind the throne, the one who ultimately ran the political machine of which her husband was the titular head. It's possible that Elijah, knowing this, really did have something to be afraid of with her, which was not the case with Ahab. But that does not leave us without questions which, in turn, lead to some possible speculations. For instance, what experiences did Elijah have as a boy and young man that shaped his unconscious responses to particular interpersonal encounters, such as those with an angry, domineering woman? Considering Elijah's sudden behavioral shift, we have reason to consider that he is "remembering" when he flees Jezebel's wrath. We could surmise that his implicit memory was overwhelming even his capacity to take in the full weight and meaning of what he could recall explicitly—yesterday's firestorm. His implicit responses took over and began to create his imagined future. He began to consider a more pessimistic outcome. The only future he saw had him in a pine box.

Our lives seem to be so much like that of Elijah. How is it that we somehow "forget" what God has done in our lives and regress to old ways of living? Even though we have felt Jesus' forgiveness, why do we have trouble granting that same absolution to family members who have mistreated us for years?

Even when we know the facts about God's grace, we still often feel ashamed and inadequate. Even though we love our children, we still pick the most inopportune times to lose our tempers with them, shaming them with the backwash of our own unresolved hurts and fears. Like Elijah, we sometimes focus on more pessimistic outcomes for our lives, unaware that our implicit memory is taking charge of how we consider our future.

Yet there is great hope to be found in Elijah's story. That's because God went out to meet Elijah at the cave where he was hiding. He sent the angel of the Lord to comfort and care for him. Then, instead of immediately telling Elijah what to do or solving his problem for him, God asked him: "What are you doing here?" (1 Kings 19:9).

When Elijah admitted his fears, God did not dismiss, minimize, or ridicule him. And while he promised to pass by Elijah, he didn't reveal himself to his prophet in the mighty wind, earthquake, or fire that Elijah saw. All these fierce acts of nature would likely have driven Elijah back into the deep recesses of the cave—both in the mountain and in his mind and memory. Rather, God called to him in a gentle whisper. He did not overwhelm him but answered Elijah's terror and hopelessness with a quiet voice that transformed Elijah's experience. As a result, Elijah's remembered future was changed.

Once God had Elijah's attention by gently calling him out, he inquired again, "What are you doing here?" (v. 13). He then gave Elijah an assignment: the prophet was to go back the way he came and, along the way, carry out different, more confident actions that reflected the truth about the state of the political as well as spiritual landscape. In fact, Elijah was not alone but was one of seven thousand who had remained faithful to Yahweh and whom Yahweh promised to preserve (vv. 15-18).

God does this with all of us. First he comes to our deserts and lonely mountains. He asks us questions, sometimes difficult ones that may initially drive us deep into the caves of our own minds, into the recesses of old neural pathways and ancient, repetitive memories. His probing may leave us exhausted, famished, and terrified. His queries may even elicit the very feelings we try so hard to avoid. Often the question is simply, *What are you doing here?* He never asks with scorn or derision but always with hope and anticipation. He asks with the tone of a God who is eager for us to retrace our neural pathways, to eventually take a different route and create a new end to our story. To "remember" our future differently.

Sometimes we are not paying attention, but God does not cease his pursuit. He whispers again, inviting us to meet with him, to wrestle, to complain, and to weep. When we are finished, he gently asks again, *What are you doing here?* Each time he asks, we tell our story differently, for now it must include the experience of hearing a Voice telling us that we are not alone. And hearing that voice will change our memories and the way we live our futures.

And we have even more reason to hope. While it's true that established neural networks are most likely to fire, it's equally true that recent research demonstrates that our brains were created with beautiful and mysterious plasticity. That means our neurons can be redirected in ways that correlate with joy, peace, patience, kindness, goodness, faithfulness, gentleness, and self-control. Instead of automatically following the wired sequence of our old memory, with reflection, we can choose to create new pathways. There is one requirement: we must pay attention to how our memory is manifesting itself by answering questions like, *What are you doing here?*

Chapter 6

EMOTION:
THE EXPERIENCE OF GOD

W hat do you feel?"

As you might expect, I ask my patients this question—or a variation of it—almost every time we meet. Though the way I phrase the question doesn't vary much, the responses do:

"I don't feel anything at all."

"I'm feeling anxious."

"I feel like my boss does not understand me."

"I feel like leaving my marriage."

"I feel confused."

"I don't know" (which is perhaps the most common response of all).

Those who are unable to identify their emotions often see them as a nuisance, an obstacle to clear thinking that needs to be tamed by rational processes. Patients frequently tell me they wish they did not feel angry. Others admit they feel needy, which reinforces their feelings of being weak. Then they feel guilty because they're sure God is not pleased with them feeling—let alone being—weak.

"If we could just dispense with all these . . . *feelings*," people lament when they're dealing with depression, grief, and shame, "the world would be a better place. At least that's how I feel."

This disdain toward our emotions often influences our life with God.

That's because emotion is the very energy around which the brain organizes itself. Without emotion, life would come to a standstill. It is the means by which we experience and connect with God, others, and ourselves in the most basic way possible.

My patients are often surprised when I suggest that emotion is much more important and vital to God than it has been to them. They are equally surprised to discover that God is very interested in our emotions, and (among other things) experiences us through them. I am not implying that God needs any created thing apart from himself. But what if emotion, or something similar that is even deeper, wilder, and more real, is an essential element of who God is? What if emotion, as we understand it, is a reflection of what God experiences in his heart? Wouldn't we do well to attend to this aspect of our minds, since doing so would mean paying attention to a part of us that reflects God's being (albeit ours is a less intense version)? Does this sound far-fetched? Allow yourself to take in the following passages of Scripture.

> Though the mountains be shaken
>> and the hills be removed,
> yet my unfailing love for you will not be shaken
>> nor my covenant of peace be removed,"
>> says the LORD, who has compassion on you. (ISAIAH 54:10)

> How can I give you up, Ephraim?
>> How can I hand you over, Israel?
> How can I treat you like Admah?
>> How can I make you like Zeboyim?
> My heart is changed within me;
>> all my compassion is aroused.
> I will not carry out my fierce anger,
>> nor will I devastate Ephraim again.
> For I am God, and not a human being—
>> The Holy One among you. (HOSEA 11:8-9)

Imagine, if you will, what this tells you about what God is *feeling* as he speaks these words through the prophet. More specifically, from the context as well as the language itself, imagine what you sense God sounding like, looking like—his demeanor or what you imagine his facial expression would be. Some who read these passages may sense the longing in God's queries while others may not. Reflect on your response to the notion of God's compassion being aroused, or the image of his fierce anger. Are your thoughts limited to your "thinking about" these feelings, or do you also notice feeling something yourself as you ponder what you are reading?

Now look at this verse from the first book of the Bible:

> The LORD regretted that he had made human beings on the earth, and his heart was deeply troubled. (GENESIS 6:6)

This is one of the most poignant sentences in all of Scripture. Not only does it describe God's emotional experience, it connects his emotional response directly to humankind. It's one thing for us to contend with the deep, painful emotions of another human. But how do we feel as we reflect upon and connect with God's experience of pain and sorrow in light of his having made us? Such passages reflect how the people of God have experienced him over the centuries and illustrate how powerfully emotion links us to God.

What is this phenomenon we call emotion, anyway? How are we helped by paying attention to it? How can we begin to connect emotion to how and what we remember? How will being more aware of its forms change our experience of relating with God and with others? These are important questions, for we will see how, if we ignore emotion, we do so to our peril, for to ignore it is to ignore the voice of God.

THE BOTTOMLESS WELL OF EMOTION

One reason we underestimate the importance of emotion in our relationships with God and others is that we have an incomplete understanding of its role, specifically how feelings are experienced and expressed. Before we look more deeply into how to strengthen our emotional connection with others, therefore, let's define what we mean by emotion. (By the way, I'm not suggesting that there is a unifying, static definition of emotion. For one thing, as with all areas of brain function, our knowledge about emotions is constantly growing. In addition, researchers from various fields emphasize different aspects of emotion when they use the term because they are examining different characteristics of emotion. However, I do believe it's helpful to have a working definition for the particular facets of emotion we'll examine as we explore the role of emotion in our seeking for God's Kingdom.)

When asked to describe emotion, most of us refer to it in terms of sadness, happiness, shame, fear, anger, guilt, or other feelings. We can all relate to these states of being, and most people (though not all) can readily distinguish one feeling from another. We know that feeling guilty is qualitatively different from feeling joy or sadness or anger.

How do our brains enable us to make these distinctions? Many people assume emotions are tied to external events alone—we feel guilty because we have hurt a friend or we feel joy because someone has praised us. Terms like *ashamed, guilty,* and *afraid* are helpful, but we also experience and express our emotions in ways that we do not commonly consider. Before we are consciously aware of a particular feeling, our bodies have already begun to react.

Down deep: primary emotion

Imagine for a moment sitting with friends in their living room. The sky is bright outside their picture window, and you're immersed in a warm, friendly conversation. You are comfortable and relaxed, with a conscious awareness of feeling contented and happy in the presence of your friends. On some level, you are aware that you are "pleased with feeling pleased."

As you talk, you and your friends hear something rap on the window. How do you react? Your initial response is driven by primary emotion. When startled, parts of your peripheral nervous system respond without your conscious awareness. That means your breathing and heart rates, along with your blood pressure, muscle tone, and sweat rate, elevate. In addition, your brain signals your adrenal glands to increase the production of stress hormones.

Brain time is measured in microseconds to nanoseconds, so long before you become consciously aware that something has hit the window, your central nervous system is collecting and synthesizing data from several sources and preparing your physical response. To prepare your body for action, it sends signals to your peripheral sensory nervous system, including your auditory, muscle, and internal organ systems.

Throughout this process, your brain experiences a surge in energy, changing its pattern of energy flow—the electrical firing patterns of the neurons. The right hemisphere registers electrical impulses as it senses both distinct and subtle changes in your state. Neurons in this region also register any primal emotional responses you might experience but neither be aware of nor find easy to put into words.

The energy shift involves multiple parts of the brain, including the left hemisphere. This process integrates the brain, electrically connecting different parts of it—in this case, integrating the two hemispheres and the lower, deeper regions with higher cortical ones. This process is largely removed from the parts of the brain that register conscious awareness or rational thought. Your brain does not "think" of this event initially in terms of something hitting a window so much as it registers a cumulative shift in the patterns of electrical firing throughout the various neural networks that have been activated in response to this particular stimulus.

Actually, what happens next will depend a great deal on what has hit the window. Let's say a small bird accidentally flew into it and glanced off the glass. You might all briefly turn your attention to the noise, but if the bird flies off unharmed, your attention will quickly return to your conversation and your physiologic readings return to normal within a few seconds.

How does your response differ if, instead of a bird flying into the window, the rapping noise comes from another friend greeting the rest of you just before he enters the house and joins you in the living room? In this case, your primary physical/mental responses are likely to be more lasting and eventually lead to a predictable feeling of pleasure at the arrival of your friend. Long before you are consciously aware of feeling pleasure, however, your body is sending the basic signals that predispose you to have that particular feeling. The duration and intensity of these primary sensations are significant enough that your brain is able to compare this particular state (happiness) to other times when you have experienced it. It *remembers* those occasions through the circuitry responsible for implicit memory and ultimately brings you to the point of awareness of pleasure at seeing your friend.

But what if the knocking comes from a stranger wielding a handgun? You experience an entirely different set of emotions in this scenario. Those emotions quickly cascade into a state you might describe as fear. Your body registers signals that lead to feelings caused by fright, comparing your fear to other situations that stirred up this feeling.

These three examples—the bird, your friend, and the stranger with the handgun—display the two important stages of primary emotion. The first stage in this progression is called *initial orientation*. This refers to the orienting process that occurs when your attention is drawn to a stimulus. This happens quickly, and your attention shift is the first indication of a surge in energy.

Following this initial orientation, your brain, through the many networks that represent implicit memory and incorporate the brain stem (fight-or-flight mechanism) and the limbic circuitry (emotion, fear recognition, etc.), moves to assess the stimulus in terms of relative levels of safety and/or attraction. Is this something that you need or want to continue to attend to? This second phase of primary emotion is called *appraisal and arousal.*

Your brain (again, using layers of neurons that are often not connected with consciousness) appraises the setting and arouses the rest of your brain/body system for appropriate action. You either become more fully drawn to the stimulus (because it is important to pay attention to, either because you like it or dislike it a great deal) or you disregard it. Different settings will create very different primary emotional responses.

The brain is constantly monitoring the landscape, both internally and externally, even when you are sleeping. It is an anticipation machine, comparing what it is experiencing in the present moment with what has occurred in the past (using both implicit and explicit neural memory), in order to prepare it for future action. This constant monitoring and shifting in energy is the activity around which the brain organizes itself. This is emotion. The origin of our word *emotion* is grounded in the idea of e-motion, or preparing for motion. That is why the phenomenon of emotion is deeply tied to ongoing action or movement. We cannot separate what we feel from what we do.

When faced with an unexpected event, we may also be aware of mental activity that may not be fully expressed in the form of clear thoughts or words. These sensations accumulate quite quickly. They are preverbal and not necessarily linked with physical awareness. These perceptions, while difficult to describe with words, may form as images or diffuse, amorphous impressions that create a deep awareness of *something shifting* within us. This shift leads to either an enhanced or diminished sense of well-being, as well as an enhanced or diminished sense of being connected within ourselves and others.

Again, much of this activity is correlated with deeper, lower regions of the brain, such as the brain stem, thalamus, limbic circuitry, and lower temporal cortex, that are responsible for activity that does not immediately reach our conscious awareness. Such emotion originates from areas of the brain that we do not consciously control and that resemble the brains of lower mammals and reptiles, keeping us connected to the rest of creation. At the same time, an integrating, oscillating wave of electrical activity is continuously moving back and forth across the entire brain. This wave may be one way that the brain brings together its disparate areas into a convergent whole, creating our overall sense of what we feel.

Primary emotions are experienced through your sensory perceptions (such as heaviness in your chest or tingling in your hands or feet) and more diffuse mental imagery; they are further expressed by other physical behaviors. For example, as part of your primary response, you may cross your arms, set your jaw, or tighten the muscles in your back or neck. You may lift your eyebrows, groan, frown, or smile. These physical phenomena in turn reinforce the sensory feedback loop by sending messages back to the brain that inform it of its ongoing state.

On the surface: categorical emotion

Eventually, as these moments expand into longer, more intensified time periods, we become aware (if we are paying attention) of the qualitatively distinct states of feelings we call *categorical emotion*. These are what we generally mean when we talk about emotions. They include shame, guilt, anger, sadness, joy, and fear, to name a few. At this time researchers don't know specifically how we become aware of these particular states. We speculate, though, that they develop, not only out of our inner neural and experiential activity, but out of our interactions with the neural and experiential activity of others' minds.

THE REALITY ABOUT EMOTION

As we've seen, emotions go much deeper than feelings that we can readily name like joy, fear, and sadness. What else do we know about emotions that will help us relate better to God and other people?

1. *Emotion is something that you regulate* and *that regulates you.* Your awareness of it—how much you pay attention to it (there you are again, paying attention to what you are paying attention to)—enables you to harness it for the purpose of growth in your relationship with God and others.

2. *Emotional states are not influenced or created in isolation.* Your emotional states have a profound impact on others—especially your children. The more you pay attention to your primary emotional states, the more you are able to truly and effectively perceive others' emotional states as well.

3. *Emotion is not debatable.* If your daughter senses the feeling of joy, shame, disappointment, or some general form of distress, that is in fact what she feels. She may not easily have words for the affect, but she does sense it. If she cries because she was cut from the basketball squad, there's no sense in telling her, "You shouldn't be sad about not making the team. Lots of people were cut." And it would be very counterproductive to say,

"Enough of the crying already! I might expect that from your four-year-old sister, but not from you." This would shame her for expressing the emotion she senses.

In both cases, it is important to realize that your daughter's primary and categorical emotional states *are not opinions to be countered. They are true experiences that require attention.* Here again I will point out that it is through the brain's medium of emotion that God most frequently addresses us. If we ignore, deny, or debate these feelings, we are ignoring God's messengers. This does not mean that emotional states *are* God and therefore have the right to have dominion over us. No, rather they are nondebatable communiqués that require a mindful, attentive, and balanced response.

4. *While categorical emotions are universal across time, cultures, and gender, primary emotion does not always present itself in the same way.* You experience the same sensations of categorical feelings as everyone else. What is intriguing, however, is that you may express your primary emotion differently than other people having the same categorical emotion. When you witness an expression of primary emotion in someone else (whether a facial expression, a sigh, a tone of voice), that response may mean something very different to you than it does to the one who is expressing it. This can lead to all sorts of interpersonal disconnection.

EMOTIONAL DISCONNECT

Let's say you are meeting your wife at the train station after work. As you walk up to her, you notice her facial expression. Immediately you sense a tightening in your jaw and neck muscles as your brain quickly adjusts to your interpretation that she is angry or upset with you. You have seen this expression a thousand times before, and you know exactly what it means. It is the universal sign for *I'm angry at you, you insensitive slug who's trying to pass as a human male, and now is the time to grovel.* You suddenly and automatically (with the assistance of implicit memory input that you are unaware of) employ the appropriate countermaneuver that consistently eases her (and your) pain: you look at your shoes.

You believe this action will create the distance and time your wife needs to forget that you exist and that she is angry with you, at least for the next few minutes. This seldom works. And the reason it doesn't work is this. Although you have seen this expression a thousand times, most of those times it wasn't coming from your wife. It was coming from your mother, who was in fact angry with you. She may not have been very effective at paying attention to your emotional states, perhaps due to her lack of awareness of her own emotions. For that reason, she did not notice how her anger affected you. In order to cope with the unpleasant feelings her anger caused you, you may have learned to distance yourself from her gaze. You would do this by—that's right—looking at your shoes. Since no one helped you process what you were feeling, you never learned how to address what you felt in a conscious way. In fact, you might not even be aware that you felt hurt, afraid, and ashamed.

But since looking at your footwear effectively reduced the intense primary feelings you experienced at the time, you continue to repeat this behavior. Your brain (especially your right hemisphere) is wired in such a way that whenever it captures this same set of stimuli from nonverbal signals, it reacts with a similar, virtually automatic neural network firing pattern that leads to the behavior of avoidance.

You have little awareness that your actions toward your wife have anything to do with your relationship with your mother. Essentially, you are experiencing implicit memory responses translated through your primary emotional states. These make sense in the context of your relationship with your mother, but not your wife. What you interpret as her expression of anger may actually result from her feelings of anxiety or fear. Perhaps she is not angry with you at all. Instead of feeling upset and distant, she may feel needy and want greater closeness. Looking at your shoes in silence with your heart rate increasing does not calm her anxiety. Instead it heightens it (along with the slug-value she assigns to you).

In this case, paying attention to your primary emotional responses and connecting them to your implicit memory can bring freedom in your relationship. Instead of automatically reacting to your wife's facial expression by gazing at your shoes, you might ask her what she is feeling. Once you respond based on her true feelings rather than the signals you receive from your own brain's circuitry, you are likely to respond much more effectively. This is not easy, however, and it takes practice; often it requires the presence of another mind, as Erin found out.

THE VALUE OF FEELING FELT

Erin came to see me to get help with her depression. She was an architect, committed to her husband and to God. Although quiet and constitutionally shy, she was easily likeable. On the surface I could identify no obvious tragic elements in her life story.

But one day I asked her to tell me the narrative of her childhood. As she began, her face, usually fairly expressionless, changed, as did the tone of her body posture. She talked about her parents' heated arguments and the sharp memory of her intense fear that they would divorce. Although the details of those fights were fuzzy, she recalled with precision the distress she experienced, though she had no recollection of her mother or father ever acknowledging her pain. As she moved further into her memory of these events, her voice grew quiet and words failed her. Tears welled in her eyes. She stopped talking and averted her gaze. Her arms were crossed and her fists clenched.

In earlier sessions, I had sometimes asked Erin what she was feeling. She often pondered her answer before stating helplessly, "I'm not sure." On this occasion, I asked her not what she felt, but rather *where* she was feeling anything. When she gave me a quizzical glance, I clarified, "Where in your body do you sense yourself feeling anything?"

Erin thought for a moment and then declared with a slight sense of growing discovery that she felt tightness in her chest and a constriction in her throat. I wondered aloud if she noticed feeling anything in any other places. I pointed out her body posture and facial expression. I acknowledged her tears. I told her that it must not be easy to feel what she was feeling, given how she appeared. In addition, I noted how frightening and painful it must have been—not only when she was a young girl, but also right at that moment as she shared her story with me—to be so worried about her parents and not have anyone to talk with about it.

As I remarked on her story and what I was observing in her, I noticed changes in my own emotional state. I, too, felt a heaviness in my chest. Tears came to my eyes as well. In addition, I not only sensed what she sensed, I *sensed her sensing my sensing what she felt*. She was having the experience of what Dan Siegel describes as *feeling felt*. Her response to my observations and to my feeling what she was feeling was a visible relaxation in her body posture and facial expression.

I then encouraged Erin to consider how she would describe the feelings she had been experiencing up to that point. She was able to articulate that she felt afraid, sad, and embarrassed. These words represented categorical emotional states that she was previously unable to imagine in words in her mind. With no small sense of liberation she first admitted her awareness of these physical manifestations of emotion; when I asked what she felt (not what she "thought") after I had acknowledged her primary emotions, she said she felt relaxed and relieved.

Notice that for Erin to come to a place of greater "integration," both our brains must work in concert. From two minds emerges a process that leaves her feeling more connected and coherent, less alone, and most important, less fearful of being present with the emotions she has just experienced.

That I felt what Erin felt indicates that my feelings and actions were *contingent* upon, or influenced by and dependent on, her own feelings and behaviors. This required that I first *attune* to her. This is another important aspect of emotion. Our fluctuations in energy are highly influenced by the fluctuations in other people's minds. Our brains tend to look for and influence each other, even when we are not paying attention. Our right hemispheres tend to capture and respond to nonverbal stimuli that originate from the right hemispheres of others' brains, often without us even noticing.

This connection can be both good and not so good. It is what marketing and advertising executives count on. They count on our *not* paying attention to how their nonverbal (as well as verbal) stimuli are shaping us. This is good for Madison Avenue. It's not always so good for relationships. If I don't pay attention to my friend's body language (and my reactions to it, both internal and external) I may find myself saying and doing things that can be hurtful.

The fact that the brain responds in such an interdependent, contingent manner reminds us that there is no such thing as a true individual. Each of us is influenced, whether we are aware of it or not, by the contingent emotional experience of others around us. It is not possible for us *not* to influence others or *not* to be influenced by others. Our brains develop, and as such so do our communities, relative to our level of attunement to the emotion that moves within and between us.

Thus it is no surprise that the whole of Scripture points to the idea that God is not first and foremost intending to save us as individuals. His desire is to redeem the entire world, and we *as a body of people, inextricably connected by emotion* are being saved in the process. Thinking of ourselves as individuals is common in the West, but such thinking is much more limited to a left-hemisphere way of the mind rather than a more integrated way. To live in the way of love requires that I pay attention to the fact that my mind, through the process of emotion, longs to be connected to others. Paul as much as says this in his letters to the churches at Corinth and Colossae, as we will see in later chapters. Thus, what we are learning about the brain in terms of emotional attunement and contingency points to what the Hebrews and followers of Jesus have believed for over three thousand years.

FEELING LIKE GOD

While we often miss cues about others' emotional states, we generally pay even less attention to our emotional response to God and his response to us. And when we do sense his feeling toward us, it's often not good. We "believe"—cognitively assent with our left brains—that God feels good things about us even as we suspect that he is disappointed in us.

Numerous Scriptures show something quite different. Does the following verse sound as if it comes from a distant, hostile deity?

> Yet the LORD longs to be gracious to you;
>   therefore he will rise up to show you compassion. (ISAIAH 30:18)

Nor is God into manipulation or force. He is into active, direct, contingent persuasion. We see that in Moses' encounter with the angel of God in the manifestation of a burning shrub. Exodus 3:3 tells us that Moses considered the bush and decided to investigate. What comes next is important: "When the LORD saw that he [Moses] had gone over to look, God called to him from within the bush, 'Moses! Moses!'" (v. 4). Notice that God's action came in response to Moses' movement. God certainly appears to have taken initiative in this story, but he did not overwhelm Moses. God's engagement was contingent upon Moses' emotional/behavioral, or mind/body state.

Later, in Exodus 32, God is seemingly overwhelmed with his own anger in response to the outrageous behavior of the Hebrews, who have begun to worship a golden calf. He asks Moses to "leave me alone"; he "relents" from his anger only after Moses pleads on behalf of the Israelites. It is easy to assume that God yielded in the face of the logical, rational argument that Moses made. Or perhaps that God had developed short-term memory loss and changed his mind when he was reminded of the facts that Moses presented.

Could it be that God responded, not only (or even mostly) to the facts presented by Moses, but to Moses' pleading? Reflect what Moses would have felt, especially in the presence of an angry God. It's not hard to imagine his fear and anxiety at God's offer to create a new nation from Moses' line. Imagine Moses' nonverbal cues: his facial expression, his tone of voice, and his gestures.

Might not God have been acting in response to Moses' emotion? If so, in a sense God's "right brain" was responding to Moses' right brain.

The point, of course, is that God attunes to us and feels and acts contingently. We influence him through our emotional states. Certainly through Scripture we see that God feels joy, hurt, surprise, delight, grief, anger, distance, and a multitude of other things in response to us. Our problem is that often we do not take ourselves seriously enough to believe we have that much influence on the One who created the universe.

David, the second king of the Hebrews, gives us a taste of one who lived an emotionally contingent life with God and who apparently believed that he affected God contingently as well. David was not simply paying theological lip service either. We are told that David was chosen as king because of his heart relationship with God. He was not chosen simply to agree with and carry out what God wanted people to do. In 1 Samuel 16 we read that God was interested not in David's stature or his accomplishments alone but in something God saw that others, including David's own father and the prophet and judge Samuel, could not see—the condition of David's heart. From a perspective of neuroscience, this notion of "heart" would largely be a subject of (but not only of) emotion.

A man after God's own heart

David is the author of numerous songs and poems, many within the book of Psalms, that give us a glimpse into his heart. But I invite you to attend to another story in which David engaged God's heart in a situation that was anything but pleasant. The incident follows David's adulterous liaison with Bathsheba, the wife of one of David's soldiers, Uriah the Hittite. When Bathsheba discovers she has become pregnant with David's child while her husband is off fighting valiantly for the king, David has Uriah killed. (See 2 Samuel 11–12 for more details.)

In the wake of David's nastiness—the abuse of power and adultery, the lying, the murder, and above all the cowardice—the prophet Nathan confronts David. Interestingly, Nathan does not address the problem directly. He does not appeal to David's left-mode, logical, linear thinking by saying, "Hey pal, as you are aware, you messed with the wrong woman. God knows all about it, and now you're going to pay." Nor does he ask an inane question like, "So, Dave, been out in the neighborhood checking out bathing women?" or "Had sex with anyone lately who wasn't your wife and then had her husband killed?" Instead, Nathan tells a story, much as Jesus would do a few centuries later. The prophet outflanks the logical, linear Maginot line in David's brain with his tale of a rich man who steals the lone lamb of a poor man.

As we have seen, the power of storytelling goes beyond the border of the story itself. It moves into the nooks and crannies of our memories and emotions, sometimes gently, sometimes explosively, revealing, awakening, shocking, calling. This is what happens to David, and his *heart* is revealed. He is caught off guard when the story brings his right hemisphere to life unexpectedly. In fact, he is undone. Nathan tells a story that pierces David to the core. His first words in response to Nathan's confrontation are simply, "I have sinned against the LORD" (2 Samuel 12:13).

Notice that David does not mention Bathsheba or Uriah. He does not speak about how to spin this situation in the newspapers or how to handle the political fallout. He speaks about what he has done to *God*. Hurt *God*. Saddened *God*. Betrayed *God*. He is broken in the realm in which he most intimately and primitively experiences God—his emotion. He puts into words what his heart feels God feeling in the wake of his actions. And although his behavior with Bathsheba is inexcusable, his response to Nathan is fully consistent with who God had known him to be from the beginning—a man "after [God's] own heart" (1 Samuel 13:14).

David's heart—his emotion—even in his guilt and shame, appears to be fully engaged with God's heart—God's emotion. Nathan's response to this is telling. "The LORD has taken away your sin. You are not going to die" (2 Samuel 12:13). In effect, the prophet is saying, "God gets you. And he gets that you get him. You are not going to be separated from him. Your life will not be forfeited because of this."

The conduit by which David was most primally and fundamentally connected to God was emotion. David did not repent in response to a logical argument. The desire to repent was first and foremost just that—desire. And desire begins in the recesses of the right hemisphere and lower, deeper brain structures that echo ancient longing for reunion with one from whom we have long been separated.

I recognize that my reflections on this interchange contain a fair amount of speculation. Yet David's poetic prayer of contrition, found in Psalm 51, expresses his emotional connection to God:

> Have mercy on me, O God,
>   according to your unfailing love;
> according to your great compassion

blot out my transgressions. . . .
For I know my transgressions,
    and my sin is always before me.
Against you, you only, have I sinned
    and done what is evil in your sight;
so you are right in your verdict
    and justified when you judge. . . .
Cleanse me with hyssop, and I will be clean;
    wash me, and I will be whiter than snow. . . .
Create in me a pure heart, O God,
    and renew a steadfast spirit within me.
Do not cast me from your presence
    or take your Holy Spirit from me.
Restore to me the joy of your salvation
    and grant me a willing spirit, to sustain me. . . .
You do not delight in sacrifice, or I would bring it;
    you do not take pleasure in burnt offerings.
My sacrifice, O God, is a broken spirit;
    a broken and contrite heart
    you, God, will not despise. (vv. 1, 3-4, 7, 10-12, 16-17)

David does not write God a letter of prose. He does not dictate a theological treatise on adultery and the proper place of confession and absolution. He does not mechanically utter some prefabricated prayer. Instead, he writes poetry. He stands up to his full emotional height, and in this psalm accomplishes the integration of the right and left hemispheres of his brain. This is what poetry does.

As we read this psalm, we can sense the weight of David's agony wash over us. With every line, we are submerged in a sea of emotion that is symbolized in language. The emotion finds the thought, and the thought finds the words. Psalm 51 explains what David really means when he tells Nathan, "I have sinned against the LORD."

I suggest that those who organized the canon of Scripture knew what they were doing when they placed the psalms in the center of the Bible. From the perspective of neuroscience, this book is in the perfect symbolic position, pointing to the full integration of the mind as we bring together both language (left hemisphere) and emotional states (right hemisphere) in the beauty of poetry.

ATTENDING TO YOUR OWN FEELINGS

We can't describe with certainty David's emotional life when he finds himself on his palace roof watching Bathsheba bathing rather than out on the battlefield with his men. Clearly, though, he isn't paying attention to it. The biblical record of David's family life includes an earlier incident involving David and his wife Michal, daughter of the king he supplanted. As David dances before Yahweh in a worship celebration, Michal is embarrassed. When David comes home, Michal shames him, and he sharply defends himself. It appears things have not been good at home for some time. It's not surprising to find David, years later, acting out his emotional states in a manner that has long-term ill effects familially, socially, and politically.

As David's experience illustrates, what you do with emotion shapes the communities in which you live, be they your immediate family, church, neighborhood, or school. It is emotion that initiates the revelation that you have sinned and have been sinned against. It is emotion that moves you to confession and repentance. It is fundamentally only in response to emotion that a spouse or friend will be open to the invitation for change. Emotion is the part of creation that God uses to get your attention and to create the family he so longs to come to full maturity. It is certainly not the only thing God uses. But it seems to be the place he starts, from the perspective of the brain.

To what degree are you attuned to your own emotions? to others' emotions? to God's? How much attention do you give to how you respond to those emotions? For instance, do you attune to your child's emotions, or do you act only in response to your own as you react to your child's behavior? When your son mouths off after a hard day at school, do you immediately ground him for disrespecting you? Or do you not only correct him for his sassiness but also invite him to talk about what he's feeling about his struggles at school?

The same question can be asked of any interpersonal interaction. The more you pay attention to primary and categorical emotional states, the more you see that most of life is about responding to shifts in emotional states either from other minds (your spouse, your boss, your pastor) or from your own. In short, life is fundamentally about emotion. If you do not attune to it, you will eventually respond to it anyway, but in forms of thought, feeling, and behavior that bring you closer to shame than to glory.

Furthermore, the more attentive you are to emotional states and the more you actively reflect on them and talk about them with a trusted friend, spiritual mentor, or psychotherapist, the more you will literally integrate the neural circuitry of your brain. What is more, when you pay more attention to your own emotional states, you become more familiar with the states of others' minds. This enables you to assist in the integration of their minds as well.

I noted above that primary emotions are those you can learn to regulate (you can, if you practice, relax your facial muscles when you are anxious) and that regulate you (the sensation of the gentle touch of someone's hand on your shoulder creates a cascade of warmth and relaxation throughout your entire body).

The problem is that, like Erin, you may be virtually unaware of those primary emotions. Yet if primary emotion is one of the most important means by which you comprehend your experiences in life, *including your experience of and with God*, what does it say about that very relationship if you are not paying attention to those emotional patterns?

A second problem is that you may not have much practice putting into words those categorical emotions that actively shape your life. Perhaps you grew up in a family whose members seldom engaged in conversations about what they felt (not just what they thought). As we have seen, if you do not attend to categorical emotions like joy, anger, and shame, your relationship with God will be limited. Not only will you be unable to share your feelings with him, but you'll be functionally disconnected from his feelings.

A third problem is that you may find it difficult to identify feeling states in others. When you try to identify them, you may frequently misread them. That's why I often ask patients what they feel me feeling. The question can be somewhat puzzling at first. They may initially tell me what they think I am thinking. With more probing, they may tell me what they think I am feeling. But feel what I am feeling? How can they do that? How does one actually feel another's feelings?

I usually point to their own primary sensory experience of what they witness in me. I ask them to consider my nonverbal cues, along with the words that I am using. What do they notice about my body posture, my facial expression, how relaxed I appear, and the tone of my voice? Based on these cues, what do they feel I am feeling?

I also ask them to describe what they feel as they pay conscious attention to my nonverbal cues. In other words, they have to learn to pay attention to what they are feeling in response to what I am feeling. And if they misinterpret anything that I know I am or am not feeling, I will usually clarify so we can explore the differences between what I feel and their interpretation of my feelings.

But what do we do with the question, What do you feel God feeling when you are in his presence? Again, people are quick to give stock answers. Often they tell me what they believe God thinks. It comes in some form of analysis: even though they may use the language of emotion, the force of their statements indicates the importance of God's assessment of them—his "left-brain" function, if you will:

"He thinks I need to pray more."

"He isn't happy with me."

"He feels sad about my choices."

"He's disappointed with me because I haven't done enough to please him."

"My life has been pretty hard, but I shouldn't complain. I think he's angry with me because I'm really ungrateful and that just can't be good."

It is not easy at times for us to allow for God to have a "right hemisphere"—to attend to his emotional state. This is not surprising, given how little we pay attention to our own. As we've discovered in earlier chapters, though, reading Scripture and paying attention to, writing, and telling our own narratives are life-giving means to integrate our minds, which will help us attend both to our own feelings and to God's.

Why can it be so difficult to connect with God emotionally? Simply put, our emotional response to God is often clouded by our own stories and implicit memory activity. My neural pathways representing those well-encoded states of shame or guilt leave little room for the new pathways of joy and delight. This is why we need to be attentive to what others have experienced that reminds us of the way God *is*, not the way our implicit memories and primary emotional states make him out to be. But remember, God does not want to leave any part of us distorted or incoherent. He is ever about turning over every stone to reveal all that needs to be healed—especially those densely wired, ancient, implicit neural networks that represent emotion that is not integrated into the larger part of our mind's landscape.

We sometimes fail to grasp how important emotion is in the shaping of our relationship with God. For some of us, much of our exposure to life with God has been centered on belief systems that depend heavily on "being right" theologically. We believe that if we know things to be true in the logical, linear, factual sense, we can then proceed in life with confidence, both in terms of how we behave as well as how we believe others, whether or children, our friends, or our enemies, "should" behave. Unfortunately, this mode of thinking, which is largely driven by the activity of the left hemisphere of the brain, is unable to account for or enable us to live with the parts of life that don't follow these logical guidelines (which often feels like most of it).

This does not mean that the left hemisphere's vital function of logical thinking is unimportant. In fact it is just as important as the experience of emotion. We live in a world, however, that encourages us to take an unbalanced approach in the way we engage God and the way we engage others about God. Emotion usually is given an honorary but lesser seat at the table. No, our relationship with God is not only about emotion—far from it. Yet emotion is where it begins. And if we do not pay attention to the beginning of the story, it will be difficult to comprehend it in its fullness.

FEELING GOD'S DELIGHT

If considering God's emotions feels foreign to you, you may want to engage in an exercise that may help bring you closer to feeling what God feels. First, consider your feelings when you encounter this passage:

> The LORD your God is with you, the Mighty Warrior who saves. He will take great delight in you; in his love he will no longer rebuke you, but will rejoice over you with singing. (ZEPHANIAH 3:17)

Take a few moments in a quiet and comfortable place, free of distraction, and simply imagine, the best that you can, being in God's presence *while he is feeling delighted to be with you, while he is quieting you and rejoicing in your presence.* Imagine God singing about you. Until I wrote that sentence, I don't think I'd ever actually thought of God singing. Is he a baritone, a tenor, a soprano, an alto, or perhaps some blended combination of vocal beauty that is impossible to describe? The point is, he's performing the opera in your honor because he takes so much pleasure in you.

Still don't have the picture? Think of U2 holding a concert just for you. In your honor. But now imagine that instead of Bono, it's God. Too cool. We often consider how we *should* feel when in God's presence. But have you ever imagined how he feels in *yours*? Do you feel Jesus feeling delight, joy, and peace? If not, what do you feel him feeling instead? What do you imagine he looks like? How does he sound? What does he say? What is the tone of his voice? And then, what do you feel yourself feeling as you respond to these initiatives of God?

This exercise might take five to ten minutes. Do it once or twice a day, every day, for six weeks. Monitor what you feel (what emotion is evoked in you) in general, and what you feel specifically when your thoughts turn to God. Notice how your general body tone, as well as your general level of distress and anxiety, changes over that time.

Keeping an emotional inventory may also effectively help you discover what you feel. It is simple and can be done in a matter of two to three minutes. Every day, at least three to four times per day, for at least six weeks, stop for those few minutes and consider what you have been feeling for the last three to four hours. Write this on a three-by-five card and keep a record. Once or twice a week, review what you have written. Begin to pay attention to your trends and how they correlate with the events of your week.

As an alternative you might meditate prayerfully on a passage from Scripture, such as Psalm 26:2-3.

> Test me, LORD, and try me,
>> examine my heart and my mind;
>> for I have always been mindful of your unfailing love
>> and have lived in reliance on your faithfulness.

Here the psalmist is asking God to reveal to him the content of his heart, as the writer pays attention to and feels the love God has for him. He wants to know what is in his own mind, *and is asking for another mind to assist him.* He is not fearful of coming into contact with what he will find there, especially when he is surrounded by love to begin with. Neither should you be afraid.

Chapter 7

ATTACHMENT: THE CONNECTIONS OF LIFE

What do you crave most in life?

Chocolate? The Ferrari F430? A vacation in Fiji? Sex?

Actually, there is something each of us wants more—even more than the air we breathe:

Connection.

While connection may not be our top need for immediate physical survival, our Creator has formed us in such a way that there is nothing more crucial to our long-term welfare. In fact, virtually every action we humans take is part of the deeper attempt to connect with other humans. Even when it terrifies us. Even when we suspect at some inscrutable, preverbal place in our minds that we will be betrayed. Even when we have spent years perfecting our deftness at avoiding connection or carefully protecting ourselves from all but the most controlled forms of it. We find ourselves drawn to it, despite our occasional repulsion by it—especially in relation to particular people.

Another term that reflects this idea of connection is *attachment*. As we continue to focus on particular functions of the mind, we turn to attachment research. Once again we'll see how God uses an important function of creation, that of attachment, to point us to himself and to a life of depth, mercy, and justice. Attachment theory supports the supposition that there is no such thing as an individual brain, not even an individual neuron. In fact, researchers have discovered that the way we attach shapes the neural networks that are the vehicles of the attachment process itself. Those neural networks then reinforce the same interpersonal dynamics, which leads us to attach to others in much the same way as we did to our parents.

Connection begins with a newborn's first breath. She wails into a universe that she hopes will respond to her with comfort and strength to reverse the course of her distress, whether from cold, hunger, pain, or exhaustion. The parent who is attuned to this piercing cry moves to touch, soothe, search for, and quell the discomfort—even at 3 a.m.

At other times, the child delights simply in being noticed and affirmed. Suppose this precious bundle lies quietly, shifting only her small mop-covered head as she gazes and blinks. Suddenly, she moves her limbs in such a way that she momentarily startles herself. She notices you noticing her, and the faint curl of the muscles of her lips, chin, and mouth form her prototype tooth-less smile. You return the favor, albeit with more teeth, and her whole body contorts as she squeals with glee—although an abstract concept like glee is something her small brain may not yet distinctly recognize.

Connection between an infant and an adult is transmitted and translated first through her physicality. Yet it is only the beginning of the oscillating dance between the child who is seeking solid relational ground on which to stand and her parent who, ideally, attends to her, mindful of her needs (at times even before they are expressed). In the process, the parent also provides the child with the necessary matrix to navigate the world.

In the same way that each baby enters the physical universe through the birth canal, so we enter the world of relationships through the portal of attachment. The passageway is uniquely sculpted through the cooperative effort of the child and his or her mother and father. It is the result of literally dozens if not hundreds of experiences every day that are expressed, received, and interpreted through the mind/brain/body matrices of the participants.

Of course, since the linguistic, logical reflecting realm of the infant's left hemisphere is still relatively underdeveloped, the newborn cannot consciously reflect on this process. He cannot think to himself, *Hey, this relationship has been working out pretty well for the past fifteen days or so. I feel secure and safe, and there's great room service. I'm so proud to be their son.*

But the neurons in his right brain, along with deeper subcortical structures, are veritably scrambling over one another, connecting and pruning like so many bees in a hivelike network. They soak up the incoming sea of non-verbal cues emanating from within the child's own body as well as the bodies of his caretakers. In other words, the infant can sense equally the frivolity of laughter and the tension of irritability. His body will absorb his mother's anxiety simultaneously with the milk from her breast. He will distinguish the relative gentleness or roughness—or for that matter, the very presence or absence—of his father's physical touch. He will notice the timing and intensity of his parents' responses to his pleasure as well as his distress. His brain will begin to register the general level of safety, tranquility, or chaos generated in the presence of each primary figure with whom he connects. In essence, his brain begins to wire in accordance with his experiences. In fact, the nature of his relationships with his parents shapes the neural networks in a fashion that will have lifelong implications.

Much of this attachment process is mediated through the lower brain structures and the right hemisphere. These systems, which are responsible for how children (and eventually adolescents and adults) regulate themselves, are being contoured by the very interactions they are having. And so, even as we confess that God has "created my inmost being [and] knit me together in my mother's womb" (Psalm 139:13), we also see that God appears to be very interested in partnering with us to bring the creation process to full maturity. Yes, he knits each infant together in the uterus, but he then gives parents particular freedom and responsibility to shape the neurological wiring of their children.

Although attachment as a formal domain of scientific study is relatively new, the concept is not, as the creation narrative in Scripture makes clear. At the dawn of creation, being connected was as natural and as necessary as breathing, and a reflection of God's own state of being—one of community, integration, and connection. Genesis 2:18 reveals that God, with his hands having been deep in the mud into which he exhaled life, senses the man's lack of completion, declaring, "It is not good for the man to be alone. I will make a helper suitable for him."

Not long after this beautiful picture of connection, though, we read about the first man and woman's choice to disconnect from God by violating his instructions. Their choice's horrific consequences, which are spelled out in Genesis 3, illustrate how desperately humans need each other—but how difficult it is to maintain loving, vital, courageous intimacy. It is not surprising, then, that the story of the Bible is ultimately one of Immanuel, God *with us*. God is present and connected in the face of our resistance and our terror. Jesus loves us in the quagmires of shame and desolation that we have created.

As Scripture shows, attachment has been kneaded into the most primitive fibers of our being. Even in moments of despair and darkness, even when our behavior is repulsive and hurtful, we are desperately trying to regain our course and act on the inescapable longing for the attachment that was lost in Eden. The neuroscience is clear: the concept of a single functioning neuron or a single functioning brain simply does not exist in nature. Without input from other neurons, a single neuron will die. Likewise, without input from other minds, a single mind becomes anxious, then depressed, then hopeless, and then dies, either by intentional means (suicide) or more passive forms of poor self-care. It is not good for a man or woman—or a neuron or a brain—to be alone.

The term *attachment process* refers specifically to an interpersonal occurrence between a child and his or her primary caregiver in which the immature infant brain relies on the adult brain to help organize itself. Technically, this describes the way a child attempts to connect with her parent, not the other way around. This is not to suggest that the parent plays no role in this process—quite the contrary. In fact, as we will see, the parent's response to the child's temperament is what molds the child's attachment pattern. From the moment of birth, the infant brain seeks connection. It is like a miniature radar system, scanning the surrounding environment, searching for something—someone—to help bring coherence to its emerging sense of life.

Each child is born into the world with a certain genetically predetermined temperament to which the parent reacts. This parental reaction then elicits the particular attachment pattern that the child tends to develop with each parent. That explains why no two siblings ever really grow up in the same home. For no two children have exactly the same temperament, so each elicits different emotional reactions from his or her parents.

Infants tend to develop a particular attachment with each individual. This means that a child develops a certain style of attachment with his mother, but perhaps a different style with his father. An attachment pattern, therefore, is relationship specific. As an adult, you may tend to relate to people who behave like your mother in the same way you relate to her and relate another way to people who reflect behaviors like your father's.

Attachments can form as early as seven months of age, the result of the brain, especially the right hemisphere, engaging the world through multiple layers of neural networks and the formative experiences of emotion and memory. The brain is capable of being wired in response to the interactions an infant has with parents. Given these realities, it is not surprising that nearly all infants attach, though only to a few people. They do not indiscriminately connect with anyone who walks in the room, but rather to those with close emotional and social proximity.

How much influence, then, do genetic factors wield in the development of attachment? Some research indicates they play very little role. Rather, the profound relational dynamism that exists between the child and parent (and teacher, youth group leader, or coach as the child ages to adolescence) shapes both brain and behavioral changes. Our chromosomes are the material stuff from which the rest of our bodies emerge. But a great deal of what those genes do is contingent on the experiences presented to them through our vast, interconnected nervous system.

ATTACHMENT RESEARCH

In the late 1960s and early 1970s, the British researcher John Bowlby began developing the attachment theory. His book *Attachment* was the first of several groundbreaking works in this area. He explored the formation of close emotional bonds between infants and toddlers and their primary caregivers, usually their mothers, and the effect on those children when those bonds were prematurely broken. Many of his initial observations were based on the outcomes of children who had been separated from their parents during World War II.

He contended that the manner and degree to which these primary relationships were formed and either sustained or interrupted significantly impacted the emotional and behavioral vitality of the children. He postulated that the parent-child relationship could provide a "secure base" from which children could explore the world around them with confidence and security. These children could then develop emotional elasticity in the face of stress, build healthy relationships with peers, and establish a sense of emotional equilibrium within their own minds.

Researchers now know that secure attachment has far-reaching and positive implications for a child's future cognitive, social, and emotional development as well. Healthy attachment also helps develop the fundamental matrix of the mind around which children, when grown to adulthood, form a coherent narrative. They are better able to make sense out of their lives and form mature, secure relationships with other adults.

One of Bowlby's colleagues, Mary Ainsworth, advanced his work to the point of demonstrating that there are particular patterns of attachment, certain styles that have corresponding behaviors and attitudes. These patterns have been replicated in numerous rigorous studies. These styles tend to be stable, in that they continue to be operational in people's lives even into adulthood, unless they encounter alternative emotional experiences that shift the pattern to another. Following Ainsworth, Mary Main and her colleagues at the University of California at Berkley diligently tested and applied the previous findings to develop an even more robust formulation of the theory, including ways to comprehend attachment as it is manifested in adulthood.

While at Johns Hopkins, Mary Ainsworth conducted research to examine the child-rearing practices of twenty-six couples, all of whom were parents of a newborn. For twelve to eighteen months, from the time the infants were born, she and her assistants observed daily interactions between the infants and their primary caregivers, usually the mothers. When the infants were one to one and a half years old, each mother and child took part in an experiment called the Infant Strange Situation, conducted in a small laboratory room equipped with age-appropriate toys.

The experiment was intended to more formally explore and measure the range of the children's reaction to several different relational shifts. Initially, the parent and child were together in the laboratory room by themselves. Next a stranger entered the room and began to engage the child in the presence of the mother. At some point the mother, and then the stranger, would leave the room. Within a short time the mother would return to the room and attempt to engage the child.

The investigators observed these interactions throughout a twenty-minute period. They noted several important sequences of behaviors, including the child's capacity to explore the room and toys while with the mother; the child's reaction to the presence of the stranger, both in the presence and absence of the mother; the child's response to the departure of the mother and stranger; and the child's overall reaction to the mother's return to the room. Some of their most important correlating findings were between the parenting styles they had observed over the previous months and the behavior of the children during the Strange Situation, especially their reactions upon their mothers' return to the laboratory at the conclusion of the experiment. These correlating findings were the basis for the four distinct attachment patterns that Ainsworth and Main eventually identified:

Secure attachment
Insecure attachment—avoidant
Insecure attachment—ambivalent/anxious
Insecure attachment—disorganized

These four patterns, which I'll define shortly, demonstrate various ways a child may approach the world based on the patterns of interaction and responses with his or her primary caregiver. In the population at large, secure attachments occur most often, about 65 percent of the time, though a child may develop different forms of attachment with different caregivers. Usually a child develops a dominant form, with smatterings of other styles accompanying it. In this sense, the child does not follow the same pattern when relating to all individuals.

Over the last twenty years, researchers have studied adult attachment to determine whether there is any connection between the attachment pattern of infants and the way they connect to people as they mature into childhood, adolescence, and adulthood. Mary Main and her colleagues developed the Adult Attachment Interview, or AAI, as one tool in this study. The AAI is a twenty-question interview administered to a patient that takes between sixty and ninety minutes to complete.

Since attachment is reflected in the way we tell our stories, the AAI attempts to evaluate adults' positions toward attachment by exploring the way each tells the narrative of his or her life. Questions explore the subjects' experiences with their own parents and other attachment figures, relevant losses or traumatic events, and if applicable, parenting experiences with their own children.

The interview assesses the *coherence* of the narratives. In other words, the therapist is not merely seeking information or facts about subjects' lives but is evaluating the manner and style in which patients tell their stories. Do the incidents of the subjects' stories and the emotions they display while telling their stories seem to fit together? Do the subjects ask for clarification of questions they do not understand? Do they provide what the examiner is actually requesting? Do they seek to be understood, elucidating their comments along the course of the dialogue? Is it clear that they are thinking about the process as it proceeds, aware that the interview is a collaborative effort?

Four definable profiles have emerged from this research. These include autonomous or free; dismissing; preoccupied or entangled; and unresolved trauma or loss. At least three important discoveries have come to light using this interview technique:

1. The attachment status of adults predicts *with an 80 percent degree of confidence* the attachment pattern that their own children will develop toward them—even if they are not yet parents. This tells us that the adults' status is not greatly influenced by the presence of their own children.

2. Attachment patterns tend to be stable over time; the way an infant attaches or connects in relationships is consistent through adolescence and into adulthood. Strikingly, each of the four classifications of childhood attachment strongly correlate with the corresponding AAI description of adult attachment:

    secure child ⟷ free adult

    insecure-avoidant child ⟷ dismissing adult

    insecure-ambivalent/anxious child ⟷ preoccupied adult

    insecure-disorganized child ⟷ adult with unresolved trauma or loss

    In other words, the way people learn to manage emotional states as children will follow them into their adult friendships, marriages, and work relationships. It is possible for a person's attachment pattern to change at any age (from insecure to secure or vice versa), but this will *not* occur without a significant influence from an outside relationship or a dramatic shift in circumstances. In fact, those who seem to have matured to connect in healthier ways are said to have developed "earned secure" attachment. (Later we will discuss the significance of this finding.)

3. Adults with dismissing, preoccupied, or unresolved orientations toward attachment generally have a much more thorny course when navigating the unexpected twists and turns of life, particularly in interpersonal relationships, than do those who are securely attached.

MENTALIZING

Not surprisingly, adults with secure attachments are generally more empathic than others. Empathy is not something people are "born with." Rather, they develop this quality through what researchers call mentalizing, or mentalization—the imaginative mental activity that enables us to sense and interpret the feelings, desires, and intentions of another person. This process is dynamic and flexible, evolving in healthy or unhealthy ways, depending a great deal on the newborn's caregiver.

When a baby is born, she interprets her sense of self, and by extension her sense of her own mind, by what she sees, hears, touches, feels, and experiences from her primary caregivers. She does not independently have a sense of her own mind. She will acquire it—but it will be based on how she sees herself in her mother's eyes, so to speak. And what she "sees" will depend on what her parent sees in the first place. If her mother mentalizes well—attunes and responds in a healthy way to her baby's needs—the infant will develop a particular sense of herself and of the mind of her mother. She will see her mother seeing her in a loving light. If her mother does not mentalize well, the baby will experience a different outcome. Either way, she will see herself *and come to understand herself primarily through what she witnesses in her mother's responses.*

As infants become toddlers and older children, they must depend upon their own ability to read the minds of others as they wander farther away from the more predictable, secure base of their primary caretakers. The child will begin to "read" what others around him are intending, and when feeling uneasy will likely conjure up images, thoughts, sensations, and feelings of being in his mother's thoughts to create a sense of calmness. Early in the life of the developing infant, this process depends heavily on lower and right-mode processing functions of the brain. As left-mode function gradually comes online, children develop ways of putting right-mode function into linguistic form. They don't simply "sense" another's mind, they begin to translate what they sense into thoughts:

I'm an idiot!
I'm pretty good at that.
She hates me.
She thinks I'm cool.

Like memory (to which it's closely connected), mentalizing is understood as being either implicit or explicit. Implicit mentalizing uses neural tracts that operate quickly and rely largely on implicit memory. In practical terms, this means we interpret others' intentions quickly, automatically, and out of the implicit models of our memory, with little consideration of any alternative understanding of what the person intends. So when you hear a coworker use a tone of voice that sounds angry, you assume that person doesn't like you rather than considering the possibility that he or she is simply tired.

Explicit mentalizing is conscious and reflective, and it is more easily accessed in nonthreatening environments. It tends to use neural pathways that require longer firing times because of the extra recruitment of cortical fibers responsible for contextualization. Using explicit mentalizing, you can *contextualize* (or shape and influence) what you imagine is in your coworker's mind by reflecting that she, although her voice sounds irritated, has also just completed a harrowing day in which she dealt with multiple complications. You can conclude, not that she hates you, but that she is exhausted.

The degree to which a child learns to mentalize in a healthy manner is directly related to the competence of the child's parent to mentalize in the first place. If a parent does not read his or her infant in an attuned manner and respond with wisdom to the baby's needs, the child will develop distorted methods of signaling his or her own needs and intentions to others. For this reason, mentalizing is a major force that influences the attachment process and shapes its outcome.

GOD AND ATTACHMENT

Our attachment patterns, translated into and through our neural networks, not only affect our relationships with other people, they are one of the primary forces shaping our relationship with God. Whatever our dominant patterns tend to be, we will relate with and assume things about God through those same neural networks. (After all, he created our brains and doesn't bypass them when he invites us to a personal encounter with him.)

Remember that *assuming things about God* does not simply mean what we *think logically* about him. Our brains, through the forces of various emotional states and implicit as well as explicit memory, *construct our experience* of God—sometimes in ways that contradict what we assent to theologically. In this way, paying attention to our attachment means we are invariably paying attention to our connection with God.

THE FOUR PATTERNS OF ATTACHMENT

Secure attachment

People who have made coherent sense of their own stories enable their children to attach securely as well. They provide the soil in which the seed of a child's story can germinate, moving toward security. In fact, of all the variables that influence the formation of a child's attachment pattern, *the single most robust factor is whether or not the parent has made sense of her or his own life.*

Parents of securely attached children are emotionally attuned, perceptive, and responsive to their needs. The mother is a steady, dependable presence in her children's life. She responds consistently with compassion, patience, and kindness to the needs of her children, which leaves them feeling that the world is predictable and safe. The father pays attention to aspects of the children's behavior that are largely mediated by the right brain, such as their emotional states and nonverbal cues. This invariably requires the father to be aware of his own right hemispheric functions as they resonate with those of the right mode of his infant or child. These children feel understood and connected, and the universe makes sense to them. By demonstrating the healthy form of mentalizing, the parents create the potential for the child to develop this quality as well.

This mindful approach to the emotional state of a child literally prepares a template at a neurological level that enables the child to grow into an awareness of a God who also cares about his or her joys, hurts, fears, and mistakes. It also lays the groundwork for the child to experience God as trustworthy and responsive and to see the world he has created as ultimately and infinitely safe, despite surface evidence to the contrary. As the child grows, he or she can more easily imagine a God with whom a substantive relationship is possible and desirable.

At the conclusion of the Infant Strange Situation (ISS), when the mother of a securely attached child returned to the laboratory room where her infant had been alone for several minutes, she would find the child distressed and often tearful at being isolated. Upon seeing the mother, the child would immediately approach her and would find comfort and assurance. Within a brief period, the child would demonstrate a suitable level of recovered emotional equilibrium and tended to leave her mother to once again explore the toys in the room. In essence, such a parent has established an emotional environment in which the child has a secure base from which to wander off and encounter the world without fear.

Children whose dominant pattern of attachment is secure tend to develop into adults whose Adult Attachment Interview (AAI) reveals an autonomous or free orientation toward attachment. These people are likely to pay attention to others' feelings, value relationships, and be well integrated socially, emotionally, and cognitively. Others describe them as being cooperative but not milquetoast, either a good leader or follower, and willing to resolve conflicts (not avoid them). They are not without insecurities but are willing to engage and address them. They are also likely to parent in a way that fosters secure attachment in their own children.

Recall that the AAI is focused on measuring how people tell their stories, not on the facts of those stories. Since storytelling form is a hallmark of attachment, the AAI evaluates the coherence, fullness, and richness with which the person presents the events of her life. A person with a secure attachment tells her story with a robust awareness of the emotional landscape of her life as it is interpreted and understood through that very story.

Parents who are mindful of their children's needs and flexible in their interactions with them are literally assisting the neural wiring process in their children's brains. This enables their children to be open and receptive to the image of a God who is interested and delighted in them, compassionate and full of grace when they stumble, yet willing to discipline them without simultaneously shaming. As they grow older, when life feels less integrated, more disconnected—when they want juice but are offered only milk; when they have a fight with their mom over the environmental disaster area they call their bedroom; when their first love breaks up with them; when their marriage feels insufferable; when their own children demand more than they believe they have to offer; when they develop cancer—they will still retain *in their neural circuitry* the imprint of a God who is *there*. A God of bone and blood. A God of strength, mercy, and mystery. A God of history, acting in their lives, the proof being in what they feel in a manner that is undeniable, rooted in their very bodies. And they do not simply have an awareness of this being "true" as a *fact* (an explicitly encoded, dominantly left hemisphere function), but rather as an existential, emotional, remembered experience *as a recalled autobiographical memory* (one that requires the integration of the left and right, as well as lower and higher regions of the brain).

HOW TO ENCOURAGE SECURE ATTACHMENT IN YOUR CHILD

A secure attachment does not mean you give your children only what they seem to want any time they want it. As children move into the second year of life (or even before), they require physical limits. But wise parents who are attuned to their young children recognize that when their toddlers do not immediately respond to their commands, the children are not so much "disobeying" as responding from immature neural networks.

Imagine a dad watching his son play in their backyard. When the boy plucks a leaf off a bush, the father walks over to get a closer look. Seeing the boy lift the leaf up to his tongue, the dad admonishes the boy to "take the leaf out of your mouth." The boy may not respond, not out of disobedience but at least in part because the exploding array of neural networks in his brain make

ATTACHMENT: THE CONNECTIONS OF LIFE

the transition from picking the colorful green leaf off the plant to putting it into his mouth to taking it out and handing it to his father a somewhat bumpy ride. Yet if the father is implicitly and almost instantaneously able to sense the child's predicament, he can provide emotional buffers for that transition.

Dad will monitor his tone of voice and body movements as he approaches his son to retrieve the wayward vegetation. He will consciously shift his facial expression to one of warmth and gentleness, which will reduce his son's likelihood of responding in a defensive manner (e.g., running away with the leaf, squealing while eating it as fast as he can)—which, incidentally, might be done with little conscious awareness.

The same can be said for how a mother interacts with her adolescent child as she provides limits having to do with driving an automobile, developing sexual standards, and navigating impulses toward risky behaviors. The teenager, whose own explosive brain growth leads him to believe he is invincible and immortal, needs his parent's wise guidance. While there is less physical engagement with teenagers—you likely won't have to keep your sixteen-year-old from eating begonia leaves—hopefully there will be more verbal interaction between Mom and her son as together they tackle the complex shaping of the son's neural networks in the context of dizzying hormonal and metabolic changes.

Parents attuned to their children's emotional states provide the basis of secure attachment. Of course, no parent will be able to read his or her child perfectly in every interaction. Peter Fonagy, a British psychoanalyst and researcher in the field of attachment, suggests that even the most sensitive parent accurately tracks with his or her child only about 45 to 50 percent of the time. But over time the child will have the experience that his emotional states matter, even when his parent makes a mistake that disrupts his emotional equilibrium.

God does not expect parents to be perfect. He does, however, long for us to be perceptive. He does not expect that we will never make mistakes, but he cares that we are attuned to the mistakes we inevitably will make. God cares that we are honest about our blunders, but not so that we will beat ourselves up until he is satisfied that we have been sufficiently shamed for our behavior. God is interested in integration, in connection. And telling the truth—both verbally and nonverbally—about our mistakes actually enhances the integration of the mind of the one we have hurt—and our own minds as well.

Let's say a normally attuned father comes home from a long day at work to find his twelve-year-old son's bike blocking the space in the garage where he typically parks. The dad sighs, puts his car in park, and gets out to move the bike out of the way so he can pull into the garage. His irritation mounts when he opens the door leading from the garage to the family room and sees his son sprawled out on the sofa, TV remote in one hand and a cookie in the other.

"Son," the dad says curtly, "how many times have I told you to put your bike where it belongs? The next time that happens, you lose the bike for a week."

Only when his son turns to look at him does this father notice his son's downcast face and red-rimmed eyes. Instantly the dad wishes he could retract his harsh words. His voice softens. "Ryan, are you okay?"

"Sorry, Dad," the son says, as the tears start to fall again. "I just—it's just Matt told me at school today that his dad got a new job and they'll be moving out of state in a few months." Dad knows that Matt is his son's best friend— in fact, his only real friend—since their family moved to the area two years before.

Yet even in this situation, this chastened dad has the opportunity to build healthy, new connections. If he acknowledges to his son that he should not have automatically assumed his son had been thoughtless and then asks for forgiveness, the dad helps strengthen his son's attachment pattern. Despite wounding his son, Dad's confession of his own bad behavior enhances the resilience of the strands of emotional intimacy between the two of them.

As you pay attention and respond helpfully to the emotional states of your youngsters, they sense your regard and responsiveness. They become aware of their capacity to get their needs met. They will grow, without even the assistance of language and logical, cognitive constructs initially, to behave in a significantly interactive way with their environment. They will understand that they can effect meaningful change in their world. They will have the experience of feeling felt, and as they gradually encounter a range of emotions, you will give them language to understand and integrate these feelings into the larger landscape of their lives.

Insecure attachment—avoidant

Unfortunately, not all of our attachment experiences are secure ones. Most parents who raise children with insecure attachments, however, do love and care about their children. In fact, most would say they are very committed to their kids' welfare. The driving force behind this form of attachment is the manner in which the caregivers respond to their children's emotional states, often without the adults even being aware of the effect of their parenting. They may be very concerned that their children grow up to do well in school, obey rules, and learn to be solid members of society. They may especially desire that their children believe the "right things" about what it means to be a Christian and that they maintain the correct theological posture when considering the nature of God, Jesus, and the nature of man.

The first of the three forms of insecure attachment is avoidant. This pattern tends to arise in homes in which a parent is emotionally unavailable, imperceptive, unresponsive, and rejecting of a child's emotional states. That doesn't mean a parent is continually, actively, and knowingly saying or doing things that make the child feel rejected. Instead, these parents engender within the child the sense that feelings don't matter and that the world is an emotionally barren place. The child's mind learns not to pay attention to emotion (for he or she gains nothing by it) and finds alternative means to adapt to life stressors, such as by avoiding closeness or emotional connection.

In the concluding laboratory session of the ISS study, when the mother of an avoidantly attached child returned to the laboratory playroom, her son or daughter, who incidentally demonstrated a notable *lack* of emotional distress in her absence, treated her like a lamppost. The child tended to ignore the mother's presence, as the child had learned that she provided little comfort for his or her emotional distress. Even by this early age, it is as if these children had learned that emotional input from their brains was not reliable and that expressing this emotion to those around them did not get their needs met. Over time, such children essentially learn to dismiss awareness of their own distress, turning to other forms of behavior to cope or distract themselves.

In addition, these insecure children learn to dismiss input from their right hemispheres, including the insula, which is designed to help humans translate the emotional signals from our own bodies, as well as interpret the nonverbal communication of other people. By doing so, they literally prevent the neurons from the insula from firing and connecting with other parts of their right and left cortex that would make them aware of these physical sensations.

To compensate for these underdeveloped parts of their minds, they will often overdevelop their left hemispheres, relying heavily on the benefits of logical, linear, literal processing. They will highly value the actual words people say to them but miss the contextualizing body language, facial expressions, or tone of voice that accompanies the language. (A husband with this pattern will interpret his wife's silence to mean she has nothing to say rather than as her way of expressing hurt or anxiety.) On the other hand, others often view them as strong, thoughtful, laid-back, and perhaps unflappable.

From the standpoint of the AAI, adults with a dismissing orientation tend to tell their stories rather blandly. Their narratives will usually avoid the deep color of emotional context, mostly being concerned with the salient facts and linear progression of events. Their stories may make logical sense, but listening to them may feel a bit like watching paint dry. Then again, they may be quite accomplished in their chosen vocational fields, as left-mode processing is a valued commodity in many walks of life. He may be able to write software for a complex computer system. She may be unmatched when she argues legal precedents with aplomb. Or he may be renowned for his skill as a surgeon, as was Roger.

ROGER'S STORY

Roger's educational pedigree was impeccable. After completing his undergraduate studies and medical degree at a prestigious Ivy League institution, he trained at one of the top pediatric surgical residency programs in the country. By the time he was in his midthirties he was beginning two careers in earnest. He had accepted his first position at a teaching hospital, and he became a father. In one job he quickly ascended, a rising star. In the other he was flaming out. His wife, Joy, had come to see me when their first child, Gabriel, was about two and a half. She told me she no longer knew what to do in response to Roger's incessant impatience and harshness with the toddler.

"I don't understand it. He's one of the most respected young pediatric surgeons in the region, and he doesn't seem to know what to do with his own child," she fretted. "I want to have more children, and so does Roger, but sometimes I feel like I already have two—only one of them is almost forty years old. I'm really worried about having another baby, seeing how he is with Gabriel. Maybe it's just the stress of his work. He is really busy." I suggested that he consider coming to see me, which he willingly did.

Roger was warm, friendly, and soft-spoken. He admitted that he wanted to be a better father. He was completely flummoxed as to why he reacted to Gabriel as he did. "He drives me nuts," Roger said. "He just seems so obstinate at times. I simply don't know why I get so angry at him." This level of exasperation had begun when Gabriel was about two years old.

In our first meeting I explored the usual issues around the general state of Roger's emotional health. He denied any history of anxiety, depression, or substance abuse. He was committed to his wife and son and had a good relationship with his parents. He loved his work, even in the face of mountainous time demands. He and Joy had become involved in a local church fellowship where he found the "preaching to be intellectually stimulating." When

I asked if he had had any major traumas or losses in his life, he flatly, though thoughtfully, said no.

Next I asked about what life was like for him as a very young boy. He told me he couldn't remember anything with clarity before his seventh or eighth grade year in school. In addition, he acknowledged that his family never talked about emotion or feelings. His father was quiet and his mother was anxious; but apart from their emphasis on their children doing well in school and being well-mannered citizens, they tended to stay out of their children's lives. He remembered spending much of his middle school and high school years either in his room reading or working at the local grocery store. He had friends in high school and college, but most of his energy was consumed with academics.

Given that he used a paucity of words to describe his emotions and that he recalled so little of his younger years, I invited him to participate in a simple exercise called a body scan. This relaxation exercise uses a technique commonly referred to as guided visual imagery. The patient positions himself in a comfortable posture, closes his eyes, and then systematically, at my direction, focuses his attention on different parts of his body, beginning with his feet and then proceeding through his lower limbs, ascending throughout his body to eventually shift to his abdomen, back, neck, head, and face, respectively, culminating with focusing on his breathing. This task enables the participant to enhance his awareness of his bodily sensations, and enlarge his awareness of how his emotional states are translated through them, and provides a way for him to release the stress and tension he feels in each area of his body. It also has the capacity to evoke implicit memories as a person attends to parts of his body that have encoded and retrieved those memories. Surprisingly, when Roger reached the point in the exercise in which he was focusing on his abdomen, he suddenly uttered a low groan, furrowing his eyebrows. I asked what he was experiencing, and he was able to stammer, "I–I see something. I'm remembering something I haven't thought about in years."

He went on to describe, at first with a vague, shadowy awareness, what he was seeing in his mind. He recalled a time when he was about eight or nine. He was standing in his driveway at his family's home in New Jersey, glancing at the point where the driveway opened to a busy highway. His mother and brother, who was two years old, stood there. Suddenly, his brother bolted into the street before his mother could stop him and was hit by an oncoming car. He succumbed to head injuries a few days later. By this time, as the sharpness of Roger's memory was rending through the formerly impenetrable curtain of his mind, tears were streaming from his eyes, and he looked at me helplessly, incredulous that this was his story—the one for which he had had no explicit memory when I had inquired earlier about any losses or traumas. Over the next several sessions, he gradually recalled how his life had unfolded in the wake of this tragedy.

No one ever processed his brother's death with him. His parents, themselves suffocating in grief at the loss of their toddler, could offer Roger little comfort for what he had witnessed and what he had lost. They never spoke with each other, let alone him, about his brother. The house became quiet and sad.

He began to recall a time when he had developed stomach problems. His parents took him to see a doctor, but as far as he could remember, his abdominal complaints went away on their own. He never spoke about the accident to anyone, not even his wife. In retrospect, he was aware of the *fact* that he had had a brother who had died as a result of a car accident, but he had not recalled witnessing it until he underwent the body scan. When he did, the memory was activated when he focused on his abdomen, the part of his body where his emotional distress had taken up residence after his brother's death. And since Roger's ambivalence toward Gabriel began when he turned two—the age at which his brother had died—it's likely that Roger's implicit memory of his brother at age two was being evoked by the presence of his own son.

Since Roger's parents never helped him process his feelings in ways that gave him language with which to express his emotions, Roger learned to rely on alternative means of navigating the trenches of the relational world that depended on his mind's left-mode strengths. His accomplishments as an outstanding academician and pediatric surgeon played to his strengths—until he was undone by a two-year-old who reflected back to Roger the echoes of old, painful, unavoidable implicit memories of loss and grief.

Emotion, researchers have learned, facilitates the processing of memory—how it is encoded and retrieved. A person like Roger with a lack of emotional processing often is unable to easily recall memories of events that preceded his middle school years. By neglecting to pay attention to emotion, however, people run the risk of leaving behind important parts of their lives that may return to haunt them, as was the case with Roger.

Fortunately, it was not too late for Roger to begin processing his intense feelings of grief. As he had the experience of feeling felt in his helplessness, he was able to reframe those very feelings as the normal, expected reaction of an eight-year-old to overwhelming sadness. As he experienced those feelings of grief and confusion, they no longer felt so overwhelming. We worked together on a number of strategies he could use to relax and experience comfort in the presence of his distress. He learned to tolerate what only a few weeks earlier he had found intolerable—the feelings that unknowingly were activated when his son tried his patience or seemed inconsolable. He found himself becoming more empathic with Gabriel as he was better able to sense what his son was feeling.

Insecure attachment—ambivalent/anxious

The parental hallmarks of children with ambivalent attachment are the caregivers' inconsistency and intrusiveness. The parents often seem unable to read their children, because they themselves are so consumed with anxiety. When it comes to availability, perception, and responsiveness, therefore, the child cannot predict the parent's behavior. Sometimes Mom attends to her daughter, and sometimes she does not. Sometimes Dad will be sensitive to his son's needs, and sometimes he will not. At times Mom will engage her child when the child is content to be left alone. For instance, an infant may be quietly playing with a toy when the mother quite unexpectedly sweeps in, disrupting the activity. This lack of sensitivity and predictability leads to elevated levels of anxiety, uncertainty, and insecurity in the child. She concludes that the world is an emotionally unreliable place.

Those with this attachment pattern filter the Bible through their own spiritual stories, making it likely that their *actual, experienced sense* of God will be understood in those emotional terms. When anxious, they will more likely sense God to be unpredictable and unreliable, with little sensitivity; their mental images and emotional sensations convey God's intrusion into their lives and his displeasure with them. They comprehend with their left brains the "facts" they read in the Bible that they are instructed to "take on faith," but their right brains, due to lack of neural associations, may not incorporate the attendant emotional qualities associated with those facts.

In the ISS, a clear pattern develops with those infants who have formed ambivalent/anxious attachments. In the absence of her mother the baby displays evidence of distress, indicating she does indeed value emotion. When the mother returns to the room, the child immediately returns to her for comfort, but unlike the infant who is securely attached, she is not easily consoled and is quite reluctant to move away again to explore the toys. It is as if the infant fears that Mom, her source of comfort, could vaporize at any moment. Although the mother is at one level a potential wellspring of consolation, she also creates an emotional weather pattern that enhances in her child the very anxiety she is attempting to resolve.

In the AAI, adults who as children had ambivalent/anxious insecure attachments will tend to reveal a preoccupied or entangled orientation toward attachment. They are likely to be easily overwhelmed by doubts and fears about relying on others and will at times be "flooded" by right brain processing. Elements of their implicit memory intrude into their left-brain processing, at times unannounced and seemingly unprovoked by external circumstances. Thus, they become "entangled" or "preoccupied" with elements of their minds that interfere with a fluid, coherent narrative process. This makes it very difficult for them to attend to others' needs, given that their own emotional states take over in ways of which they are often unaware.

The manner in which stories are told in the AAI suggests that the right-mode processing circuitry overwhelms that of the left. The person is flooded with feelings that are not easily placed in a linear flow of understanding, so the story may sound disjointed. The boundaries between past and present events often seem blurred and confusing to the listener. In addition, the storyteller often appears preoccupied. The left brain does not have adequate access to make cohesive sense out of the emotional payload that is being foisted upon it in such unannounced, unpredictable ways.

LYDIA'S STORY

At seventeen, Lydia was persistently anxious and despondent about her future. She was wary of crowds and ruminated constantly about what others were thinking of her. She found herself consumed with concern about making sure she said the right thing. After most interactions with other people, she would mentally review the conversation and critique her performance, invariably feeling discouraged when she perceived she had "performed poorly"—said too much or too little, or tried to inject humor that seemed to fall flat.

Most of her classmates, friends, and acquaintances would have been surprised to learn of her anxiety. She was physically striking, articulate, and poised; her parents reported that although she had only one or two close friends, everyone who knew her found her delightful, albeit somewhat shy; she was a straight-A student; and she was a gifted violinist who had already performed before audiences of several hundred people.

However, once I witnessed Lydia's interactions with her mother, I had a better sense of the cause of her anxiety. Hovering and worried, Lydia's mom appeared to be even more anxious than her daughter, though she claimed that her apprehension was solely due to her daughter's plight. As I observed their relational style, I noticed the degree to which Lydia would respond to her mother's emotional oscillations, seeming to obtain little comfort from her mother's attempts to be helpful. This came as no real surprise, since most of her mother's nonverbal cues, including the way she asked questions of Lydia, signaled her own elevated level of angst.

As Lydia and I explored her relationship with her mom, she acknowledged that although she was certain that her mother loved her, she never knew when her mother was going to be calm enough to listen to her without becoming "stressed out." She desperately longed for her mother's comfort, and at times this was available, but more times than not, she just wasn't able to count on it, which left her feeling even more anxious.

"It seems at times that life is really all about her," Lydia mentioned. "I don't know how to get her to stop worrying so I can stop worrying."

As we talked over several weeks, it became clear that although Lydia was a deeply feeling adolescent, she had had little practice attending to her own emotions because she was so frequently monitoring those of her mother, and by extension, those of her peers.

Lydia's mother was the director of the women's ministry at her large suburban church. Yet her anxiety over her daughter was not doing much to convince her daughter of Jesus' desire to comfort her—despite her mother's appeal to biblical admonitions to trust Jesus, to be anxious for nothing, to remember the lilies and the birds in the Sermon on the Mount. Lydia's mentalization of God largely was a patchwork of mental images and emotional sensations representing his intrusion and displeasure with her. It seemed not to matter when she heard that Jesus invites everyone who is heavily burdened to come to him for rest. Lydia simply did not have the template in her mind for that kind of Jesus.

Whereas Roger needed to become more familiar with his emotional states and less dominated by his left-brain mode of processing, Lydia benefited from engaging her left hemisphere so that it could moderate her unpredictable right mode. For several weeks we talked not only about how she felt, but also about how those feelings were translated in terms of how her brain was working.

She began to pay more attention to particular states of mind, especially those that caused her heart to race, her breathing to shorten, or her mind to ruminate about what she had said to her friend. As soon as she noticed any of these signs, she would imagine what her brain was doing in the process. She learned, for example, to picture the amygdala (the fear center) taking over her limbic circuitry (her emotional modulator) and her brain stem (her fight-or-flight center) while bypassing her prefrontal cortex—the part that would normally regulate all of the above in a more flexible fashion.

Using guided visual imagery techniques I helped her practice—while she was calm—seeing herself in possible scenarios in which her mother was distraught (which normally tempted Lydia to follow her lead). Lydia would then imagine her brain and body becoming more tranquil as she used deep breathing techniques. This gave her a more tempered, thoughtful awareness of the event, and her mental processing became less disrupted by the intrusiveness of her mother's anxiety. Eventually, Lydia's anxiety subsided as she trained her brain in the context of our relationship.

Insecure attachment—disorganized

The third form of insecure attachment is a category that emerged from observations of a particular group of children that behaved in oddly tragic ways in the ISS. When their mothers would return to the laboratory after an absence, these children would engage in strange, sometimes chaotic, and at times even self-injurious behavior. They would become frozen with trancelike expressions; hit themselves or bang their heads on the floor; spin around in circles; cautiously move toward the caregiver while looking away from her; or move away to a corner of the room, often with a terrified look. They appeared virtually unable to calm themselves and certainly did not find their mothers to be a source of solace.

These children find the world to be a frightening and muddled place. They have few coherent means of organizing their minds in the presence of stress. This leads to abrupt, erratic affective shifts, along with impulsive, excessive behavior. The AAI profile of an adult who grew up with this form of insecure attachment is termed unresolved trauma or loss. Their narratives tend to be quite incoherent, sometimes punctuated by gaps in the stories where they omit portions of traumatic experience. Their expression of linguistic and emotional flow can be disjointed, reflecting the incoherent mental processing they experience as they recount their stories. Telling stories in such a jumbled fashion correlates with the lack of connection of neural networks in parts of the brain that are responsible for social organization. When they become parents, they in turn have a high likelihood of engendering disorganized attachment patterns in their own children.

The parents of children with disorganized attachment are often frightened themselves and/or frightening to their children. Their behavior tends to be disorienting and alarming to those in their care. They may abuse their children emotionally, physically, or sexually, or they may suffer from significant emotional disorders such as schizophrenia, severe bipolar disorder, or drug or alcohol abuse. They may also have experienced severe emotional deprivation in their early developmental years. Most of these parents report that they deeply love their children—but they appear oblivious to how their actions prevent their children's minds from formulating a coherent sense of the world.

The ways stories are told by people with this form of attachment suggest chaotic, disorganized neural network processing. Not only is the left mode occasionally overwhelmed by right-mode processing and the circuits responsible for implicit memory, their neural networks are so disorganized that inchoate behavior emerges. The process of healing for these people is often slow and arduous, but it is not hopeless.

Because their attachment has been so pummeled by trauma, those with disorganized insecure attachment may find it difficult to rest in a steady impression of God's love. In fact, because of their disorganized right-brain circuitry, they may sense only that God is often displeased or enraged with them. They may be uncomfortable getting close to God anyway because of their discomfort with intimacy.

EMILY'S STORY

Emily recalled her father's strange nighttime behavior. Until she was about seven or eight, her dad would run along the hallway outside the children's bedrooms soon after she and her siblings were put to bed. He would shout in an attempt to frighten her and her sisters, "as if he was trying to act like a scary monster," she said.

Emily begged her father to stop, but he would become indignant that she and her siblings were upset, claiming, "I'm only having fun with you."

As she grew older he began to explode with anger for no discernible reason. He would occasionally hit her, and once he threw her down the basement steps. During her teenage years he also began to goad her verbally, lacing his words with sarcastic invective to reduce her to angry tears. When she became upset he would complain that he was merely teasing her and that she shouldn't take it so personally. "You're not going to last in the real world if you're so sensitive," he told her. Her father's behavior disrupted Emily's own ability to mentalize with any degree of coherence.

Needless to say, as an adult Emily appeared unable to maintain the slightest degree of intimacy. She was quite attractive and intelligent, but by the age of thirty-seven, despite two proposals, she had never married. Both men had broken their engagements to her, each telling her he could not tolerate her unpredictable emotional swings and caustic words of criticism. In between these relationships she occasionally engaged in salacious behavior, repeatedly culminating in bouts of alcohol intoxication, shame, and depression.

"That's not who I am—and I don't know why I keep doing it," Emily said. Although she was highly educated and quite skilled in her profession, she had a chronic history of work failure due to her inability to tolerate even the slightest conflict with colleagues.

Indeed, Emily's behavior is typical of adults who as children had disorganized attachments. They are likely to display a pattern of emotional reactivity and substantial impairment of the integration of right and left modes of processing.

Emily's image of God—from the standpoint of her disorganized right-brain circuitry—is fractured; she senses only that God is displeased or enraged with her. When confronted with the idea that Jesus loves her, she begins to feel more, rather than less, disorganized because of how she responds to intimacy. Again, despite what she learns from her small group Bible study, and despite how much care its members offer her, she may interpret their attempts at connection to be disorienting and confusing.

Learning to regulate a traumatized brain often requires long, hard work. Emily continues this work to this day. She is now less fearful and less likely to cause trouble for herself at work, but she still fears intimacy and struggles mightily in her relationship with her current boyfriend. It will likely require a Herculean effort on his part to remain present in the face of the unpredictable, sometimes unfathomable, changes in her demeanor and behavior. But there is hope.

When Emily felt slighted after her boyfriend told her he couldn't escort her to a coworker's wedding due to a previous commitment, she called Amy, a friend in her Bible study, who could serve as an "emotional regulator." Emily trusted Amy when she gently pointed out that Emily's boyfriend wasn't being unreasonable at all. In fact, as Emily gets more experienced at exploring her implicit memory, she is better able to identify for herself when her reactions to minor slights are excessive. We have worked diligently to help her create a greater awareness of what it means to have an integrated mind; however, she needs frequent reminders to encourage the firing of those neural networks that represent for her the experience of trust, something she had very little of growing up.

WHY YOUR ATTACHMENT PATTERN MATTERS

If you now recognize that you have an insecure attachment, what are you to do? Will you forever be left with the residual imprints of your relationships with your parents? As a parent who may be relating in the same way to your children, do you still have time to help your children attach in a secure fashion?

We must be careful not to respond to these questions too quickly or easily with spiritually superficial or trite answers. It is not uncommon for those of us who live in the subculture of Western Christianity to expect transformation to happen if we simply recite the verses that assure us of such an outcome. We hear this in various forms from the pulpit and in the Bible studies, parenting workshops, and marriage enrichment seminars we attend. We are familiar with the language: God is faithful; God will provide; Jesus loves and forgives you. And we are admonished to live a particular life: love your neighbor as yourself; renew your mind; be perfect even as your Father in heaven is perfect; do not give the devil a foothold.

These words are helpful and true. But some parts of our minds seem numb or unresponsive to them. Theological *facts*, such as the fact of my sinful nature or other presuppositions about God or man, have great worth, but they are not very helpful on their own in getting us to live the way we want to live. They do not reflect our total experience, and alone they may not provide enough practical guidance for Roger, Lydia, Emily, and others like them. We would like to believe that our theology comes first, shaping our stories and our emotions; the opposite is closer to the truth, at least from the standpoint of how the mind functions.

Fortunately, as we'll explore in the next chapter, attachment patterns *do* have the capacity for change (leading to a state called earned secure attachment), but substantial interaction with an outside brain relationship or a change in circumstances is required for this transformation. We cannot change our stories without simultaneously changing the neural pathways that correlate with those modifications.

This is exactly what the Gospels proclaim: that in Jesus, the entire world has been introduced to a "substantial interaction with an outside brain relationship" that powerfully changes our circumstances.

As followers of Jesus, we are caught up in the vast and glorious story that God is telling—but not without coauthors. He is dedicated to creating a world of blessing and goodness—but not without our cooperation. The stories of Scripture illustrate that God is deadly serious about partnering with human beings in order to bring abundant life to the earth. He does not seem to be in a hurry to clean up our personal scandals, much less the world at large, all by himself. He is looking for serious partners.

The first partner, Adam, failed miserably, as did several others. Some partnered more helpfully than others, but only when Jesus came did we see what partnering with God really looks like. It looks like crucifixion. Like I said, God is absolutely serious about this. But it also looks like unmitigated joy, healing, mercy, and forgiveness, because it looks like resurrection.

And what has this to do with attachment? We have been invited to add our chapters and verses, to be coauthors in this Story. And the manner in which we tell our stories will reflect the degree to which we have allowed God's Story to fully intersect with our own. Healthy attachment is a means by which God creates connection between his creatures, but it is also a shadow of what our relationships with him look like when we fully enter into his Story with our own. If you identified with Roger's, Lydia's, or Emily's story, you may wonder if the hard work necessary to attain an earned secure attachment is worth it. It is if you want a deeper, richer relationship with others. It is if you want your own children to experience this security. And it is if you long to know—not just as an explicitly encoded fact but as an emotional, remembered experience—that God is loving and he is with you, acting in your life for your good. The proof of this change will be rooted in your own body as a recalled autobiographical memory (one that requires the integration of the left and right, as well as lower and higher regions of the brain) of God's love for you.

It will become real in a dimension of life that may well elude the realm of scientific inquiry. You will read Psalm 37, and the poetry will cascade over your consciousness, reminding you that

> The LORD makes firm the steps
>   of those who delight in him;
>   though they stumble, they will not fall,
>   for the LORD upholds them with his hand. (vv. 23-24)

This passage will make sense, and not simply as a left-brain function of logical, linear reasoning or assent to theological conviction. You will read Scriptures such as this and have the experience of feeling felt by God. As you read verse 24 above, you will sense the qualitative difference between *stumbling* and *falling*. God's presence will be comforting and undeniable, because he has taken up experiential residence in your mind, not least through the process of secure attachment.

Chapter 8

EARNED SECURE ATTACHMENT: POINTING TO THE NEW CREATION

Marlene is a wise woman.

Her son, Calvin, wasn't so sure of that, though, the day he asked her advice on how to handle his fifteen-month-old son, Eric. He and his wife, a high school teacher, had decided that Calvin would stay at home with their first-born, since as a successful writer, he had more flexibility in his work hours than she did.

Calvin had initially approached fatherhood with great optimism and anticipation, and for the first several months of Eric's life, he seemed to fit the role of a stay-at-home dad quite comfortably. But once Eric became mobile, everything changed. Eric was always running (there seemed to be little walking), grunting (all language was still foreign to him), or pointing and flailing, leaving a trail of food behind him. (Perhaps this should not have surprised Calvin, as this is a behavioral pattern of many males, no matter what their age.)

Eric's not-yet-developed language skills made for interesting guessing games between father and son, but no matter how hard Calvin worked, he wondered if he was temperamentally cut out to tolerate his son's energized physicality. Still, Calvin didn't want to make his wife wonder whether he was up to the job, so he decided to call his mom.

"Mom, I'm so frustrated," he said. "How is it that I can always stay on top of my deadlines but can't keep up with a toddler? I'm starting to feel so overwhelmed. How did you do it with five kids?"

Marlene's answer unnerved Calvin: "You really should talk with your father about this." Partly puzzled, partly irritated, Calvin did not understand why she didn't simply give him the counsel he sought.

"Why would I talk with him about this?" he asked. "Dad never talks with me about anything."

Which was true. His father had initiated few conversations with Calvin as he was growing up, unless he was telling him when he should be home at night from a date, asking whether he had finished his homework, or reminding him he had to get up for Mass every Sunday morning.

Calvin's father had never been unkind or harsh, merely distant. Marlene had been the one to roll up her sleeves and do the messy work of raising him and his siblings. Calvin never would have sought guidance from his father on parenting, and his mom's insistence that he speak with him only added to his confusion.

"Mom, come on. You know Dad doesn't know the first thing about toddlers. Why can't you just give me some ideas on what I should do to be sure Eric and I both live to see his second birthday?"

"Look, you're a father, Calvin," she said, "and I think you need to get advice from a father. Besides, there are some things your dad has been learning recently that may surprise you."

Of course, thought Calvin. If his father was discovering anything new, his mother would be the one to let Calvin know about it. As he told his mom, his father never talked to him. It was the family way.

Calvin's reaction isn't all that surprising, given the attachment pattern that had been forged between him and his dad. Without having the words to describe it, Marlene was hopeful that her son and husband could change that pattern.

As we hinted toward the end of the last chapter, attachment patterns can be changed, even in adulthood. Through a process called earned secure attachment, people can develop the sense of well-being and confidence that results from healthy attachment. In other words, they can finally tell their life story in a coherent, complete way. It won't happen, though, simply because they take in new factual information or have strong willpower. This transformation requires either a significant encounter with an outside relationship or a profound change in circumstances. (By the way, this chapter focuses only on the movement from insecure to secure attachment. Chronic abuse or emotionally overwhelming, traumatic events, however, can reverse a secure attachment pattern to an insecure one.)

What does it look like when someone gains secure attachment? Consider the following scenarios:

- A sensitive seven-year-old boy lives in a family in which emotion is dismissed, but he has a second grade teacher who "gets" him. As a result, his attachment can evolve to one that is no longer avoidant, but secure.
- A teen who lives in the whirl of her mother's anxiety may look up to a coach or youth group leader who asks her questions about her life without expecting her to take care of his or her own distress. As a result, the teen may begin to have the experience of feeling felt with no strings attached.
- An adult with a dismissing position toward attachment may have done pretty well on her own until she is diagnosed with cancer. Confronting her own mortality, she joins a support group and is surrounded by other patients offering her comfort—a totally new experience for her. These cosuffering confidants may invite her to tell them the story of her life from the beginning, as they seek to know her in this place of deep vulnerability.

The common denominator in these stories is that all three individuals open themselves to being known for the first time. None of them manage to alter their attachment patterns or orientations by themselves. In fact, they engage with people who are also working hard to make sense of their own lives. Remember, there is no such thing as an individual brain. Transformation requires a collaborative interaction, with one person empathically listening and responding to the other so that the speaker has the experience, perhaps for the first time, *of feeling felt by another.*

One of the wonderfully mysterious outcomes of storytelling and listening is their capacity to enable our left and right modes of processing to integrate. The left and right brain are integratively woven together in a way that doesn't happen when someone simply reads or listens to text that invokes logical, linear, right-wrong processing.

A person who listens empathically and responsively as someone else tells his or her story is able to validate the storyteller and, through questions and musing, arouse that individual's curiosity so he or she will consider alternative ways to imagine his or her story. At the same time, emotion and memory that have been buried deep in the storyteller's right hemisphere and lower brain emerge. This interpersonal interaction exposes these functions of the mind and facilitates the integration of various layers of neural structures and brain systems, which in turn creates new neural networks. The firing patterns of these networks, *though previously potentially available,* did not exist before such interactions took place.

Such an encounter is necessary because we cannot change our stories without simultaneously changing the neural pathways that correlate with those changes.

GOD AT WORK

While the term *earned secure attachment* is used by researchers to describe an experience between two people, essentially it is the process through which God wants to take all of us. The details and process will differ according to each individual's life, but by allowing his story to intersect with ours, God is moving us all from deep places of insecurity to security. The apostle Paul hints at this in one of his letters:

> Therefore, if anyone is in Christ, the new creation has come: The old has gone, the new is here! (2 CORINTHIANS 5:17)

Once again we see that creation—in this case through the evidence of earned secure attachment—points us toward the deep realities that God began in the new creation process with the resurrection of Jesus.

Jesus' resurrection is not merely (or even primarily) an event that grants believers a "Get into Heaven Free" card. God is already at work restoring his creation now. Again, Paul states specifically how this can work itself out in our lives today:

> Do not conform to the pattern of this world, but be transformed by the *renewing of your mind.* (ROMANS 12:2, ITALICS MINE)

If we suffer from insecure attachment, looking to God's story in its fullness gives us the opportunity to move to a secure means of connecting with him and others. But this is where things get tricky. Even the way we hear, understand, and attempt to enter into God's story will be colored by the hues of our own.

Making all things new

Scripture is primarily—among other things—a story. From Genesis to Revelation it is the story of God's desire and practice to be with us, culminating in the life of Jesus. God is *present* with us. But not merely "with us" physically. He is that to be sure, and even closer, in the presence of the Holy Spirit. In Jesus, God comes not simply to be in the same room, but rather to walk right up to us, look us in the eye, touch us on the shoulder, and speak our names out loud, smile, and share a drink with us, all the while engaging, persuading, challenging, inviting, convicting, and empowering each of us, loving us into new creation.

And in the process, *our neural networks are changed.*

Healthy attachment, as we know, emerges from contingent communication, in which two individuals, through both their spoken dialogue and non-verbal cues, each affirm the other as they interact. This reflects the postulate that there is no such thing as an individual brain. In orthodox creedal life, followers of Jesus contend that God is a triune social being. There is a Father. There is a Son. There is a Spirit. Therefore, within the life of God there is no single "brain." Within the Godhead, God has made perfect sense of his life, if you will. His own communal life is one of contingent communication.

That contingency is displayed no more poignantly than in Gethsemane (Luke 22:39-43). It is not too much to imagine the Son hearing echoes of the Voice at his baptism telling him who he is even as he pleads, "Father . . . take this cup from me!" As he speaks, he surely senses the Father hearing and responding to every word, every crimson drop of sweat. He feels God feeling him. He sees himself in the Father's eyes. The mentalization is as attuned and alive as it has ever been. The Son senses the Father's presence, and the Father's persistent invitation to the Son to trust him. Then Jesus responds, "not my will, but yours." The Son senses the Father's presence, his love, and his acceptance.

While on earth, Jesus lived as one with the Father, with an infinitely secure attachment to him. Jesus was able to trust the Father with his life, even if that led to death. With that much confidence in his relationship with God, it is no wonder Jesus was so free of anxiety that he was able to do all that he did: heal, turn tables, speak with wisdom and conviction, calm stormy weather, withstand torture, and snuff out the sting of death through the power of his own death and resurrection.

But we, viewing the universe through the lenses of our insecure attachments, have a difficult time believing that God gives us absolute security as well. Oh, we at times "believe" it with our left brains. But the avoidant, ambivalent, or disorganized patterns in our childhood development tend to lead us to cloud, distort, or ignore God and respond to him in ways that leave us disconnected from the life of joy Jesus describes in the Gospels.

How is it that despite our "belief" in God's love for us, we don't experience that love transforming our inner lives or our relationships with friends, parents, children, spouses, or neighbors? We assent to the idea of the Holy Spirit's capacity to transform us as theological dogma imbedded in the neural networks of our semantic memory. But often we don't sense God's transforming power comprehensively with our mind's right mode of being. In fact, our right mode is often overcome by our left mode's systematic tendency, so that when we're asked how God views us, we automatically respond with words like *sinful, depraved,* and *wicked.* And we can refer to particular passages of Scripture to prove it. We're really good at that. But *that* is not always good for *us.*

Engaging with the story

Scripture is many things, not least a lightning rod evoking and revealing the various parts of us that are wounded, healed, delighted, resentful, affectionate, or sad. Our reactions to the Bible, then, are rooted in our stories.

Perhaps you have been gently bathed, forgiven, and enlivened in the waters of its story of grace and adventure. You may breathe it in daily like oxygen, a practice first mediated by a mindful spiritual overseer, parent, or friend. On the other hand, maybe you've been on the receiving end of Scripture used as a bludgeon by an overassertive parent or authoritarian church leader. If so, you may want to scream (if only under your breath) at the very mention of it, given the memory, explicit and implicit, of the role of "religion" in your history.

I say all of this to emphasize that the way we approach and react to God's story as it is told in the stories of the people of the Bible is itself biased by our stories, our brains and all that their neural networks represent in terms of memory, emotion, and attachment, and the degree to which our minds are more or less integrated. This does not mean that we only hear through those particular headphones, but our spiritual auditory system will be influenced by them.

With that in mind, let me encourage you to be open to the possibility that God is in the business of changing your story from poorer to richer, from harsher to gentler, from rigid to flexible, from sadder to joyful, from shameful to confident and free—and by extension the story of those with whom you have intimate emotional contact. Telling your story to an empathic listener is one means through which he works. Scripture is another. But, in order for God's story to penetrate yours, you must do something that is not always easy for you to do. You must pay attention.

With its different authors, forms of literary style (e.g., history, poetry, instruction), historical expanse, and more, Scripture is both a simple and complex story. It recounts how God got involved in the lives of a particular people, a people who were not necessarily great partners, for the purpose of collaboratively saving the world from itself and establishing God's Kingdom of justice, mercy, and goodness.

But this is no fairy tale. Naturally, given that the story involves real people, it's messy. Also, since it involves God, you get the sense that the story is not so much about how to simply clean up the mess, but how creative you can get with the mess you have. This is what God seems to be up to—creating good, mysterious things out of messes.

We all must pay attention to those aspects of God's story that we often, with our particular neural networks, ignore, are unaware of, or are distressed by. For instance, how often do we read right over the passages in which God expresses his "delight" for us? Or how often do we stop to consider what the writer of Hebrews means when he writes: "For the joy set before him he [Jesus] endured the cross, scorning its shame" (Hebrews 12:2)? After all, most people feel shame at some level; very few stop to consider its corrosive effects. Sometimes these tendencies are reflections of our own insecure attachment; but God is also in the business of drawing those with secure attachments even more deeply into security—in the words of Paul, deeper into faith, hope, and love. It is not just those with insecure attachments who desperately need a Savior. We all do.

Over the course of the remaining portion of this book we will examine different themes of God's story as they press up against our own. To begin, I invite you to consider one simple vignette that both illustrates and vitalizes the change we long to experience by being known.

In Luke 3, we encounter Jesus at his baptism. (This story is recounted in other Gospels as well). Luke records that

> When all the people were being baptized, Jesus was baptized too. And as he was praying, heaven was opened and the Holy Spirit descended on him in bodily form like a dove. And a voice came from heaven: "You are my Son, whom I love; with you I am well pleased." (vv. 21-22)

This passage focuses on Jesus and his experience of hearing God's voice. The Voice centers its attention on Jesus and the fact that he is loved and is pleasing to the Father. The presence of the form of a dove highlights the activity of the Holy Spirit in this drama and is a reminder that the Father engaged Jesus through a physically sensed phenomenon, not an idea limited to an abstraction in his mind. In John's Gospel we also read that John the Baptist witnessed this dovelike form descending to envelop Jesus, which told John there was something unique and remarkable about his cousin (John 1:32-33).

While we rightly focus on Jesus' experience and this validation of his public ministry, I invite you to consider the possible additional layers and textures of this story. Good narratives, like great symphonies, often contain one major theme on which several movements are developed. The anchor melody is never far from the surface, and this one is no different. Consider an additional thrust of this narrative, a supporting movement if you will—Jesus being the revelation of the Father's inherent nature.

Let's examine the possibility that the focus in this story is as much on Jesus' experience of *God* as it is on telling us something about *Jesus*. Yes, we see that Jesus is loved and is pleasing to God. No doubt the writer, given the context of the entire Gospel, is attempting to demonstrate this, and it confirms what Luke records just a few paragraphs earlier, "As Jesus grew up, he increased in wisdom and in favor with God and people" (Luke 2:52). The progression is rather straightforward: Jesus lives his life in a way that is pleasing to God; God's pleasure follows Jesus' behavior. This is a major theme. But we don't want to miss the important undertones Luke is composing that give deep, supportive resonance to the symphony.

What if this is a story that rings with subtle yet clear tones the melody that Yahweh is a God who, from the earliest moments of Jesus' awareness of him, is, by his very nature, pleased with him. That *before Jesus even began to behave* in a pleasing manner, he sensed the presence of God and that presence was dominated by a sense of God's pleasure with him. Sort of like Eric Liddell in *Chariots of Fire*, feeling God's pleasure before all the running.

What if from his earliest days on the planet, Jesus was deeply aware that God's fundamental orientation toward his entire creation, humans especially, was one of deep, compassionate affection? What if he sensed that the Father was prone to outlandish behavior such as taking the ridiculous risk of persuading and urging, rather than forcing us to love and sacrifice, patiently waiting for us—for millennia—to partner with him in the task of blessing the earth and all of its peoples?

Practice Being Known

If you'd like to try the meditation exercise based on the story of Jesus' baptism in Luke 3, find a quiet place where you will not be distracted or interrupted. Allow yourself to be in a comfortable posture, with your eyes closed.

Take a deep breath and begin to imagine yourself in a physical environment that is peaceful and calm. You may visualize yourself beside the ocean or a lake, in a forest or a meadow, or surrounded by mountains—anywhere that exudes beauty and tranquility. Allow yourself, now, in your imagination, to take a few moments to be aware of your surroundings, simply taking in what you sense visually, tactilely, and auditorially.

Next, allow yourself to sense God's presence. There is no right or wrong way for him to appear or be revealed. You may even perceive his physicality to the point of being in bodily form.

Now, if you are a woman, imagine hearing God clearly say to you directly, calling you by name, "You are my daughter, and I do so love you. I am *so pleased* with you and that you are on the earth." Or if you are a man, you would imagine hearing something like, "You are my son whom I love. I am *so pleased* with you and that you are on the earth."

Sense, if you can, God looking you directly in the eyes as he says these words. Do not turn away from his gaze. Do not resist his voice. Allow yourself to be in his presence for several minutes. Do not leave this place in your mind quickly. What do you feel? What do you feel God feeling as he looks with tenderness and strength into the windows of your soul?

Remember that people have different reactions to this exercise. There is in fact no right response, only a true one.

I invite you to practice this meditation—it may take only a few minutes—each day for six weeks. If you do, remember that you are not simply engaging with some abstract dimension of your mind; you are in fact, changing the neural networks of your brain. Practically, this exercise may lead you to a deep awareness of being known and cared for by your Father. Initially, this may take place only during the meditation. Eventually, however, you will find that you can quickly access the positive images, feelings, sensations, and words you hear during moments of discomfort in everyday life, altering your response to an anxiety-provoking event.

What if Jesus' life was first and foremost a *response* to his acute awareness of Yahweh's affection, to the depth of being known and loved by his Father? In this sense, the progression is reversed: Jesus' behavior follows God's pleasure. First, before anything, God is infinitely pleased—he's just that kind of God to begin with—and then Jesus responded with behavior that was reflective of one who is supremely confident that he is infinitely loved by God. In this sense, as he grew, Jesus increased in his awareness of God's pleasure. He did not simply grow in what he knew *about* God, but in his *felt awareness of God's pleasure with him, God's joy in* Jesus' *presence.* Jesus' life was a living, breathing, fearless response to his experience of a God who contingently pays attention to his creation and takes great joy in its presence.

Consider the following passage written by King David, with which Jesus would have been quite familiar:

> You have searched me, LORD,
>> and you know me.
> You know when I sit and when I rise;
>> you perceive my thoughts from afar.
> You discern my going out and my lying down;
>> you are familiar with all my ways.
> Before a word is on my tongue
>> you, LORD, know it completely.
> You hem me in behind and before,
>> and you lay your hand upon me.
> Such knowledge is too wonderful for me,
>> too lofty for me to attain.
> Where can I go from your Spirit?
>> Where can I flee from your presence?
> If I go up to the heavens, you are there;
>> if I make my bed in the depths, you are there.
> If I rise on the wings of the dawn,
>> if I settle on the far side of the sea,
> even there your hand will guide me,
>> your right hand will hold me fast.
> If I say, "Surely the darkness will hide me
>> and the light become night around me,"
> even the darkness will not be dark to you;
>> the night will shine like the day,

> for darkness is as light to you. . . .
> How precious to me are your thoughts, God!
> How vast is the sum of them!
> Were I to count them,
> they would outnumber the grains of sand—
> when I awake, I am still with you. (PSALM 139:1-12, 17-18)

Imagine Jesus taking in David's experience. He comes to know a Yahweh who is intimately involved in the life of his individual creatures. This is mentalizing of the most profound nature.

If we lived as if we believed this was true, would we, too, not be free from anxiety and fear? Would we not be comforted? Would we not feel deeply cared for and protected? Yet as a consequence would we not seek justice and peace? Would we not rather give generously than hoard? Would we not be more patient with our spouses? Would we not be better behaved parents at our sons' and daughters' baseball and soccer games? Would we not remember the Sabbath more often and live less harried, less frenzied lives? Would we not be more creative in our handling of punishment for criminals and third world debt? You know the answer.

It is no wonder, given his immersion in the life of this kind of God, that from Jesus would emerge the Sermon on the Mount, the multiple healings, the longing and weeping over Jerusalem, the crimson sweat of Gethsemane, the journey to Golgotha, and his ultimate trust in God's vindication that came with the brilliance of a Sunday morning.

NO INVISIBLE MEN—OR WOMEN

Even the Old Testament reveals a God who always tracks with people. Here God is no flat, two-dimensional drawing. He is constantly on the move, but never hyperactive. Oscillating in his comings and goings, but never inattentive. Intimate, but never controlling or controllable. Dangerous, but never insensitive to the fact—or apologetic for it. Loving, but never patronizing. In Genesis 16 we are introduced to Hagar, the maidservant of Sarai, Abram's wife. (God had not yet renamed them Abraham and Sarah.) Abram's narrative is already muddy; in his fear that God will not follow through on his promise to provide a son through Abram's wife, he has succumbed to Sarai's suggestion that he have sex with her slave in order to guarantee offspring. After Hagar conceives, she shows contempt for Sarai, who in return begins to abuse her. (This behavior is from the family intended by God to bless the entire world.)

Hagar, in her desperation, flees Abraham's mobile estate to the only place she can go: the wilderness. What is striking is that before Hagar shows any evidence that she is interested in God's assistance, *he* is looking for *her*:

> The angel of the LORD found Hagar near a spring in the desert; it was the spring that is beside the road to Shur. And he said, "Hagar, servant of Sarai, where have you come from, and where are you going?"
> (GENESIS 16:7-8)

Notice that *he finds her*. God is watching, looking, and finding. The text gives no indication that she says anything before he acts. He asks her a question, as if he is not certain of what she is about to think or do. He is seemingly quite aware of where she is *now*. Her nonverbal expressions tell it all. But he seems to desperately want her to have the experience of being known by him, not just for her to know information about her future, but to be felt and seen by the God of grace. This is the kind of God he is. But notice that God is no kindly grandfather who merely observes. When Hagar admits she is running away from her mistress, he gives her the following direction:

> Then the angel of the LORD told her, "Go back to your mistress and submit to her." The angel added, "I will increase your descendants so much that they will be too numerous to count."
> The angel of the LORD also said to her:
>
> "You are now pregnant
>   and you will give birth to a son.
> You shall name him Ishmael,
>   for the LORD has heard of your misery."
> (GENESIS 16:9-12)

God requires Hagar to turn back into the very pain from which she has fled. He leaves no stone of her broken life unturned. But without flinching, God adds that he will not only preserve her pregnancy but make her descendants "too numerous to count." He will ensure her security, despite her status as an Egyptian, a slave, and a woman. In her time, in her position, she is less valuable than a domesticated animal. But God is speaking to parts of her heart that only she would have, could have known:

> She gave this name to the LORD who spoke to her: "You are the God who sees me," for she said, "I have now seen the One who sees me." (GENESIS 16:13)

Hagar has the experience of being *seen*. And in her exchange with God, she sees the One "*who sees me.*" God meets her and she is known. And this changes her life—and the history of the world—forever. It is in her being known, seen, heard, and felt that she is able to return to Sarai.

Too often we feel invisible, most notably when God is in our presence. We don't feel seen or known by our spouses, our parents, our friends, and especially our enemies. We long to be seen, sensing that when that happens, we will move with courage, kindness, and strength. Jesus, immersed in stories such as these, lived a life as one who was *seen*, as one who was *known* by God. He did not simply know *about* a God who knows. Jesus was *known*, just as Hagar was.

God wants the same for you. Even our parents, no matter how well they relate with us, "hit the mark" only about 50 percent of the time with us. But God hits the mark *every* time. In the language of attachment, our heavenly Father mentalizes at peak capacity—he lovingly senses and interprets our feelings, desires, and intentions at all times.

This is not to suggest that we are not sinful or wicked. For indeed we are. I am suggesting that this often is not a very helpful place to begin. The place to begin is the beginning. And in the beginning God was, and is, pleased. As we will see in chapter 10, our brain is easily drawn to pay attention to the source of sin. But what if we begin to pay attention to God's mentalization of us on *his* terms?

IN TUNE WITH GOD

I introduced Roger (insecure avoidant), Lydia (insecure anxious), and Emily (insecure disorganized) in the last chapter and told you about some of the different ways I worked with each of them. Though my approach varied depending on their form of insecure attachment, I had them all do one of the same exercises. This form of guided visual imagery used Scripture to help them pull together their feelings, perceptions, and sensations in a coherent way.

Regardless of how broken their stories, I wanted them to be able to hear the voice of God telling them that they are safe, that they are loved, and that they have been called to new life, new vitality, and new adventure.

When each was seated comfortably in my office, I invited them to close their eyes and picture themselves in a peaceful, calm environment. Once they visualized an actual setting, whether by the ocean, in the mountains, or on a quiet forest path, I invited them to take in the beauty around them. Then I asked them to allow themselves to sense God's presence, without telling them what that might look like. Next I asked them to imagine God calling them by name and saying, "You are my child whom I love. I am so pleased with you and that you are on the earth." I asked them to be open to his voice, to linger in his presence. Then I asked them what they felt as they allowed themselves the experience of feeling God looking at them with tenderness and love.

Roger, Lydia, and Emily each had a different reaction to this exercise. There is in fact no right response, only a true one. However, their reactions revealed the manner in which each tends to respond to emotional intimacy.

Roger actually found this exercise very difficult. Because he had grown up paying virtually no attention to his feelings, it was difficult for him to sense much of anything. Adding to his discomfort, I asked him to visualize, which required him to engage an underutilized right mode of operation required for visuospatial orientation and emotion.

Lydia, whose mother had passed on her anxiety to her daughter, worried that she might be "manipulating God" by creating her own version of what he might say to her. She was clearly uneasy at first, admitting her concern that she might be doing something "wrong." Her left-mode, right-wrong dimension was dominating her experience, creating more anxiety. Because she was easily distracted by these thoughts during the exercise, I suggested she engage in frequent shortened versions of this exercise, which enhanced the likelihood of new neural networks being formed. Gradually, she was able to remain present with her sensations for longer periods, gathering what her body was telling her without the interference of other brain signals.

Emily was distressed by my explanation of what we would do during the meditation—even before it began. She sensed at a level she could not put into words that to do this would be too unsettling, too frightening. She felt somewhat disoriented and confused by the idea of engaging God in such an intimate way, even if it was only an imagined encounter. For that reason, we engaged in other, more gradual approaches that allowed her to slowly encounter emotion without becoming completely undone by the process.

One of these exercises was the body scan, which I also used with Roger (see page 125).

Although each of their stories was different, eventually each reported feeling peaceful, loved, and cared for when they engaged in this exercise. They also reported experiencing relief and a sense that their distress, anxiety, and fear had been replaced with a palpable tranquility.

They had experienced a clear revelation of God's deep joy in their presence, which is true all the time. This is God's fundamental posture toward us . . . always. I am not suggesting that this is the only thing God feels in response to us. Scripture is clear: he feels angry, sad, grieved, and the like—but all of these and other more noxious emotions are undergirded by his deep covenantal agape, one quality of which is deep joy in our presence. What would your life be like if you were completely aware of the Father's deep awareness of and pleasure with you throughout all of your waking hours?

This exercise is not limited to comforting those parts of us that are fearful or wounded. It also speaks to those insecure behaviors that are anything but examples of peace, patience, faithfulness, gentleness, kindness, or self-control. It is not afraid to set limits. As the writer of the letter to the Hebrews reminds us:

> "My son, do not make light of the Lord's discipline, and do not
> lose heart when he rebukes you, because the Lord disciplines those
> he loves, and he chastens everyone he accepts as his child." Endure
> hardship as discipline; God is treating you as his children. For what
> children are not disciplined by their father? (Hebrews 12:5-7)

Therefore, do not fear the comprehensive nature of the Father's voice when he tells you he is pleased with you—even in the face of discipline.

God never connects with us simply to make us feel safe or loved. His transformation always includes a command (a word against which our tendency is to rail) to follow him to the remaining places within ourselves and the world where darkness, cruelty, injustice, and rebellion persist. He invites us to go into ever deeper places within ourselves and within the world, both ventures requiring a greater degree of faith, hope, and love. He is a God, as C. S. Lewis noted, who is good but not safe; easy to please but hard to satisfy.

Regardless of the situation, God wants you to know you are his child in whom he takes great pleasure. Will you pay attention to this, and how will you respond? With frequent practice of this exercise (and others like it), when you face a difficult temptation or situation, you can envision Jesus with his arm firmly around your shoulder, reminding you that, "You are just the right person for this dilemma. Your friend [spouse, child, boss, etc.] needs just what only you can bring to the table." Or, "You are mine. It is time to give up this wandering, avoiding, frightened behavior [this gossip, this sloth, this shame, this arrogance, this mindlessness] that you use to cope with your mind and your world. It is time to join the adventure." (We will deal with the issue of shame more explicitly in chapter 10.)

HOW TO ENGAGE WITH SCRIPTURE

As Roger, Lydia, and Emily found, we can be changed by allowing God's story to intersect with our own. When we tell our stories or listen to another person's story, our left and right modes of processing integrate. This is why simply reading the Ten Commandments as a list of dos and don'ts has so little efficacy. The same can be said for Jesus' admonitions during the Sermon on the Mount or the apostle Paul's instructions to the early church communities. Isolating commands for right living apart from their storied context is at best neurologically nonintegrating and, at worst, disintegrating. This is why telling our stories is so vitally important.

But narratives are not the only instruments within Scripture that can help us integrate our minds and lives. Poetry is another powerful literary tool. It has several distinct features:

- By activating our sense of rhythm, poetry accesses our right-mode operations and systems.
- Reading poetry has the effect of catching us off guard. Our imaginations are invigorated when our usual linear expectations of prose (that one word will follow obediently behind another on the way to a predictable end) don't apply. This can stimulate buried emotional states and layers of memory.
- Finally, poetry not only appeals to right-mode processing, but to left mode as well, given its use of language. This makes it a powerful integrative tool.

Appropriately, then, the Hebrew psalter lies at the center of the Christian Scriptures. One hundred and fifty poems and songs were collected over hundreds of years, bound into a canonical book that is whole in itself. The psalms are not to be approached (as we moderns tend to do) merely as a collection of unrelated poems. Yes, each one speaks with its own peculiar rhythm and authority; but we only understand it in the context of the entire psalter and then only in the context of the entire Bible.

Here in the middle of the muddle—between the stories of exile, homecoming, rebellion, kingdom building, further exile, prophetic warning and wooing, the coming of the Messiah, death, resurrection, the building of God's Kingdom, and a future hope—lies a series of poems that bring it all together and bring our minds along for the ride. Perhaps the psalms are so appealing in the first place because of their power to integrate so many disparate layers and systems of our brains. They point us to the story of God as a whole, which in turn points us to Jesus. And this, I suggest, can move us from an insecure attachment to a secure one, and from unhealthy to healthy mentalization.

For example, consider Psalm 6, in which David hints that the human drama of connecting, beginning with parents and offspring, is a reflection of what we do as children of God:

> Have mercy on me, LORD, for I am faint;
>   heal me, LORD, for my bones are in agony.
> My soul is in deep anguish.
>   How long, LORD, how long?
> Turn, LORD, and deliver me;
>   save me because of your unfailing love.
>   (vv. 2-4)

Can you not hear the peal of the infant in all of us as we cry out these words? Who hasn't at some point felt these words and longed to say them? Next we read the psalmist's experience of God's response:

> Away from me, all you who do evil,
>   for the LORD has heard my weeping.
> The LORD has heard my cry for mercy;
>   the LORD accepts my prayer.
> All my enemies will be overwhelmed with shame and anguish;
>   they will turn back and suddenly be put to shame. (vv. 8-10)

The poem expresses David's anguish, followed by his deep awareness of God's deliverance. He *feels felt* by God—God has heard his weeping, recognized his cry and responded, so the child feels accepted. As a result, his understanding of his circumstances and his vision for the future are revolutionized. This does not happen merely as a result of the writer's simple assent to a new set of facts; rather he experiences an existential shift that occurs because a need has been met. This exemplifies the psalmist's mentalizing God as one who considers him, who compassionately responds to his distress.

David, the warrior and eventual king of Israel, wrote many psalms while on the run from Saul and others seeking his life. But he was also a musician who imagined and embodied his experience with God through poetry. His verse reflects David's sense of God's mindfulness of him, perhaps expressed most powerfully in Psalm 139 (see pages 144–145).

David feels searched, perceived, sought out, and protected. He senses the complexity and intimacy in which he was made—and that God was there when he made him. He senses himself in God's mind and senses God's thoughts toward him. Like a child who, when faced with adversity, pictures his mother thinking of him with comforting, assuring thoughts, so David does with God.

When we read this poem, the Spirit uses it to facilitate the integration of our brains and to demonstrate God's mentalizing posture toward us. If we allow ourselves to be immersed in the form as well as the language of this song, we are overwhelmed with feeling felt, the awareness of being known. This is not merely a litany of facts about God. Although deep, left-brain theology infuses these words, the power of David's experience of God is delivered via the right-brain activating force of poetry. David's memory and understanding of God's action in Israel's *story*—in *his* story—infuse him with the sense of feeling felt—being known—by God. Putting this lyric into the form of music brings neural networks together, knitting David's heart into a quilt of coherence.

Not perfection, mind you. David's life was anything but neat and tidy. Reading about the dynamics in his family of origin in 1 Samuel 16 and 17 indicates he may have been insecurely attached. When God directed the prophet and judge Samuel to the house of David's father, Jesse, where he was to anoint a replacement for King Saul, Samuel asked Jesse to call out all his sons. Jesse seemed not to remember (or was he protecting?) the youngest of his eight sons.

The arrival of David appears to have been an afterthought. Jesse called him in from the fields only when Samuel, after being restrained by the Spirit from choosing any of the older seven men, asked him if he had any other sons. Tending sheep was a job that usually fell to the socially insignificant in that culture, but that was David's job. How was it that David seemed so easily forgotten? Clearly, he did not occupy the same status in his father's mind as did his brothers.

In the next chapter, we read that David's brothers were sent off to fight the war against the Philistines, while David was sent to assist King Saul, who was wracked with some sort of mood disorder, perhaps manic depression. David's skill with the lyre comforted the king while his brothers battled the Philistines. Then, Jesse sent David with food provisions for his brothers, telling him to bring home news of their welfare at the battlefront. Eliab was not happy to see his little brother talking to some of the other fighting men:

> When Eliab, David's oldest brother, heard him speaking with the men, he burned with anger at him and asked, "Why have you come down here? And with whom did you leave those few sheep in the wilderness? I know how conceited you are and how wicked your heart is; you came down only to watch the battle."
>
> "Now what have I done?" said David. "Can't I even speak?"
>
> (1 SAMUEL 17:28-29)

Apparently not all was well in the house of Jesse. Perhaps Eliab was keenly sensitive at having been passed over for Samuel's blessing, and for a shepherd at that. Perhaps David provoked some of the discord himself. But there's no doubt that Jesse was not contributing to a family environment of emotional safety, understanding, and grace. At some level David, even in his own home, was the target of ridicule and dismissal. It is reasonable to wonder about his attachment pattern (which we can't know explicitly) and the degree to which he endured a father's dismissive or perhaps indulgent orientation toward him, as well as angry, perhaps even disorganizing behavior from his siblings.

Many of us can easily resonate with various parts of this story. Conflicts with parents and siblings who don't get us. Ridicule from those whom we expect to watch our back. The feeling that people outside our families are more accepting of us than those within.

Yet at some point God met David in ways and through relationships that bridged the emotional and neural gaps caused by old family wounds and insalubrious mentalizing. Perhaps David sensed God's presence during his time alone as a shepherd, surviving by his own wits. Perhaps his friendship with

Saul's son Jonathan or the mentoring he received from Nathan the prophet gave him a sense of well-being.

In his psalms, we get a picture of a man who, though he intimately knew the feeling of being wounded, ashamed, and afraid, held this pain simultaneously with a deep awareness of God's presence, attunement, and affection. David felt felt, and so he remained flexible, confident, and courageous in the face of adversity.

As we permit his poetry to embrace us, to sing to our hearts—our minds, our brains—we come to a deeper place of integration and wellness too. It places us in position to perceive God's presence through a process that activates neural firing in both right and left hemispheres, in lower and higher brain areas. It facilitates the connection of the hemispheres in ways that mere left-mode systematic inculcation of facts about God does not.

In the coming chapters, we'll delve into classical spiritual disciplines, such as meditation, that will enable God's story to wrap itself protectively around us. We may find this a challenge, though, if we begin with dominantly dismissive, entangled, or unresolved traumatic postures toward attachment. If so, we may either avoid capturing the emotional depth of the psalm, filtering out any and all distressing feelings (such as the several passages in which anger, shame, revenge, or complaining are front and center), or be overwhelmed by those very same passages, our right mode smothering that of the left.

THE REST OF THE STORY

I opened this chapter by suggesting that Marlene, Calvin's mother, is wise. Why would I say that, given that she advised her son to talk to his father, the last man Calvin wanted to emulate as a parent?

Her counsel didn't make much sense to Calvin, but because he had a lot of faith in his mother—and because he didn't know who else he could talk to—he reluctantly arranged to meet with Ed, his dad. Their discussion would be the beginning of Calvin's remembering his future differently.

When they met for breakfast one Saturday, his father, a man in his early sixties, began to share details of his own life that Calvin had never known. Ed's father, who had died before Calvin was born, was a violent alcoholic. Ed had sworn that if he were to have children, he would never treat his children the way he had been treated. And he would never tell anyone about his early childhood, fearing that to do so would increase the risk that Ed would repeat it—not to mention how ashamed he felt simply reflecting on his life in his home growing up.

As an adult, Ed retreated whenever emotional issues arose in the home. He allowed Calvin's mother to take over at those times. He was just too fearful that he would eventually strike out in anger and someone would get hurt. Unfortunately, Ed's fear kept him from sharing virtually anything emotionally with his children, even the joys and victories of their many accomplishments. His children thought Dad was disinterested; he thought he was doing them a favor by keeping his distance.

But when Eric, his first grandchild, was born, Ed began to feel deep sadness, even to the point of despair. He so longed to have a connection with the little boy—he was less fearful of hurting him, because he was not directly in charge of his welfare. But he simply did not know how to do it.

When Ed shared his desire with his wife, she suggested he come to see me. Over time he began to tell his story of fear, shame, and grief. Ed had been reared in a religious tradition in which God seemed as angry and disappointed as his own father. Church attendance was very important but tended only to reinforce his sense of guilt and shame. He developed a dismissive form of insecure attachment.

After our initial meetings, Ed began to meditate on particular psalms, employing various contemplative prayer methods. This practice, along with experiences in therapy, gave him the sense of feeling felt. He then began to imagine and make sense of his story in new ways. Ed no longer was overwhelmed by the memory of his father's anger. He was less terrified of intimacy, no longer worried about his own anger.

Ed learned to imagine God as one who is pleased with him, who isn't waiting for him to fail so that he can shame him. As he read over Scripture with a newfound thirst, Ed began to see the whole scope of God's story. He was able to imagine God attending to him with deep love and affection. The apostle Paul's proclamation that "if anyone is in Christ, the new creation has come: The old has gone, the new is here!" was no longer simply a metaphor of a mental process; it reflected real changes in Ed's mind/brain, new synapsing networks that represented his transformed experience. These eventually led him to be willing to take more risks with his family, including initiating emotional closeness with his grandson.

What he hadn't expected was for his son, Calvin, to take the first step. Nor was Calvin expecting what he got from his father when he did. When he heard his father's story of transformation, especially in the spiritual dimension of his life, Calvin was stunned, relieved, and, at first, somewhat disoriented, given that neither he nor his dad had much practice sharing emotions with each other.

Calvin later told Ed how hearing his father's story gave him a sense of relief; before their subsequent conversations, he assumed his father was distant because he was not interested in him. This had made Calvin question his adequacy and made him less confident. Now he was discovering that his father had only been frightened, convinced that by keeping his distance from his children he would protect them from the parts of him that might wound them.

For his part, Calvin found himself, over time, becoming less and less anxious about his relationship with Eric. He noted that as his father spoke with him in tones and body language that had been absent and for which he had so long hungered and thirsted, he became gentler and less urgent with Eric. Life seemed less harried. And Eric, even at his young age, seemed to respond by being less reactive to Calvin.

And what of Ed and his grandson? Eric, I assure you, will never be the same. What neuroscience is pointing to is that as one person makes more coherent sense of their narrative (Ed, in this case), he or she has the potential to change the brains of those with whom he or she has intimate contact by activating new neural networks. Eric's brain circuitry will largely be shaped, given his age, by the nonverbal, right-mode communication emanating from his father. Calvin's mindfulness of Eric's states of mind and his consequent attunement to his son's nonverbal cues will help the little boy attach securely to his father.

Do you ever feel as if it's too late for change? Ed shows that it never is. God is always at work. If you worry that you messed up your children years ago and now all you can do is pray for them, I want to assure you there is hope. But this hope comes from you making sense of *your* story first, not your child's. Even if your own parents are unwilling to write a different ending to their story, don't despair. Rather, consider how God's narrative is calling to yours with a voice and demeanor that is easy to please and equally hard to satisfy. As each of us diligently works to make sense of our lives, and as we allow for God's story to intersect and transform ours by placing ourselves (through various practices including meditation and reflection upon the Scriptures) in positions for him to do so, we become examples and agents of the new creation, with the experience of earned secure attachment pointing the way.

Chapter 9

THE PREFRONTAL CORTEX AND THE MIND OF CHRIST

The prefrontal cortex (PFC), along with our language centers, is the part of our neurological system that sets us apart from all of God's other created beings. Attention, memory, emotion, and attachment all come together and are integrated at the PFC. That's why I often refer to this part of the brain as the Grand Central Station of the mind.

I recall vividly (though thankfully she does not) where my daughter and I were standing in our kitchen the morning when the trains in my mind's Grand Central Station crashed and I couldn't find a conductor anywhere.

Rachel was about three and a half years old on this early Saturday morning. Her mother was sleeping, and I was already busy getting some things done while it was quiet. Rachel, it seemed, had other plans, believing that tranquility is fine if you're asleep, but once awake all bets are off. Now, I have to say that had you forewarned me of what was about to happen, I would have dismissed you outright. But it did happen.

When Rachel got up, shortly after I did, she began to play music rather loudly on her little toy cassette player. I was still upstairs and hurried down the hallway to her room to quell the noise. I was intent on keeping the house quiet and my wife sleeping so I could finish some urgent matters (which now I don't even recall). I walked downstairs to the kitchen, and all remained quiet for a few minutes. Then a loud burst of music began emanating from what sounded like a Bose system coming down our stairs. Rachel, our blonde-haired little munchkin, was simply welcoming Saturday morning to our home with tunes from her toy cassette player. As she headed for the breakfast table, the train wreck began.

For reasons that I only later reflected on, I simply lost my mind. As Rachel entered the kitchen, I yelled at her, seemingly unaware that I was violating the official code of quiet I had only minutes before enacted and now felt compelled to enforce—loudly. And it was no mild enforcement. I can't quote myself, but I felt a furious rush of anger charge out of me in her direction. The trains were colliding, twisted metal everywhere.

I recall yelling something like "I said turn that off! If you can't do as I ask you, you don't need to be here. Go back upstairs!" Even as I write this, it's hard to believe what I felt and what I did. I wanted to hurt her feelings—and I turned out to be pretty good at that. Even as the words poured out of my mouth, a sliver of my mind was desperately trying to pull me back from the edge of insanity, but to no avail. I knew I was heading down the wrong track, but I couldn't—or wouldn't—stop myself. Imagine that. Me, the follower of Jesus, the psychiatrist, no less, yelling at his three-year-old for making too much noise—and being loud about it.

I saw Rachel's crestfallen face, the hurt, the puzzlement and shock at having her father shout at her for something so benign. She turned and went back upstairs without a word, shutting off her little music player as she left. What had come over me?

This (unfortunately) true story is a reflection of what we as humans do that leads to the brokenness we observe in our world. Friends, family members, members of churches or school communities, ethnic or religious groups, and even countries find ways to lose their minds, becoming the antithesis of what they claim that they desire. No doubt you encounter examples of it every day:

- your irritability in the checkout line when the little blinking light goes on and the cashier calls for a price check
- the way your teen rolls her eyes when you ask her to go up and change out of the halter top she planned to wear to school
- the insults hurled between a conservative and a liberal pundit on talk radio
- countries that go to war over a piece of land

Often in the heat of moments such as these, those involved feel as if they cannot help but respond the way they do. Yet the PFC enables us to consciously and intentionally choose our response when we are hurt, annoyed, or defensive. Could being more aware of the activity of my prefrontal cortex have prevented me from scolding my daughter so harshly and needlessly? Would it help you temper your irritation at the elderly woman in front of you who insists that a sign by the canned peaches says they're on sale for 79 cents, prompting the price check? Would it help us all love God and our neighbors more sincerely?

So far in this book we have examined a number of functions of the mind that operate within and between brains. Too often they are out of balance; the good news is that God intends to intersect our story with his, which has the potential to change our minds, our brains, and our lives. When our minds are integrated, train wrecks like the one in my family's kitchen are much less likely to happen. The prefrontal cortex plays a key role in integrating these brain functions effectively.

In this chapter, we will examine how the prefrontal cortex is a specific part of the central nervous system that models *in our very brains* what Jesus has called us to be as people of God's family. We will also witness the extent to which Jesus' prefrontal cortex was integrated when he walked the earth and how he calls us to live so that we can experience the same degree of mindful integration.

ANATOMY LESSON

The prefrontal cortex contains neurons responsible for a range of complex, conscious, intentional mental activity. Its different regions correspond to different functions of the mind. (See diagram on page 32.)

For example, the dorsolateral prefrontal cortex (along with other parts of the PFC) is associated with a number of executive functions that enable us to:

- discern and decide between conflicting thoughts and feelings;
- distinguish the difference between immediate gratification and long-term consequences;
- create a mental sense of expectations and what is necessary to achieve a desired goal; and
- focus attention on various mental activities, often simultaneously.

The orbital frontal cortex is associated with our sense of conscience and social judgment. It is linked with our ability to:

- generate emotional states and cognition that temper and regulate salient, pleasure-driven feelings, thoughts, and behaviors; and
- restrain our behavior so that we don't simply act on impulse.

The anterior cingulate cortex is often associated with the feelings that drive pleasure and reward-seeking behavior. It senses and directs the activation of behavior toward the most significant external or internal stimuli.

Although these subregions of the PFC play a key role in the activities described above, it would be wrong to conclude that each function is somehow contained neatly in a particular area of the brain. Each of these anatomical locations receives extensive input from other parts of the PFC as well as other regions of the brain. A great deal of incoming sensory data from other regions of the brain converges at the PFC, creating an extensive hub from which hundreds of neural pathways extend to influence and potentially regulate other regions of the brain, particularly the brain stem and limbic circuitry.

The prefrontal cortex, therefore, functions best when working in an integrated fashion with other parts of the brain. Although it serves some of the highest functions of the human mind, it relies on other areas of the brain that serve "lower" purposes, both in terms of their location in the central nervous system and their level of conscious awareness. This configuration hints at what we will more fully explore in the later chapters of this book when we examine the nature of community and the body of Christ.

Unlike our heartbeat or our normal breathing rhythm, which are examples of automatic activity that originates from the lower brain stem and limbic circuitry, the neurons of the PFC usually require *conscious attention* to activate them.

The input the PFC receives from the brain's lower regions represents those emotional and memory states that are the bulk of daily human behavior. The degree to which the various circuits representing the disparate functions of the mind (attention, memory, emotion, language, sensory perception, etc.) are integrated at the level of the PFC in a balanced fashion will to a large extent shape our behavior and attitudes.

NINE PFC FUNCTIONS

As we've seen, different anatomic regions of the PFC relate to particular mental activity. However, in his book *The Mindful Brain*, Dan Siegel offers another equally valid way of describing and interpreting the role of the PFC. He lists nine functions for which we heavily depend upon the prefrontal cortex.

In fact, secure attachment is highly correlated with the first eight functions listed below. These attributes are quite robust in people who are securely attached. The nine functions include:

1. *Body regulation.* Based on information it receives from the sympathetic and parasympathetic nervous systems, the PFC can influence our response to situations that have triggered our flight-or-fight response and other automatic impulses.
2. *Attuned communication.* The PFC enables us to connect with another person's mind as well as aspects of our own. It enables us to wonder and speculate (without judging) what another person is thinking or feeling and be consciously aware that we are doing so at the time.
3. *Emotional balance.* The PFC regulates the limbic circuitry so that our perceived emotional lives are vibrant and dynamic, yet not overwhelming.
4. *Response flexibility.* Humans have the capacity to demonstrate restraint, to allow enough time between what we sense emotionally and how we choose to act. During this time, we reflect and deliberate, considering consequences of our behavior and alternatives to our first impulses.
5. *Empathy.* This is the quality of feeling what another is feeling, without being consumed by those feelings. This requires the activation of resonance systems that "read" another's nonverbal cues, as well as data from our own internal bodily sensations that are transmitted to the PFC via the (right) insula.
6. *Insight.* We begin to "make sense of our life" as we connect the past and potential future to our present. This ability relies on circuitry involved in memory and emotion that provide ever-enlarging contextualization to our emerging story.
7. *Fear modulation.* The PFC, through neural extensions to the limbic circuits, especially the amygdala, has the capacity to calm the frenzied activity of the "fear factories" of our brains. Even though we may have developed fears at a young age that are imbedded into ancient parts of

our minds, the PFC can override these fears so they do not control our actions and thoughts.

8. *Intuition.* The sensations we receive from our viscera, or hollow organs (heart, lungs, and entire gastrointestinal tract), register with the PFC via the brain's insula. We learned earlier about the extended brain; here we see it arcing back to the brain, dominantly in the right PFC, to provide us with holistic convictions about everything from the feel of a room to the feel of a person.

9. *Morality.* The PFC has been shown to be actively involved as we construct our sense of morality in the world, considering not only our own good but the welfare of others as well. Studies have revealed that those with a damaged PFC demonstrate impaired moral judgment.

Siegel has proposed that an integrated prefrontal cortex leads to a life that is flexible, adaptive, coherent, energized, and stable—symbolized by the acronym FACES:

> *Flexible*: Behavioral and emotional resilience in the face of stress.
> *Adaptive*: The capacity to adjust and change, incorporating new growth and learning into our mental matrix.
> *Coherence*: The means by which we include nuances of emotion and implicit memory into our narratives, giving them a much more distinct and comprehensive texture. This characteristic corresponds with the changes we undergo when we are fully mentalized and "feel felt."
> *Energized*: Living with a sense of vitality, expectation, and hope.
> *Stability*: The deep awareness of security and predictability that enables us to connect with others while simultaneously maintaining boundaries of safety.

Whenever I work with patients, I inquire often how their lives are reflecting FACES and in what ways they desire to expand their growth in each of these dimensions.

THE MEETING PLACE

The comprehensive and complex degree of mental activity undertaken by the PFC is particularly evident in the manner in which we access our awareness of our narrative. This occurs as we synthesize and process our attention; memory; emotion; logical, linguistic processes; and ongoing sources of sensation and perception, whether outside or inside the body.

Ultimately we make sense of our story within the PFC, especially as neural regions of the left and right hemispheres and the upper and lower brain domains are coordinated and integrated. The prefrontal cortex, then, is not so much a structure that does something special (although that is true) as much as it is a place where multiple important but separate neural networks potentially intersect to make us who we are continually becoming. This dynamism, manifested in the PFC, correlates with the ongoing emergence of our narrative and by extension how we relate to others and ourselves.

The way we understand and make sense of our story is reflected in the wiring of our brain. This networking (via Hebb's axiom: neurons that fire together wire together) tends to reinforce our story's hardwiring, in this case at the location of the prefrontal cortex, and will continue to do so unless substantially acted upon by another outside relationship.

As you reflect on the functions of the PFC, you may begin to see how much we depend upon adequate, balanced integration of the prefrontal cortex to become the people we claim we want to be. If we cannot override our impulses, if we are not attuned in our communication, if we are not empathic, and so on, we find ourselves wandering in a barren, conflict-ridden relational landscape. Or, in my case, standing in my kitchen yelling at my daughter.

LOW AND HIGH ROADS OF FUNCTIONING

We find ourselves on the low road of functioning, according to Dan Siegel, when the integrating function of our prefrontal cortex is not adequately balanced, as when I overreacted when my daughter played her music. An array of routes lead to the following roads:

> We lose our patience and then our temper.
> We give our spouses or our children the silent treatment.
> We passively act out our anger.
> We indulge in food, alcohol, drugs, sex, or work as a way to cope with our inner conflicts.

Or we can be subtler, especially in the church. In our land of consumption, we often behave like consumers of church. It is always easiest simply to leave one congregation for another that "better suits our needs" rather than do the hard work of integrating our minds and hearts within themselves and with our fellow parishioners. (Of course, many times our fellow churchgoers don't even know we're disgruntled because, despite our hurt feelings over what they said or did, we say that all is fine. Or at least we assume it will be when we find another church community.)

The low road, therefore, represents a *dis-integration* of the prefrontal cortex. Essentially, important data that would help us assess and respond appropriately to our situations is left outside our conscious awareness. Either we're operating predominately through automatic, bottom-up processing (with the limbic and brain stem neurons running the show) or by implicit memory tracts.

Essentially it is a way in which we *hide from the truth.* As in my interaction with Rachel, much of this truth is emotional in nature. We are either overrun with emotion (as I was), not allowing for alternative, helpful neural tempering (as when I simply let my fight-or-flight mechanism have its way) or we ignore it, shutting out valuable emotional input that would better inform our behavioral choices. When we hide from what we feel—from emotion—we hide from the truth. Remember that emotion is not a debatable phenomenon. It is an authentic reflection of our subjective experience, one that is best served by attending to it. When the PFC is essentially off-line, neglecting to provide proper context so we can sense emotional states in a balanced way, we miss the truth of what our brains are attempting to tell us.

Traveling on the low road

We set out on the low road of behavior by way of experiences that activate a distressing emotional state. This can be an internal or external event, thought, or other feelings. It can be a concrete or abstract event that elicits a shift in us that we may or may not sense. This trigger can be anything from a glance to a tone of voice, to the news that you have just been laid off from your job. It could be your husband requesting to connect with you sexually or your wife turning you down for the same. It could be the sermon you heard, the throbbing headache that the pain reliever didn't seem to touch, or the phone call you didn't receive in a timely fashion. The initial stimulus can lead to either a gradual or quite rapid descent to even lower regions of the low road.

We may, after a period of several hours or only a few seconds, if we are attentive to it, notice shifts in our physical status—that our heart rate or breathing is changing, or that our thoughts begin to race or feel jumbled. If the tension increases further, we move to a place where we feel we may "lose control," which means different things for different people. Finally, we may plunge to depths of intense feelings, from which we have difficulty finding our way out.

At this point, we may begin to feel stuck, our mental wheels mired in the ruts of feelings and thoughts. Feelings of vulnerability, hurt, shame, or threat often lead to anger; when this is not sufficiently addressed we devolve to the experience of resentment. This ultimately leads to contempt. Marriage research indicates that one of the most powerful predictors of a marriage's failure is the degree to which either of the partners expresses contempt for the other. I suggest this is not restricted to marriages but is true for all significant relationships.

When we find ourselves on the low road, metaphorically the PFC has come unhinged. Neurologically it has become less efficiently connected to the other parts of the brain that are sending messages to it. On the low road we do not regulate our bodies well; we do not attune to others' emotional states; our emotions are unbalanced and our responses are rigid. We leave no space for empathy and therefore limit our insight; fear becomes our gyroscope, overwhelming our capacity to attend to our bodies and making it impossible for us to intuit internal and external situations with wisdom. Ultimately this leads to poor moral choices. This entire process gives new meaning to the expression "He flipped his lid."

Getting off the low road and back on the high road takes a great deal of energy—particularly the further along the low road we have traveled. First, we must become aware that we are on the low road; second, we must take adequate steps to shift our physiologic states in order to change the trajectory of our minds' course.

One simple yet surprisingly effective way to begin shifting our mind-set is to change our physical position; for example, by sitting if we've been standing (this tends to relax the body) or by moving from one room to another to discuss a conflict calmly.

Sometimes gaining additional information can help us change the way we are thinking about a situation. Asking ourselves the who, what, where, when, and how about a situation can tell us a lot and enable us to step back from the intensity of our feelings.

Notice I did not include the question *why* in the list of questions above.

That's because many times *why* is intended not so much as a question as a statement. When your spouse asks you, "Why are you wearing that shirt?" she is not asking you anything. She is telling you something. And you know what it is. The shirt has to go.

More seriously, you might ask yourself, *Why am I so depressed? Why am I so anxious? Why am I so lonely? Why do I lose my temper so easily? Why am I still unemployed? Why did you betray me? Why did you forget my birthday? Why does my mother or father still treat me like a child? Why did God allow me to develop cancer? Why is my church falling apart? Why is there evil in the world? Why, why, why . . . ?*

It's not that *why* questions are irrelevant or unnecessary or unhelpful. But one has to consider, would it be helpful to have the answer to "Why did my daughter die?" In most cases, it wouldn't. When we ask the question "why?" we're not so much looking for a left-brain explanation (that is generally an answer to a "how" question) as we are seeking validation for feelings that feel far too overwhelming to be understood.

We use *why* as a substitute for the difficult work needed to integrate our right and lower brain emotional states with our left hemisphere linguistic function. If we are not practiced at putting into words those "groans" that Paul speaks of in Romans 8, we are bound, like Job, to put our language to God and others in the *why* category:

> Why did I not perish at birth,
> and die as I came from the womb?
> Why were there knees to receive me
> and breasts that I might be nursed? . . .
> Or why was I not hidden away in the ground like a stillborn child,
> like an infant who never saw the light of day?
> (JOB 3:11-12, 16)

Such *why* questions are generally not helpful when we're trying to get off the low road.

One other caution: as we attempt to make the shift to high-road functioning, we are vulnerable to quickly descending back into the canyon of mindlessness. Perhaps during an argument with our friend or spouse, we are trying to correct our course when the other person says something that immerses us back in whiplash fashion into the same emotional vortex from which we had almost escaped. This also helps explain why it is so difficult to overcome a pattern of substance abuse or sexual addiction. During their initial period of abstinence, abusers often find themselves flooded with emotions they do not yet have the mental or spiritual maturity to regulate, and as a result, quickly return to their old habits.

Regaining and remaining on the high road

Carolyn knew it was coming. Her husband had that look. His body was stiffening to a hickory hardness again.

"You seem angry," she said.

"I'm not angry," he replied. No, of course not. He was *never* angry.

Then Raymond clammed up. Typically his silence would last an entire afternoon, leaving Carolyn feeling disoriented and confused. Her heart pounded in her chest, and thoughts swirled in her head. She could feel the reservoir of tears brimming just behind her eyes, pressuring to overflow. She knew she wouldn't be able to concentrate on the tasks she had planned to accomplish that day.

She could sense the first wisp of the downward spiral not long afterward. The coils of depression, perceived in her mind as a lack of motivation and in her body as fatigue, wrapped themselves around her, threatening to take her down even further. She feared that later that evening she would explode, yelling at her husband in a final attempt to get Raymond's attention.

When she had looked back on this pattern in the past, she had wondered where Jesus was when all this was happening. Where was the advertised power of the Holy Spirit? She had prayed so often for her marriage over the last several years, but the answers seemed distant and hollow. These moments were especially shaming now that she was leading a Bible study for young mothers. What if they found out about her marital struggles?

She wondered if this afternoon's encounter with Raymond could be different. Over the past several weeks, Carolyn and I had been reviewing her narrative. We had explored her attachment patterns to see how her way of paying attention, remembering, and managing emotion had developed.

Memories of conflicts with her mother were painful. From the time Carolyn was little, whenever her mother was angry with her, she responded by not speaking to her daughter—sometimes for up to a week. It is not hard to imagine how disorganizing and disturbing this was for an eight-year-old, let alone a teenager. As a child, Carolyn had become quite sad and withdrawn. As a teenager, she became easily enraged, screaming at her mother, who would eventually turn on her with harshness and ridicule. While this shamed

Carolyn further, at least her mother had acknowledged Carolyn's presence. To some degree, this reduced Carolyn's sense of barren isolation. Most of the time, however, Carolyn just tried to ensure that her mother would not become angry in the first place.

As we talked, Carolyn was able to make the connection between her own narrative and her marriage. She became more aware of how her husband's silence mimicked that of her mother in her mind, activating implicit memory responses. She grew to understand how Raymond's silence threw the nine functions of her PFC off-line. As his silence triggered her verbal explosion, her PFC became increasingly disintegrated. She saw more clearly how her behaviors devolved to the low road—and why she remained there.

If this disintegration of the prefrontal cortex keeps us stuck on the low road, any activity we can employ to enhance its differentiation and integration is an on-ramp to the high road. Ancient Scripture texts address this process and illustrate how God is at work to integrate our individual minds, as well as the community as a whole.

In Psalm 86:11, David writes:

Teach me your way, LORD,
    that I may rely on your faithfulness;
give me an undivided heart,
    that I may fear your name.

The psalmist initially asks God to "teach me your way." This is not a request for a list of dos and don'ts. This is not about memorizing the Ten Commandments. It is a request for God to reveal what true living is all about, for God to teach David how to love him, as Jesus commanded, with all his heart, with all his soul, and with all his mind.

In your life, God's "way" is about loving him and loving your neighbor with all the parts of you. And this is hard work, especially for those parts of your "heart, soul, and mind" that have not had much practice doing that—the wounded parts, the weak parts, or the functions, such as memory or emotion, that you may not pay much attention to. As God teaches you to love him and others with all of these parts—as he teaches you his way—you undergo, in the dialect of neuroscience, differentiation, or the strengthening and maturation of each particular aspect of your heart, soul, and mind.

Notice that David's first request points to the greater hope of deeper relationship ("that I may rely on your faithfulness"). Next, he requests that

God create in him an *undivided* heart—one that is united, knit together, or, again in the language of neuroscience, *integrated*. The first two lines of this verse indicate that this knitting together is a process involving two minds, God's and David's. Notice that David is not asking God to make him more independent, but rather to enable him to connect with God. He desires God to actively create an undivided heart within him. The heart—our deepest emotional/cognitive/conscious/unconscious self—is manifested most profoundly at the level of the prefrontal cortex.

Last, the psalmist reveals his understanding of the natural direction in which his petition leads: "that I may fear your name." In this context, the word *fear* does not refer to our brain stem's predominant reactivity to threat, or our mindless fearful implicit memory. Instead, this refers to being overwhelmed with awe in the presence of God's power and beauty. This beauty is so deep that it would be painful were it not tempered by reliance "on your faithfulness" to create eyes to see with "an undivided heart."

The contemplative tradition suggests that to be so acutely aware of God's beauty in anything leads to awareness of God's beauty in everything, save that which is evil. Thus, we see God's beauty and presence even in those people whom we consider to be our enemies, as well as in the brokenness and chaos of this world. And we are compelled to become agents of mercy and justice where they are so desperately needed. It is not difficult to see how a differentiated, undivided heart leads to differentiated, undivided communities.

The creation of an undivided heart, an integrated prefrontal cortex, leads to justice, mercy, and humility. While we might imagine any number of other characteristics of God's Kingdom, none are more fundamental than these. Journeying on the high road, therefore, is not an exercise limited to what happens in our individual minds. It affects us as groups of people.

The great myth of modernity as it applies to neuroscience is that we can pull ourselves up by our own bootstraps. We can attain ultimate mindful peacefulness and, by extension, cultural utopia without an Ultimate Other to save us from ourselves. The ongoing terrorism, global warming, mounting third world debt, along with our own proclivity for insatiable consumption, should quickly wake us from that daydream. As Scripture points out,

> The heart is deceitful above all things
> and beyond cure.
> Who can understand it?
> "I the LORD search the heart

and examine the mind,
   to reward everyone according to their conduct,
      according to what their deeds deserve." (JEREMIAH 17:9-10)

The general tendency of our hearts—especially the PFC—is toward deceit and hiding the truth (the depth of our emotion, memory, and relational patterns, as well as the reality of a God who loves us beyond belief) from ourselves and others. Its general trajectory, when left to its own volition, is to disconnect within itself and from other hearts.

Just as the second law of thermodynamics says that entropy always occurs to matter in a closed system, when our hearts remain a closed system, they tend toward a greater state of chaos and disconnection. This keeps us oblivious to disparate elements of our minds that God very much wants to use to get our attention and then knit back together. The King James translation of verse 9 above calls the heart "desperately wicked," its variation of "beyond cure." We indeed are desperate and sick ("sick" being one of the more common meanings of the word *wicked* in the Bible).

In addition, God claims in this passage that *he* actively searches our hearts and minds. Some of us moderns (and postmoderns) have difficulty fully comprehending what it is like to be searched and examined—to *be known* by God. We know that our narratives, especially through our attachment patterns, tend to predispose us to be more or less open for this to happen.

Both David and Jeremiah make clear that we are unable to integrate our minds on our own. This is a creative process that God must initiate and vitalize—and has. With God's resurrection of Jesus from the dead, Jesus' ascension to his place as Lord of this world, and the outpouring of the Holy Spirit, God has released the power to integrate our prefrontal cortices. These new neural networks reflect and point to the new heaven and earth that will reach their culmination in the appearance of Jesus but whose shadowy forerunning is already emerging in our lives. God's Kingdom shows up whenever redeemed people do justice and love mercy in our families, communities, businesses, and physical environment.

All well and good. But how on earth could Carolyn learn to integrate her mind in the middle of Raymond's silent treatment? Here is where centuries of spiritual wisdom and recent neuroscience discoveries converge, offering insights into how we open ourselves up to receive what God has to offer. Below are several means by which Carolyn began to experience a greater sense of integration of her mind, her life, and her brain—and translated these into her life as a follower of Jesus.

ATTUNEMENT TO THE BODY

Developing a deeper awareness of our bodies and what they are telling us on a continual basis is the first step back to the high road. In chapter 7, I described the body scan, a guided visual imagery exercise that enhances people's awareness of their emotional states as translated through their physicality.

After leading Carolyn through her first body scan, I encouraged her to practice it at least once a day (ideally more than once) for at least six weeks and then regularly thereafter. As Carolyn practiced this exercise, she reported greater attunement to her feelings not only during the meditation but throughout the day. She noticed primary emotional shifts much sooner and anticipated where they might lead.

Movement exercises, such as yoga and tai chi, are additional means by which you can enhance your awareness of your body's sensations and breathing. Doing so enhances the integration between circuits from the insula and the prefrontal cortex.

AUTOBIOGRAPHICAL NARRATIVES: WRITING AND TELLING YOUR STORY

The low road is fraught with repeated firings of old neural network patterns that represent our limited understanding of our narrative. We then reflexively cycle through the same patterns on our way to disaster with our spouses, children, employees, friends, or enemies.

Writing and telling our stories to a trusted friend or counselor can help us change our understanding of our narratives and help us make sense of our lives (see pages 79–80). As Carolyn wrote out her life story by hand, read it to herself, and then read it to me, she began to notice things she had never seen before, such as the connection between her life with her mother and her life with her husband.

She began to make sense of her implicit responses to Raymond when he was silent. She saw them not simply as reactions to a man who didn't seem to care about her feelings but as responses one would naturally expect from a little girl or a teenager whose mother intentionally ignored her deep distress.

She was ashamed of her angry tirades aimed at Raymond, and she was convinced that God was even more ashamed of her. She was able to use her narrative to provide some distance in her mind between herself and her feelings of embarrassment, recognizing that they were what you would expect from a child who was being treated this cruelly. She also began to see herself in God's eyes as a child who needed comfort rather than as an angry, shameful daughter.

THE EXPERIENCE OF FEELING FELT

Sensing validation. Being understood. Feeling felt. We value few experiences more, especially when we're in a distressing, noxious emotional state. When we carry within our minds an awareness of this sense of validation, we are put at ease and able to respond to stress more flexibly. Just as young children are more likely to explore new territory and try new things if someone is consistently and empathically attending to their needs, so we will be more confident if we nurture a similar state of mind in ourselves. When we face uncertain, anxiety-provoking situations, our inner compass of validation and security enhances emotional balance and response flexibility (among other of the nine functions of the PFC).

During her time in psychotherapy, Carolyn became aware of feeling understood and validated whenever she described her emotions. Initially this experience surprised her, but she welcomed it with relief. She noted that as she had the experience of feeling felt more often, she was more empowered to regulate her own emotional states as well. Thinking about our sessions, she reported, reminded her of things I had said and the sense of comfort and stability she experienced then. She transferred this to times she began to feel overwhelmed, and her escalating physical responses tended to quiet.

The neuroplastic triad

Neuroplasticity, as you may recall from chapter 3, is the brain's ability to create new neurons, make new neural connections, and prune those it no longer needs. The neuroplastic triad of aerobic activity, focused attention exercises, and novel learning experiences all play vital roles in increasing the brain's level of malleability.

For this reason, I encouraged Carolyn to begin a form of aerobic activity that suited her. She began a regular regimen of brisk walking four times a week, working up from ten minutes to fifty minutes on each outing. Eventually she asked Raymond to join her, which he did. This shared activity had a lasting positive impact on their relationship.

Neuroscience research confirms that mindful meditative exercises that stretch and challenge the attentional mechanism of your brain enhance the integration of the prefrontal cortex. For that reason, I guided Carolyn through a body scan as well as a mindful attentiveness exercise, which required her to

Integration Exercises

Throughout the book you've been introduced to several exercises to help you foster the integration of your PFC. They are explained in more detail below.

Autobiographical narratives

Consider gathering with a group of two to three trusted friends. Encourage each other to write your individual autobiographies, and then share them with each other. For this to be successful, you may need to meet together for sixty to ninety minutes weekly or biweekly over several weeks or months. There is no perfect formula. What is important is that you are in a group of committed folks who are willing to share their stories as they are. As you proceed, invite God to reveal to each of you not only more about your story, but more about his story—his feelings, thoughts, and images of his mind—as well.

Pay attention to the nonverbal as well as verbal aspects of the stories that are being read. Participants also need to pay attention to what they feel—the emotions that are evoked within them as they hear each other's stories—and to honor those feelings, being careful never to ignore them but rather permitting these feelings to generate questions they might ask the storyteller.

Use the five forms of interrogatories mentioned on page 165; *who, what, where, when,* and *how*. Each question seeks information the listener does not know; more important, expressing them adds to a storyteller's experience of *being known*.

When listening to another's story, asking these questions opens the door for the storyteller to reflect on particular facts without becoming emotionally activated by the more charged query of *why*. Both the storyteller and his or her listeners are able to create deeper bonds of intimacy in a predictable, trustworthy, and safe fashion.

Attention exercise

This simple, five-minute exercise can be done just about anywhere (except, of course, while operating a car or heavy machinery). While sitting comfortably in a chair, take a deep breath and then allow the focus of your attention to find the center of the room (not the center of the floor or ceiling, but the center of the entire room's volume). Maintain this for about thirty seconds. Then, without interruption, allow the focus of your attention to shift to an area on the wall opposite where you are sitting; allow your attention to remain there for approximately thirty seconds. Next, again without interruption, allow the focus of your attention to return to the center of the room, holding it for thirty seconds. Then, without using your hands as a visual guide, allow the focus of your attention to shift to the space in front of you, the distance from you at which you would hold a book to read it, holding this space in your attentional frame for thirty seconds. Finally, allow the focus of your attention to return to the center of the room, holding it for thirty seconds.

I encourage my patients to practice this exercise daily as often as they can. More frequent, shorter sessions (four to five times a week for five to fifteen minutes) of mindful attentiveness exercises provides greater PFC interconnectedness than do longer, less frequent sessions (once per week for forty-five minutes).

This demonstrates to my patients that they actually can control their attention, while illustrating how difficult it can be to create something and then focus on that same something in your mind. The "center" of the room is an example of this and can be challenging at first. This exercise is a good beginning mindful meditation practice. The body scan is a more immersed form of this practice.

Centering exercise

One simple attention exercise that doubles as a helpful meditation practice is to choose one of the nouns listed as the outgrowth of a Spirit-filled life in Galatians 5:22 (love, joy, peace, patience, kindness, goodness, faithfulness, gentleness, and self-control). Focus your attention on that word daily, throughout the day. Feel free to create images in your mind that represent that word.

Dedicate seven consecutive days to focus on each word, continuing to cycle through all nine on an ongoing basis. Whenever you encounter another person or sense an emotional shift that tempts to take you down the low road, allow yourself to be immersed in your awareness of your word for the day. Be mindful of how that word is calling you to reflect and manifest it in that moment—especially when your mind is screaming for you to do just the opposite. Ask yourself how you can be a conduit of joy, peace, patience, or gentleness in this moment. This exercise will not only facilitate the integration of your own prefrontal cortex, you will be doing the same for those around you by creating space within which they can feel felt.

consciously hold and then shift her attention for thirty seconds from one spot in a room to another several times. (To read how this exercise works, see pages 173–174.) I encouraged Carolyn to practice these exercises regularly at home. As Carolyn became more proficient at them, she noticed that not only was she more aware of her feelings, but she was also more mindful of the feelings of others, including Raymond's.

Finally, Carolyn also began a pottery class, something she had been longing to do since she was in college and had taken a course in sculpture. This novel learning activity provided an outlet for her deep and undiscovered passion for creativity—something that is built into all of us as God's image bearers.

Spiritual disciplines

Attunement to the body, writing our stories, feeling felt, and engaging in the neuroplastic triad help us reenter the high road and stay there. Long before neuroscientists began advocating these approaches, believers engaged in spiritual practices that foster the mind's development—whether we call it an undivided heart or an integrated prefrontal cortex.

These practices, which are usually called spiritual disciplines, include the inward disciplines of meditation, prayer, fasting, and study; the outward disciplines of simplicity, solitude, submission, and service; and the corporate disciplines of confession, worship, guidance, and celebration. In many ways, these disciplines, when practiced faithfully (but without burden), do the very things that we have been discussing to help integrate our brains. Richard Foster's book *Celebration of Discipline* and Dallas Willard's *The Spirit of the Disciplines* offer excellent, in-depth discussions on each one; for our purposes, we'll consider just a sampling.

MEDITATION

Meditation, as Foster suggests, is a place to begin since it prepares us for other disciplines. As we practice listening to God and ourselves through our perceptions, senses, emotions, and thoughts, we learn to pray. The Psalms frequently reflect and promote this practice. The writer of Psalm 119 refers to this meditation numerous times:

> I meditate on your precepts
> and consider your ways. (v. 15)

Cause me to understand the way of your precepts,
that I may meditate on your wonderful deeds. (v. 27)

My eyes stay open through the watches of the night,
that I may meditate on your promises. (v. 148)

The practice of meditation, which David also mentions in verses 23, 48, 78, 97, and 99 of this psalm, puts us in position to be open to God's search of us. It enables us to be aware of our bodies and how God may be speaking to us through them. It does not simply help us focus on something else (God's law, precepts, or deeds) but facilitates the process by which we focus on Someone Else focusing on us. When we look deeply into someone else's eyes, we not only see the person's eyes, we see our being seen by them. This reflects the experience of being known.

God will search the inner rooms of our hearts. That, however, does not guarantee that we will be present where he is looking and challenging. It is one thing for God to search. It is quite another for me to *feel searched*. It requires me to be present, which requires work. This is where the practice of meditation can help.

PRAYER

Meditation naturally leads to prayer. Paul admonishes us to be *devoted* to prayer (Colossians 4:2); not only should we long to pray, we should be aware that it, too, will require hard work. This is particularly true of contemplative prayer, which requires us to be aware of God's activity in everything. This, in turn, makes us more likely to sense his movement as he guides, directs, and comforts us. Prayer in turn leads us, like the psalmist, to answer God with our prayers of petition and praise as we become aware of the depth of his love and beauty. We do so with cries of language, but also with deeply felt expressions emanating primarily from the right hemisphere that are both primal and deeper than linguistic symbolism.

The following Scripture has a meaning grounded in our brains and the way God created us:

In the same way, the Spirit helps us in our weakness. We do not know what we ought to pray for, but the Spirit himself intercedes for us through wordless groans. (ROMANS 8:26)

We cry out to God without discernible words when what we long for, what we fear, or what we desire is beyond language. This is an example of how the Holy Spirit actively engages the right hemisphere, as feeling and intent come together in expressions that lack linguistic structure but are deeply full of meaning. If we do not attend to our emotional states, the Holy Spirit is restricted from engaging in this aspect of his work in our lives.

FASTING

The discipline of fasting, abstaining from food for a set period of time, puts us deeply in touch with our bodies. We are never so aware of our impatience to satiate our hunger as when we know that our next meal is at least eighteen hours away. We realize how much our emotional ballast depends on physical comforts and how often we use these comforts to quickly and automatically shut off distressing emotion triggered by implicit memories.

STUDY

The discipline of study includes writing and reading, both of which knit together the right and left hemispheres as well as the lower and upper regions of the brain. Study should enable us to connect factual information with the emotional realms of the right and lower areas of our brains. Many people find that keeping a written prayer and reflection journal helps them do this.

Other areas of study that can lead to integration of the PFC include observing the natural world and engaging in new activities. Spending regular, intentional time with creation—at a pace that permits our attention to be captured by it—makes us aware of the beauty outside of us as well as the emotional states that are generated when we engage with the natural world. Studying the various expressions of art (sculpture, painting, music) also helps integrate our minds.

CONFESSION

Confession, like other outer and corporate disciplines, enlarges our hearts and minds by moving us from our inner worlds to the world outside us, including the earth itself, and eventually to the inner worlds of other people. Confession illustrates that as we open our lives—our narratives—to trusted friends or a spiritual director, we make way for the story of our lives to be told differently. Through this practice, we walk along with others to find healing for our sins and the sorrows of our past.

It also prepares us to undergo the experience of feeling felt and being encouraged to move in the direction we deeply long to go. In the language of faith, we call this repentance. We will consider this in more detail in chapter 10.

DISCIPLINES: MAKING SPACE FOR GOD

A couple of caveats to consider: First, we don't earn brownie points with God for engaging in spiritual disciplines. They're valuable because they line us up to be more available to hear the Spirit of God when he speaks. They create space within us for God to work. He is more than willing to do this work, but not without our cooperation.

Second, engaging in spiritual disciplines simply for the sake of becoming more mindful is not the equivalent of having the mind of Christ. Plenty of people who are drawn to the idea of mindfulness will not necessarily like the idea of a King who demands their uncompromising allegiance. And Paul is quite specific about what followers of Jesus are to pay attention to and how to do that:

> Those who live according to the sinful nature have their minds set on what that nature desires; but those who live in accordance with the Spirit have their minds set on what the Spirit desires. The mind controlled by the sinful nature is death, but the mind controlled by the Spirit is life and peace. (ROMANS 8:5-6)

The degree to which we set our minds on—pay attention to—those desires of the sinful nature tends to dis-integrate our minds by encouraging a state of mindlessness. One—if not *the*—primal sinful "desire" is the urge for instant reduction of distressing emotions. We tend to turn away from unpleasant emotional states toward inner or outer mental or behavioral means that will disconnect us from or eliminate those very states.

When we do this, we pay less attention to what is happening in our minds. We then tend to respond to internal or external events with sinful thoughts and behaviors. When our minds are set on these things, it does not lead *to* death. According to Paul, it *is* death. Death is that state of dis-integration, disconnection, and isolation that leads to everything that is wrong in the universe. And according to Paul, you don't have to be without a pulse to be dead.

All of the spiritual disciplines both require and support the skill of mindful attention, which enables us to set our minds on the Spirit. When we pay attention to what we are paying attention to and when God's voice (telling us we are his sons and daughters whom he loves and in whom he takes great pleasure) is the most resonant tone to which we are listening, our minds—specifically the prefrontal cortex—tend to be more integrated.

And, as Paul writes, an integrated mind *is* life and peace. This was Carolyn's experience. As she began to implement a consistent life of fasting and meditation, she reported a greater subjective awareness of God's presence. Her prayer life took on a less verbal, more gutteral quality at times, which enabled her to feel freer to experience emotion of a wide variety in the presence of God. She gathered weekly with two other friends for prayer and confession. Carolyn became less reactive to Raymond's silence, and instead of allowing her sympathetic nervous system's fight-or-flight response to ramp up when he became quiet, she focused on hearing God's voice reminding her that she belonged to him, especially in those moments when she felt very little like she belonged to her husband. Her feelings of shame, though still present, were less distressing.

She began to ask Raymond questions about his life and what he felt. When he would become impatient with his own ignorance, Carolyn found herself responding with patience that even Raymond found surprising. Eventually, she asked him to join her in therapy, which he did. They continued their regular walks as well.

And so on that afternoon when Carolyn sensed that Raymond was angry but he denied it, she was able to ask him if they could move to a different room to continue their conversation. He agreed, and they sat together in the comfort of their family room. Carolyn told him she was feeling sad and wanted to be connected to him. She acknowledged that she knew he might be feeling uncomfortable with her observation that he might be angry, but she was asking it because of how frightened she used to become when her mother gave her the silent treatment years ago. He accepted that; although he still did not know what he felt, he assured her he would think about it and would talk with her about it later that day, which he did. There was no explosion and there were no tirades in their home that day. Just life and peace.

The mind of Christ

So what does it mean to have the mind of Christ? Paul discusses this in his first letter to the church at Corinth, in which he identifies the Spirit as the One who can impart the power and mystery of God to us:

> The Spirit searches all things, even the deep things of God. For who knows a person's thoughts except that person's own spirit within? In

the same way no one knows the thoughts of God except the Spirit of God. We have not received the spirit of the world but the Spirit who is from God, that we may understand what God has freely given us. . . . The person with the Spirit makes judgments about all things, but such a person is not subject to merely human judgments, for,

"Who has known the mind of the Lord
  so as to instruct him?"

But we have the mind of Christ. (1 CORINTHIANS 2:10-12, 15-16,
ITALICS MINE)

In this passage, Paul is not touting the integration of neural networks as the way to develop the mind of Christ. Instead, he is describing what happens to our minds when we have the Spirit of God dwelling within us. The Spirit unveils to us mysteries of God's heart and mind that we cannot know apart from him. To have the mind of Christ, therefore, requires that we encounter an integrating Spirit who searches us and allows us to know him as we are searched—as we are known.

God longs for us to pay attention to that Spirit who is dwelling within us. Anything that we do to strengthen our capacity to do this will be helpful. Submitting to the spiritual disciplines is one way to put ourselves in the position to hear his voice. He may, in fact, call us to places we may at first be very much afraid to go, for as C. S. Lewis observed, he is not "a tame lion."

Spiritual disciplines have been practiced in the lives of deeply integrated followers of God for over three thousand years. Interestingly, they can facilitate the very things neuroscience and attachment research suggest are reflections of healthy mental states and secure attachment. Furthermore, these disciplines can strengthen the nine functions of the prefrontal cortex.

In short, the disciplines enable us to pay attention to our minds in order to pay attention to the Spirit who is speaking to us through that very medium. *Jesus' mind, I suggest, reflects the most integrated prefrontal cortex of any human of any time.*

His deep awareness of God did not happen automatically. In fact, no one has ever worked harder at knowing and being known by God than Jesus. He made himself available through the same spiritual disciplines we have at our disposal and committed himself to being known by God so he might know the mind of God. In other words, he paid attention to what he was paying attention to.

TEMPTED TOWARD THE LOW ROAD: JESUS FACES HIS DEMONS

As fallible people, we have difficulty imagining that Jesus could ever understand how hard we work to avoid the states of mind that lead to the low road. We may pay theological lip service to Jesus' humanity with its emotional travail, but given our (nonbiblical) Platonic and Gnostic tendencies to view our lives in dis-integrated ways, separating the "more valuable spiritual" from the "less valuable physical," we often overlook just how close to the low road Jesus came without actually setting foot on it.

In the Gospels (Matthew 4, Mark 1, and Luke 4), we are given a glimpse into Jesus' mind. Immediately following Jesus' baptism, the Spirit leads him into the desert. During the next several weeks, Jesus fasts and prays. After forty days, Satan comes to tempt him, suggesting Jesus turn stones into bread to feed his hunger; jump off the pinnacle of the Temple to demonstrate his charisma; and worship Satan, with the promise that Satan will hand over political control of the kingdoms of the earth to Jesus. Essentially, Satan suggests that Jesus use his gifts as coping strategies in the face of anxiety. Doing so, however, would have cut Jesus off from various parts of his own mind—his own prefrontal cortex. Satan is asking Jesus not to trust in God's faithfulness but to act alone and as if he were afraid.

It's significant that, just prior to his period in the wilderness, Jesus had heard the words that would carry him through his ministry: "You are my Son, whom I love; with you I am well pleased." Now it is this voice that he listens to during the onslaught of thoughts and feelings that tempt him to take easy, convenient ways around the mountain he senses he is compelled to climb.

As he wards off Satan's attacks, Jesus appears to draw on a range of feelings and memories, relying not just on text (he quotes Scripture) but on what his experience of the text tells him, paying attention to what has bathed him in strength and comfort for at least three decades. He does not need to test a God in whom he has ultimate confidence and trust.

From the perspective of neuroscience, Satan was tempting him in ways that encouraged Jesus not to pay attention, to be mindless toward his emotional states and memories, and to essentially live in the way of a dis-integrated prefrontal cortex. He tempted him to pay little attention to his narrative and the times he had heard his Father extol him and lavish his affection on him, revealing to him the true nature of his vocation, that of Messiah.

In this encounter with Satan, Jesus was tempted to dis-integrate his prefrontal cortex and head down the low road—to follow the same road we too often end up on:

> the road to quick fixes for himself and his people
> the road to instant gratification
> the road to flamboyant displays of personal magnetism to compensate for the destabilizing effect of shame
> the road to impatience, emotional isolation, contempt, greed, lust, and the like
> the road that tries to avoid suffering, whether in ourselves or others

In other words, the conflicts that arise in our minds are the same ones Jesus faced in those forty days of hunger and thirst in the desert.

One can imagine that in the face of the inner work Jesus did in that desert and during all the late nights and early mornings when he went away alone to pray, he was continually integrating his prefrontal cortex and becoming more skilled at picking up even the slightest nonverbal cues of those around him. And as he became more aware of the integration of his own mind, so his attention surely turned to issues of justice and questions of what to do about institutional evil—ultimate forms of dis-integration. (For us today, this translates into what we do with matters of politics, business, and ecology.) No wonder, then, that Jesus so often exposed the hypocrisy and pride of the religious leaders.

When we travel with Jesus, our brother and our King, he bids us to join him on the adventure of a lifetime. First, he calls us to a place of deep integration within our own minds, a practice he models for us in Scripture. He also invites us, through the power of the Holy Spirit, to assist him as he ushers in his Kingdom of justice and mercy for all who will receive it.

Chapter 10

NEUROSCIENCE: SIN AND REDEMPTION

The Bible does not provide a dictionary definition of *sin* the way Webster does. However, it frequently uses the term to refer either to the state of being separated or disconnected from God or to behaviors that lead to or exemplify that condition. (The Greek and Hebrew words used most often for *sin* in Scripture mean "missing the mark.")

Sin severs your relationship with God. When you are separated from God, you are separated from others and experience commensurate separation between different elements of your own mind. This was Carolyn's experience. "Being separated," then, is a metaphor for disconnection, dis-integration, and a host of other ideas that are also used in neuroscience and attachment theory.

The apostle Paul describes such dis-integrated minds in his letter to the church in Rome:

> They exchanged the truth about God for a lie, and worshiped and served created things rather than the Creator—who is forever praised. Amen.
>
> Because of this, God gave them over to shameful lusts. . . .
>
> Furthermore, just as they did not think it worthwhile to retain the knowledge of God, so *God gave them over to a depraved mind, so that they do what ought not to be done.* They have become filled with every kind

of wickedness, evil, greed and depravity. They are full of envy, murder, strife, deceit and malice. They are gossips, slanderers, God-haters, insolent, arrogant and boastful; they invent ways of doing evil; they disobey their parents; they have no understanding, no fidelity, no love, no mercy. Although they know God's righteous decree that those who do such things deserve death, they not only continue to do these very things but also approve of those who practice them. (ROMANS 1:25-26, 28-32, ITALICS MINE)

This passage includes a lengthy list of "sins." Notice that it includes both behaviors and general states that describe a depraved mind. Paul suggests that these sinful behaviors emerge as we first discard or abandon our relationship with God ("[they] did not think it worthwhile to retain the knowledge of God") and then devolve into a mind that is essentially wicked, so comprehensively and desperately sick that we may be unaware of our true state.

FROM WRECKED TO RESTORED

From a neuroscience perspective, sin is deeply reflected in the degree to which our minds are dis-integrated, or in Paul's language, depraved. In other words, what the language of neuroscience calls dis-integration offers a correlate to the scriptural language of sin.

Neuroscience also has something to tell us about turning away from sin. When we pay attention to our minds (as Carolyn learned to do), we can begin to stop the dis-integration and embrace the acts of confession and repentance that lead to redemption. No wonder, then, that Paul links regeneration with the healing, or integration, of the mind:

Therefore, I urge you, brothers and sisters, in view of God's mercy, to offer your bodies as a living sacrifice, holy and pleasing to God—this is true worship. Do not conform to the pattern of this world, *but be transformed by the renewing of your mind.* Then you will be able to test and approve what God's will is—his good, pleasing and perfect will. (ROMANS 12:1-2, ITALICS MINE)

While sin reflects dis-integration, mindful integration is an important function of redemption. In fact, the creative and integrative activity of the Spirit is reflected by the integration of the prefrontal cortex through the stimulation of neural activation and growth (SNAG), which creates new life in the form of new neural networks. Carolyn fostered this integration by beginning to take brisk walks four times a week, engaging in mindful meditative exercises, and enrolling in a pottery class. The transformation she experienced is a shadow of what is to come in the culmination of history when Jesus appears and ushers in the new heavens and the new earth, including the full creation of new bodies with new brains.

Short of perfection

Despite our desire to live integrated, Spirit-led lives, we don't always succeed. As Paul laments in Romans 7:21: "Although I want to do good, evil is right there with me." In other words, on this earth we retain our sinful nature (as opposed to our real, being-renewed selves), or that part of our mind/brain complex that represents old, dis-integrated ways of being—our old neural networks, if you will.

Let me reiterate what I stated in the introduction of this book. By exploring possible correlates of the brain as they relate to important ideas about following Jesus, I am in no way attempting to *explain* those ideas on the basis of the brain; I am not reducing them to the function of neural networks.

Nor am I suggesting that we can magically rid ourselves and the world of sin by engaging in three straightforward mindfulness exercise steps. We cannot ultimately do what only Jesus can do. There is only one Messiah, Savior, and Lord—Jesus—who is able enough to show us the way to be human and empower us to do so. But God does command that we live life as mindfully as Jesus did so we can "act justly, and to love mercy, and to walk humbly with your God" (Micah 6:8) and so extend God's Kingdom here on earth.

In fact, neuroscience suggests that, *as realities*, sin and redemption cannot adequately be described using only the left-mode, linguistic element of theology. Words are very helpful but incomplete. These words need the full-bodied assistance of what the right hemisphere can bring. The full integration of both hemispheres provides for us a better grasp on these concepts. So let's consider what neuroscience tells us about what happens to the mind when we sense a disconnection from others.

RUPTURE

The brain is constantly scanning the internal and external landscape, comparing the present to the past in order to prepare the body for the future. In the process, the brain encounters hundreds of sensations involving thousands of neural networks requiring the connections of millions to billions of neurons.

One of the more common sensations that the brain brings to our unconscious and then conscious awareness is what we might simply term distress. The word *distress* is bland, generic, and nonspecific. And in fact (to simplify a bit), when the brain initially senses that something in a relationship is amiss, this sensation initially registers as a rather generic, nonspecific stimulus. In brain time, we are not immediately aware of what exactly is wrong.

This perception of distress proceeds from our body's general sensory neural systems and then connects with networks at lower brain areas. These signals then proceed up and through both the right and left hemispheres, eventually making their way to the cortex. Only as the cortex contextualizes and consciously interprets the distress do we become aware of its source.

When it comes to relationships, distress is experienced as anything from general, nondescript and short-lived fear or anxiety to more explicit anger, hurt, disappointment, and betrayal. Distress then leads to a rupture, which occurs whenever someone perceives a decrease in emotional intimacy and connection with another person or group. Sometimes this disconnection is hardly noticed; at other times it is severely disruptive. In *Parenting from the Inside Out*, Dan Siegel explores the various forms in which we experience this phenomenon: oscillating/benign, limit-setting, and toxic.

The concept of rupture originates from studies of parent-child relationships, and in that realm refers to any instance of relational disharmony between a parent and his or her child. Ruptures, however, occur not only between parents and children but between *any* two or more minds or groups—whether couples, friends, parishioners, enemies (this could include friends and parishioners), sports teams (think hockey and baseball), races, cultures, or nations.

While the word *rupture* may sound negative, the most common forms of rupture evolve from the naturally oscillating variance of moment-to-moment and day-to-day life. This begins from the moment of birth as the infant leaves the mother's uterus, only to return to her within moments to nurse or be held. From that moment forward, the child and parent move back and forth in their orbits of interaction, at times desiring closeness, at times greater separation. We see this both in infants who are quietly exploring their toes and do not wish to be interrupted and in mothers who want to be alone with their own toes simply so they can paint their nails without being interrupted.

These vacillations create opportunities within the child's mind (or for that matter, the mind of a friend or spouse) to develop new coping strategies to weather whatever distress might arise from the shift in levels of emotional closeness. The brain will naturally recruit additional networks of neurons to assist in this process of expanding its repertoire of tools to deal with this distress.

Consider how a toddler's right and left hemispheres integrate as he learns to cope while distressed after tripping and skinning his knee:

- the insula becomes increasingly aware of his body and what actions to take to regulate it in a comforting manner
- the right hemisphere constructs images that act as tranquilizing mechanisms in times of elevated dis-ease
- the left hemisphere thinks thoughts like, *I'm sure Dad is on his way to pick me up like he always does when he hears me crying.*

This integration is more likely to occur, of course, in an environment in which a parent is mindful of—or mentalizing with—his child. How integrated and flexible the child's mind becomes as he copes with these everyday fluctuations in intimacy depends on the degree to which his parents create an environment for secure attachment.

This naturally occurring pattern of oscillating expansion and contraction of the emotional distance between two parties is present in the earliest passages of Scripture. Adam and Eve experienced God himself as one who comes and goes. Not only does Scripture portray God as immanent, it portrays God's movement both toward and away from us.

Genesis 3:8 tells us that "the man and his wife heard the sound of the LORD God as he was walking in the garden in the cool of the day." This suggests movement and implies that at times God was somewhere other than near the first man and woman in the Garden. He was not absolutely absent but rather more distant. God's movement toward and away from us is one means by which he encourages growth in our flexibility and resilience in the face of the emotional distress we sense in his relative absence.

Something similar occurs when Mom leaves her young child playing happily on the floor to answer the phone. Although from the perspective of the child Mom has "left," in reality she has only left the room but is still quite present, able and willing to respond to her young daughter. However, it takes a while for the child to learn that Mom always comes back. Often when God seems to have disappeared from our lives, we feel just like that child—abandoned and forgotten. It's only through experience and growth that we learn that God interacts with us in this way.

Benign ruptures

God relates to us perfectly; however, no matter how mindful a parent is, inevitably there will be miscues or unintentional breaks in the sense of connection between parent and child. For instance, Mom may go around the corner of a room and disappear from her infant's sight line, at which point the infant may begin to cry. Upon hearing her child's cry, Mom returns, repairing what we could call a *benign rupture*. With ongoing parental mindfulness, the child will become more resilient as he ages, able to withstand greater degrees of separation and internal distress. As his brain develops, he will comprehend that Mom or Dad requires time alone and will become increasingly competent in his capacity to self-regulate his emotions.

When the child becomes a teenager, the automobile becomes the vehicle by which the son will want to employ his desire for greater distance. Parents not only experience the pull away on the part of their adolescent child as he matures, they also engage in a certain push, encouraging the child's departure so that *the parents can begin to grow into their next phase of life.*

As the child grows into adulthood, he will respond to benign ruptures between him and his friends, employer, neighbor, and spouse based on what he learned about these naturally occurring variations in closeness during childhood and adolescence. Even two people who are emotionally connected need their space.

Benign ruptures occur between adults through accidental or even well-intentioned misunderstandings. He didn't mean to poke her in the eye with his elbow. She really thought that his plane was getting in at eleven *p.m.*, not *a.m.* He was sure she would enjoy their outing in a hot air balloon—he was not yet aware of her fear of heights.

You may become busy or overloaded with the pace and stress of life and find yourself functioning more mindlessly than you wish: you become irritable with your children when you have too many things to do and feel their demands are disrupting your schedule; you decide to play golf with your friends this weekend without consulting your spouse; you're overwhelmed with work matters at the end of the day and forget to stop at the grocery store to get the bread your spouse asked you to pick up on the way home.

These circumstances lead to minor separations in your relationships that can be repaired without too much effort. However, even these simple missteps can become more difficult to resolve if you don't have the neural templates of forgiveness that are constructed on the bedrock of experience.

Limit-setting ruptures

Limit-setting ruptures are another common form of emotional disconnection. These occur any time you set boundaries on the behavior of others, or even on yourself. Limits are necessary to create the structure you need to function. Setting boundaries is part of any close relationship, whether between employers and employees, teachers and students, coaches and athletes, pastors and congregants, or wives and husbands.

Once again, however, this form of rupture occurs first in the parent-child relationship. Early in development, the infant's right hemisphere is its dominant neurological force; eventually, the emergence of the left hemisphere helps provide logical, linear direction. Initially, however, the left brain cannot provide all the structure the child needs. Without limits imposed from the outside, the brain may be wired for impulsive, unrestrained behavior.

By beginning to set limits, parents can assist in the wiring of their children's brains so they learn restraint. This process starts through nonverbal cues, such as when parents take a child's hand away from a plant or a hot cup of tea. Eventually, they allow their children to cry while going to sleep, enabling them to grow in their capacity for self-soothing. They say no to requests or begin to set restrictions when giving their children choices ("You can have milk in the blue or the red cup, but you can't have juice"). Later they set limits on what older children can buy or movies they can watch.

Invariably these limits will create a sense of distress within children who are not getting what they want. By their very nature, these forms of rupture are intentional but not necessarily negative. In fact, these ruptures can be positive when they result from limits set by an empathic, mindful parent.

Of course, getting this right takes a great deal of energy, and we aren't always perfect. At times we send nonverbal messages we wish we hadn't or simply don't know the most helpful tactics for parenting. After all, our own implicit memory and primary emotional states activate the mental models that influence how we go about setting limits.

We see Jesus setting limits as well. During his final Passover meal with his disciples, Jesus reveals what will happen in the near future and why it is necessary for him to leave—something they very much do not want him to do:

> I am going to him who sent me. None of you asks me, "Where are you going?" Rather, you are filled with grief because I have said these things. *But very truly I tell you, it is for your good that I am going away.*

> Unless I go away, the Advocate will not come to you; but if I go, I will send him to you. . . . When he, the Spirit of truth, comes, he will guide you into all the truth. He will not speak on his own; he will speak only what he hears, and he will tell you what is yet to come. He will glorify me because it is from me that he will receive what he will make known to you. (JOHN 16:5-7, 13-14, ITALICS MINE)

Jesus tells his disciples that the Holy Spirit will not come unless he leaves. With the Spirit's help, they will grow in their capacity to trust, lead, follow, take risks, and render proper judgment. Before, when they had conflict, the disciples would turn to Jesus to fix their problems and settle their disputes. However, following his death, resurrection, and ascension, they will be compelled, through the vitality of the Holy Spirit, to work things out among themselves. They will have to *grow up*.

Toxic ruptures

Situations that lead to overwhelming or intensely painful mental states create toxic ruptures. We scream and call someone names. Or we withdraw into a vault of silence. We nurture a hurt or wound, ruminating about it, deepening the sadness or anger felt or expressed into a state of despair. We verbally or nonverbally engage in a campaign of contempt.

A cataclysmic event or wildly belligerent behavior is not always necessary to induce a toxic rupture, however. One day as you and your husband are driving in the car you pass the restaurant where he had lunch for the first time with the woman with whom he eventually had an affair. Although you both may be successfully working through that trauma that was revealed months ago, you suddenly find yourself overwhelmed with sadness, shame, and anger. You find yourself over the next few minutes becoming increasingly irritable and short with him until at one point you explode in the middle of a conversation that started out being about your son's transition to high school. Over mere minutes your thoughts, feelings, and images have converged to spill onto the dashboard, with you feeling powerless to stop the flood. You both spend the next day numbed by the interchange, worried your progress in your marriage repair has suffered an irreparable setback.

Sin hunts us on the plain of toxic rupture. It beckons us to sustained disintegration and to react to perceived injustice without mindfulness. This form of separation leads us to behave in ways that reinforce the fear and shame that are at the root of our self-destructive tendencies as a human race. Toxic rupture is so seamlessly connected with the dis-integration of our minds that it almost becomes synonymous with sin. Certainly the consequences of a toxic rupture and a depraved mind sound quite similar.

NO MORE FUN AND GAMES

Eugene came home from work to find his eight-year-old son, Will, and two of his young friends playing in the family room. It had been a long day for Eugene, and he was not prepared for the cacophony caused by eight-year-old boys shooting Nerf guns at one another. When he entered the room, in fact, one of the foam bullets hit him right on the forehead, and the trio of boys laughed in playful delight.

The scene and the noise were too much. A gasket popped in Eugene's mind. He sternly shouted, "Hey!" which got the boys' attention. They turned, startled and not a little frightened, to hear Eugene begin his rant. "Will, if I've told you once, I've told you a thousand times—I don't want you bringing all these toys out and making a mess! For crying out loud, can't you understand a simple instruction? Now get this stuff picked up!"

And then Eugene yelled, "And I don't want any more noise!" as he retreated to the kitchen. There he met the stern, worried gaze of his wife, who had come downstairs when she heard him begin his diatribe. Eugene said nothing, ignoring her quiet but irritated rebuke, and headed upstairs to change his clothes.

Obviously, something was not right with Eugene on this particular afternoon. The neural circuitries that represent the different functions of his mind were no longer talking to each other. Perhaps his outburst was caused by not getting enough sleep the previous night. Perhaps it was the curt phone call with his wife before he left the office. Perhaps it was bad traffic, or too much caffeine, or the Redskins losing *again*.

Any of these triggers might have done it, because Eugene often reacts from unresolved memories and emotions in his own narrative that he has not addressed coherently. He often finds himself so angry with Will that he feels he cannot stop his caustic outbursts. Though he feels awful as he is yelling at his son, he is still too angry with Will to pull himself away from his feelings.

During these squalls, which happen quite regularly, Eugene extends his own wounds to wound his son. He delivers the poison of shame to his wife and employees as well. Because he is a deacon at his church, he works diligently to keep any seemingly bad behavior from the view of other parishioners. He uses little restraint, though, when talking about those same parishioners at home with his family. This further embarrasses his wife. Sin is cavalierly splashed like a bad paint job all over the house.

Because Eugene rarely seeks to resolve the toxic ruptures between himself and his son, Will's mind is full of thoughts, feelings, and sensations swirling in a maelstrom of mental confusion. Physical sensations such as tension in his neck, feelings of discomfort in his abdomen, and heaviness in his chest are outward signs of this inward turmoil. Will is not sure how to cope with these disorienting experiences, so over time he will develop mental and behavioral coping strategies that will enable him to disconnect from the feelings of shame his father's anger triggers. He will think of something else or do something else to divert his attention from those intense feelings. Neuroscience suggests that this process of emotional disconnection has neural correlates that reflect this dis-integrating process.

Unless someone steps in to intervene and provide repair, Will's attachment will not be secure. In addition, he will not develop any neural template to effectively engage and regulate the feelings of hurt, confusion, and above all, shame in his life. In the future, whenever those feelings are about to be evoked, he will tend to avoid them by sheer denial or acting in such a way as to quickly diffuse them, whether through anger, substance abuse, workaholism, or even becoming obsessively neat or developing an airtight theology about his need to behave perfectly to win God's affection.

ELEMENTS OF SHAME

Toxic ruptures have at their core the element of shame. This is the weapon that Eugene wields against Will. Shame, preceded by fear, is consistently the antecedent of sin, as we will see in the following chapter. Whether we label it humiliation, embarrassment, ignominy, dishonor, disgust, or disgrace, the sensation of shame is so basic to the human condition that perhaps the most precise definition is the painfully acute awareness that something is *wrong with me*. It is the *felt sensation of deep inadequacy*. Shame is not simply an acknowledgment of perceived facts but rather an emotionally expressed and experienced phenomenon.

Shame is so off-putting that we will do just about anything to avoid sensing it, to the point of denying its presence or its intensity. The neural correlates tend to be self-reinforcing, however. Hence, we tend to feel shame in response to feeling shame.

Although the exact neural correlates for this complex emotion have not been firmly established, recent research suggests that areas of the prefrontal and temporal cortices are likely connected with it. Shame can develop in children as young as eighteen months of age; some researchers suspect even sooner. This suggests that the sensation and experience of shame is active in the mind and body of a child *before the development of language and logical, linear thought processes.*

In other words, nonverbal cues such as facial expression and tone of voice may make a child feel shame long before she can logically comprehend why she feels that way. Over time as shame is experienced repeatedly, a child will construct a narrative to explain her feelings as a means of coping with those feelings.

Guilt, by contrast, emanates as a response to one's behavior as it affects the emotional state of another, and it tends to develop in most children around the age of three to four. This emotion requires maturation of the brain to include a more distinct awareness of other people and their feelings.

SYMPATHETIC AND PARASYMPATHETIC NERVOUS SYSTEMS

In chapter 3, we briefly explored the sympathetic and parasympathetic nervous systems. These correspond to the general need of the body either to speed up (sympathetic) or slow down (parasympathetic) metabolically or behaviorally. Researchers tend to view these as the accelerator (sympathetic) and brakes (parasympathetic), each influencing the function of the three areas of the triune brain (reptilian/brain stem, limbic/paleomammalian, neomammalian/neocortex).

Ideally, the prefrontal cortical region is densely innervating all three areas, receiving input from and sending output to bodily organ, sensory, emotional, and higher/complex cognitive neural processes. Dan Siegel and others liken the prefrontal cortex to a neurological "clutch," alerting us when to press on the gas and when to apply the brake in a seamless fashion.

When children are engaged, excited, and joyfully anticipating an activity, they are in the accelerator or sympathetic mode. Their heart and breathing rates increase, as does the activity of their gut. When they become quiet and slow down, they are applying the brakes of the parasympathetic system, with respective slowing of physiologic activity. This balance between the sympathetic and parasympathetic systems is at the heart of emotional regulation.

Children require assistance to develop this balance. Usually it is not difficult for them to accelerate. Two-year-olds seem to have an endless supply of fuel, and their expanding nervous systems find delight in exploring new things such as toys, stairs, plants, scissors, and electrical outlets. At some point parents need to set limits for their children's growth and safety, as well as for their own sanity. Yet parents must also help their children learn how to put on the brakes without slamming them, so that children can eventually do so themselves without emotional distress.

Whenever a child is excitedly exploring his or her world, a parent's unexpected, harsh rebuke of "No!" may lead the child to slam on the brakes. Physiologically, the child may turn away, physically withdraw, and feel a deep sense of physical and emotional weightiness. This sense of feeling "bad" in this way is what the child eventually will describe as the sensation of shame.

Of course, to keep a child from imminent danger, this sort of action by a parent is sometimes necessary. Usually in this situation, however, a parent will quickly follow an abrupt rebuke with an expression of affection or an explanation to help the child make sense of his or her action. However, when this form of braking is not followed by a clear behavioral or logical reconnection, the child feels shame, which can lead to a barren wasteland of emotional confusion. This whiplash shift between the sympathetic and parasympathetic systems can become wired so tightly in the child that the affect of shame is automatically triggered at the slightest hint of perceived disapproval. When this occurs, the child may bring the Hebbian propensity for shame, activated through implicit memory tracts, into adulthood.

If Eugene continues his low-road behavior, by the time Will is a teenager, he likely will have developed a logical narrative for why he feels so ashamed. His explanations may include such statements as *I'm too disorganized*; *I'm not thinking enough*; *I'm not working hard enough*; or *I'm not good enough for my dad*.

Will may assume he is ashamed because he first thinks these things—and that they are *true*. However, these thoughts may be his way to cope with his more amorphous emotional state of shame; the thoughts provide a framework within which Will can cope by "working harder," "getting more organized," or doing any number of things to please his father—but most fundamentally they relieve him of his primal emotional distress—if only temporarily.

When toxic ruptures are not repaired, the residue of shame that repeatedly coats the child's mind influences virtually all of his or her responses to life's circumstances. From a neuroscience perspective, the prefrontal cortex of such a person tends to be less integrated, and the mind's dominant neural pattern involves those networks most closely associated with the feelings and behaviors related to shame. These networks are often activated by the slightest stimulus, whether a glance, a tone, or even a misunderstanding.

When we are in the grip of shame, we have a keen sense of painful isolation. We feel separated, not only from others, but disconnected within ourselves. As our multiple mental processes—attention, memory, emotion, bodily sensation, and linear, logical cognitive thought constructs—become fragmented and dis-oriented in the whirlpool of shame, we find it impossible to sense with coherence what we or the other person is feeling. This disconnection within ourselves will, in scope and range, extend to our relationships with other people, becoming a destructive force within our communities, whether they be families, churches, schools, neighborhoods, or nations. Although shame is primarily about *me*, it invariably involves others by virtue of creating greater distance between *us*. Any shaming behavior on one person's part can activate underlying shame elements in others unless they are mindful enough to resist that process.

The apostle Paul knew the power and place of shame:

> I eagerly expect and hope that *I will in no way be ashamed*, but will have sufficient courage so that now as always Christ will be exalted in my body, whether by life or by death. For to me, to live is Christ and to die is gain. (PHILIPPIANS 1:20-21, ITALICS MINE)

One measure of the abundance of his life was the degree to which he was liberated from his experience of shame. And for Paul, to be present with Christ meant to be absent from shame completely.

REPAIR

Life is full of ruptures of varying degrees involving many levels of human interaction—marriage; parents, children, and extended family; friendship; churches; communities; nations; and even between people and the creation. It can be suggested that the evidence of sin is reflected in the plethora of rela-tively toxic ruptures that exist throughout our world. Fortunately, rupture is not the final word for our lives. Regardless of its severity or duration, rupture does not have to define us. God did not settle for, nor do we have to accept, a dis-integrated prefrontal cortex or disconnection between people or between people and the earth. Instead, we can experience repair, a collaborative inter-action in which two or more parties move toward each other in an integrating weaving of minds that heals the breach in relationship.

Whether or not we experience frequent toxic ruptures, we've all experienced the feeling of being so angry that our thoughts swirl about us and we can't seem to stop them. Imagine that your favorite aunt has invited your family to her retirement party. You remind your teenage daughter that the party is tomorrow, only to hear her angrily retort, "I'm *not* going with you to that lame party, and *you* can't *make me*!" Your reptilian brain senses a primal threat and automatically tries to come to your rescue, hijacking your paleomammalian limbic circuitry and outflanking your higher prefrontal cortical networks that would otherwise keep you from losing your mind.

Your sympathetic nervous system moves into overdrive, pushing cortisol through your arteries and veins in high doses, compounding your already careening stress level. Your pulse and breathing rates elevate, and your musculature—from your feet to your face—is taut with tension. Words begin to tumble out of your mouth as you remind your daughter how self-entitled and ungrateful she is being.

Most misunderstandings can be tempered in short order if a parent mindfully notices the mild breach and engages the child verbally and nonverbally. There is one exception: even minor ruptures may prove to be major hurdles if they occur in the context of a relationship in which there is already an undercurrent of anger or distrust. The smallest slight in a marriage that is fraught with a history of contempt can be interpreted as an intentional act of treason to the relationship and flood the one who feels betrayed with intense feelings of hurt or anger.

So what do you do during those times when you feel trapped on the low road of functioning, unable to recover any sense of connection? You may be inundated with physical and mental sensations that are simply too great to turn off immediately. How, then, can you get back on the high road? Again, in *Parenting from the Inside Out*, Siegel offers helpful suggestions:

Centering. If you, like Eugene, often feel unable to avoid the low-road functioning that leads to toxic ruptures, don't give up. You do not have to give in to your responses, even if you feel powerless to resist them. First, you can learn to practice *centering*, which is simply focusing your attention on your mind and body. Doing so will enable you to regroup and shift your chaotic emotional state, which has disconnected you from yourself as well as your children, to more coherent ways of thinking.

How on earth do you "center" (and avoid saying words you'll later regret) when the centrifugal forces of the moment seem so overwhelming? It helps to begin by focusing on your body. Remember that even before inviting the Romans to transformation by the renewing of their minds, Paul encourages them to offer their bodies as holy, pleasing, and living sacrifices (Romans 12:1).

Centering becomes easier for those who regularly practice the body scan (see page 125). This exercise enables you, when you are frustrated by your teen's belligerence, to sense without much effort that part of the body that feels tense and is hijacking the rest of your mind. For instance, tightness in your shoulders or heaviness in your chest signals that you are in a fight- flight mode. You are likely behaving as if you are under threat—which you are from an emotional point of view.

An alternative way to proceed toward centering is to change your physical position and activity. You might move from a standing to a sitting position; take a few deep breaths in slow, deliberate fashion; go for a brief walk; or take a few minutes to mindfully pay attention to your body, intentionally relaxing those areas where you sense tension.

These acts can settle your limbic and brain stem circuitry, giving your prefrontal cortex the chance to catch up and begin the literal process of "gathering" your thoughts and reintegrating the disparate neural circuits that represent the various aspects of mental activities that are becoming more chaotically disconnected. These behaviors also engage the parasympathetic system that acts as the brake system, slowing down the accelerator of the sympathetic system. Your muscles begin to relax, your breathing and heart rate slow, as does the pace with which you are thinking. Essentially, you lower your overall level of anxiety and distress, making it possible to think more clearly and be more aware of the processes of your mind as well as those of your teenager.

Several spiritual disciplines, when practiced consistently, can also help you learn to center. For example, as you meditate, you can create visual imagery representing passages of Scripture or even specific words (e.g., *joy, peace, patience, kindness, goodness, faithfulness, gentleness, self-control*) that can be activated in emotionally explosive situations to help you become more tranquil and focused.

In the discipline of confession, you honestly reflect on your narrative with a well-trusted friend, counselor, or spiritual director. This enables you to be sensitive to the elements of implicit and explicit memory, along with physical and mental manifestations of emotional shifts that, if left unchecked, can easily lead you down the low road of behavior. Listening prayer deepens your awareness of God's voice as he speaks through your emotional tidal changes, directing images and thoughts toward greater wisdom and integration.

It is not easy to be committed to this kind of work. These disciplines require courage and time. However, consistently practicing them tends to wire your brain so that, during times of severe rupture, a stable neural template is already in place to help focus your attention on centering behavior.

Mindfulness. After regaining clarity through centering, you can enter a greater state of mindfulness. This enables you to be more aware of the various elements of a situation, from your own mind's processes (including your emotions and memories—both implicit and explicit—that are being activated, and the elements of your narrative) along with a more acute sense of the current circumstances that have immediately led to your adolescent's outburst over the party. This enhanced mindful state bears testimony to the regrouping that is taking place at the level of the PFC.

Attunement. Mindfulness leads to attunement to your child's mind, progressively directing your attention from your mind to the circumstances of the event as seen by her mind, reflecting on what she may be feeling and thinking. It includes paying attention to her nonverbal cues, discerning her apparent state of mind and readiness to engage in the work of repair. Attunement requires looking at your child, noticing such things as her facial expressions and signs of physical tension or discomfort. You may then alter your own posture (whether by uncrossing your arms, actively relaxing your facial expression when looking at her, or checking your tone of voice as you begin to consider the next step in the repair process).

Taking initiative. It is then up to you to take the initiative to change the course of events. When teetering on the edge of a toxic rupture or soon after you begin the repair process, microscopic relational shifts can rapidly redeploy the sympathetic nervous system and reignite your anger. In the nanosecond it takes for your teen to say something belligerent or use a disrespectful tone of voice, you may find yourself back where you were twenty minutes before when the fight began. Parents, especially those with adolescents, must not forget that as long as they are the parents, it is their responsibility to initiate and to oversee the repair process after a rupture.

But why should I have to start the process of repair? It was my sixteen-year-old who was acting like she was four! This does not alleviate children of their role or responsibility to eventually initiate the repair process, but they will never learn this unless they witness their parents modeling it and instructing their children on how to do the same.

Initiating such a repair can begin with simple statements such as "I'm sorry we had that interaction. Can we try again?" "Can we sit down in the family room and talk about what just happened?" You probably will need to apologize and admit what you have done that has contributed to the rupture: "I shouldn't have spoken to you that way. That was wrong, and I know I hurt your feelings when I said it. I don't want to do that again and promise to work on that. Can you forgive me?"

It will then be important to invite your child to enter into the repair process. This includes asking questions, particularly those *who, what, where, when*, and *how* questions we discussed in chapter 9. "What were you feeling when I reminded you about the party?" "Can you tell me more about what is making you angry?" "What feels upsetting about going to the party?" As you work to repair toxic ruptures, keep the following in mind.

1. These interactions take time, so you will need to be committed to the process of repair. To read another's body language, to move into the family room to sit down, to start the conversation over, to contain what you impulsively want to say in order to give your child time to complete her thought—all require a great deal of time and patience. We often would prefer that these interactions be over and done with in a heartbeat. But remember the brain—and your child, your spouse, your student, your friend, your employee, and most of all God—is deeply interested in connection, integration, and being known. And there is no more significant or helpful moment for being known than in the wake of a toxic rupture. The experience of being known allows for the dis-integrating process of shame to be reversed and the relationship to be reconnected in even stronger ways.

2. At times, your sense of having been mistreated will nurture within you a deep sense of injustice and a desire to be understood and validated—even by your children. You may be tempted to make the repair about being right rather than being healed. When that happens, you're in danger of dis-integrating your prefrontal cortex again, since your left hemisphere, which is driving your logical, linear thought processes as a primary means to reduce your distress, quickly begins to dominate your mental

landscape. Again, being mindful of your narrative and remembering your proclivity to insist on being right as a defense against your distress can protect you from succumbing to this destabilizing mental flux.

3. Different situations, along with children's different ages and temperaments, will require different timing and strategies for repair. The way you engage a four-year-old will be different than the way you approach a fourteen-year-old (one would hope). If your teenager whines about having to attend "that stupid party for old people" as you're walking into church, you may not be able to speak directly to her right then, but you may need to commit to having the conversation when you get home later.

   Siblings tend to have different temperaments. If your son is more sensitive than your daughter, he may require more time to work through a repair with you than she will. However, we must not be fooled into thinking that our less sensitive children have worked through things just because they don't show much distress on the outside. Careful exploration of their minds is just as important.

   As the parent, you will consistently hold the dominant position in terms of the power gradient between your child and you. It is good to be mindful that it is the relatively powerful who are in a position to initiate the repair to a rupture, as well as the fact that when a rupture occurs, variables affect when, where, and how a repair is carried out and what constitutes a successful one.

Repair can be difficult when repeated ruptures have occurred over time without consistent efforts at restoration. In marriages, friendships, or in relationships between adult children and parents in which long-standing feelings of hurt, disappointment, rejection, or shame exist, both parties may feel too vulnerable to make the first move toward reconnection. The terror of risking further rejection or shame is just too intense.

Such instances require greater effort in the centering process before one person is mindful and attuned to the feelings of the other. If you can draw support from other relationships in which you feel more connected, you will find validation for your feelings along with encouragement in your attempts to reconnect your broken relationship. Consistent corporate prayer, which we will explore in the coming chapters, can also be quite helpful.

A NEW ENDING

What about Eugene and Will? After Eugene went upstairs to change his clothes, Will was left with a heap of shattered emotions. Left to its own devices, Will's mind will do what it can to survive, which will likely include a disconnection from the feelings he is experiencing. If those feelings are left unaddressed, he will be unable to effectively deal with them in the future, either.

But what if the story ends differently? What if, after many similar eruptions, Eugene had recognized there was a problem and sought help from someone—a trusted friend, a pastor, or a counselor—to help him make sense of his behavior? In the process, he learned to pay attention to elements of his mind that he had never acknowledged before. As he told his story to someone who mentalized him empathically but with an invitation to risk living life more robustly, his narrative, his life, and his brain began to change.

As a result, while Eugene is in his room changing his clothes, he slows down enough to center his mind. He takes a deep breath and mindfully begins to think about his behavior and the preceding inertia of his day that ran him like a juggernaut into his own family room. He attunes to Will, thinking of the look of astonished fear on his face. He may begin to feel sad and sorrowful for Will and for himself. He heads back down to the family room.

Will, recognizing the padding of his father's footfalls, tenses, his autonomic nervous system and reptilian brain moving to prepare him for another round in the emotional meat grinder. But something strange begins to happen in Will's brain when he sees his father enter the family room. Eugene's facial expression is tired but kind. His voice is soft and repentant. His body language is startling in a comforting way: Eugene walks over to his son, gets down on one knee to look Will directly in the eyes, and then says, "Will, I am so sorry I said the things to you I just did. I had a bad day at work, and I took out my feelings on you and your friends. I know I really hurt your feelings, and that wasn't right. No dad should say the kind of things I just said to you, and I don't ever want to do that again. I hope you will forgive me. You guys go right ahead and play. And don't worry about the noise." He puts a hand on Will's shoulder, then pulls his son closer to him and gives him a hug. Will folds into his father's embrace, responding as much to all of the new nonverbal signals that have been offered as to anything that his father has said.

Later that night, while putting Will to bed, Eugene asks, "So how are we doing?" He invites a conversation with his son to review their conflict and the healing work that followed. In this way, he is bringing to Will's mind not only the rupture, but also the repair.

The next day when he arrives home from work, Eugene finds Will and again checks in with him. Will, being eight, looks puzzled. He may not immediately capture what his father is talking about. But then Eugene reminds him, and Will, recalling again not only the rupture but also the repair, smiles and says, "We're good." As Eugene brings the memory of repair to Will's mind, he actively facilitates the establishment of this event more firmly in Will's explicit memory; this makes it more accessible to the little boy's conscious awareness.

When Eugene admits his poor behavior and then reminds Will of the event twice, he is actually inviting his son to *pay attention* to his shame (the emotional state emanating from right and lower regions of the brain) and then gives him an explanation for it that makes sense (i.e., What *I* did caused you to feel the way you do). This explanation is consistent with Will's experience and as such he begins to feel much better.

Note that the repair is possible because Eugene first did the necessary work to integrate his own mind/brain (left-right/top-down). Next, as Eugene begins to change his nonverbal cues toward his son, his right brain begins to align with Will's right brain, enabling Will to become less overwhelmed by his own emotion and quiet his body's fight-or-flight mechanism. Then as Eugene explains his role in Will's distress, Will's right and left hemispheres become more neurally integrated at the level of the prefrontal cortex.

Current research in neuroscience suggests that every step that Eugene takes to repair the breach in this relationship activates a cascading sequence of neural networks in Will's brain. Those systems that had correlated with his overwhelming feelings of shame are now connected and wired to networks that correspond to the process of healing.

Let's assume that ruptures are consistently followed by repairs in Eugene's home. Fast-forward twelve years. Now Will sits in a college class in which a professor publicly ridicules him for questioning the professor's viewpoint. Will may sense shame, but additional neural networks in his mind, which formed during the process of repeated repair work, will be simultaneously activated. These sensations of comfort, confidence, relief, and insight act as buffers to the feelings of shame; they will not prevent Will from feeling it at all, but they will be protective. He will eventually recognize that he is not at fault for what he feels, but rather the professor, like his father years ago, is simply losing his mind. This will enable him to be less anxious overall and more creative and thoughtful in his response to the professor's inappropriate behavior.

This story of repair gives us a hint of what God is up to in the process of redemption, as spoken in the language of neuroscience and attachment. He is moving us, by virtue of his ultimate repair in and through Jesus, toward renewed, transformed minds reflective of integration. We can then extend this outward in the power of the Holy Spirit to assist in the integration of others' minds and the growing communion between minds.

In this chapter we have begun the process of conceptualizing sin and redemption using language from neuroscience. In the following chapter, we will do the opposite: with an understanding of how the brain functions, we will examine sin and redemption through the stories of Scripture, incorporating a fresh way of embracing the redemption from our sin that God has offered to us and to our world in the person and power of Jesus. We will see how this inevitably leads to the building of community and care for the earth.

Repair, among other things, is the stuff that redemption is made of.

Chapter 11

THE RUPTURE
OF SIN

Neuroscience acts like a magnifying glass, enabling us to see detail about the human condition that we might otherwise overlook. A magnifying glass, of course, is only as good as the illumination of the object we are viewing. God's narrative as recorded in the Bible is the light we will use to illumine our experience. It is important to be mindful that as Christians we believe that God's story is our ultimate authority, our source of authorship for life, delivered through our minds, transforming them in the process, judging even the magnifying glass we use to examine sin and redemption.

In the last chapter, we looked at sin and redemption from the perspective of neuroscience. Neuroscience, as we've seen, helps us recognize that sin results from not paying close enough attention to the varying experiences of our minds as mediated by the reptilian, limbic, and cortical portions of our brains—those parts of our souls by which God's voice is mediated. This leads us to act relatively impulsively, unreflectively, and (perhaps most important) *in isolation*. Redemption, on the other hand, is mindfulness in action, on both a cosmic and a personal level. (We'll examine this regeneration in the next chapter.)

IN THE BEGINNING . . .

In the second chapter of Genesis we are presented with a picture of God up to his elbows in mud, intimately involved with the construction of man's life:

> Then the LORD God formed a man from the dust of the ground and breathed into his nostrils the breath of life, and the man became a living being. (GENESIS 2:7)

From the beginning, God gets as close to us as he can. He doesn't form man from a distance—he gets in the clay and pounds out a model. And then, when it comes time to wake up the man, we read that God "breathed into his nostrils." He does the job himself. Not particularly sterile, if you think about it. But very intimate.

The remainder of Genesis 2 paints a picture of a God deeply interested and involved in the details and textures of the world he has created. He is active and having as much fun making new things as a child would. That has never changed.

And then comes chapter 3. Here we read how the first humans choose to become rebellious idolaters. Those words—rebellious idolaters—sound so . . . harsh. We live in a world that would prefer to soften those descriptors or eliminate them altogether. We sense that we have been shamed enough. No need to read the Bible to be reminded. The problem is, those words, as theological symbols, describe us to a tee.

As we'll see, Adam and Eve succumbed to the temptation of viewing God from a distorted perspective. We do the same:

- creating God in our own image through the lenses of our attachment patterns;
- forming our own gods out of any and all coping mechanisms, whether physical or mental;
- doing what we please and resisting those who suggest we do anything differently.

Some of those who leave God out of the equation of life argue that evolution alone, without the need for a loving, "dangerous" creator, offers us a picture of progress. Now while I generally comprehend evolution as part of God's creative process, you'd think that after ten thousand years of cultural evolution, we would have substantially corrected our overall trajectory of injustice and callousness. But we only need to think about the current number of armed conflicts (either between nations or neighborhoods), third world debt, political and governmental corruption, and major-league baseball on steroids to obtain a reality check.

Rupture in the Garden of Eden

If you've ever wondered how such a beautiful world can get so ugly, Genesis 3 is packed with clues. (If you are unfamiliar with this passage or haven't read it recently, I encourage you to take a few minutes to read it in its entirety.) We open to find the first created woman, Eve, talking with a snake about the nature of the world—her inner and outer ones—and the God whom she presumably trusts to have created it in a spirit of goodness.

Clearly the serpent is not there to be helpful but to engage in trickery. And being tricked always involves the subtle or blatant manipulation of fear, memory, and shame. Peer into their opening interchange and attempt to mentalize what is emerging within Eve:

> Now the serpent was more crafty than any of the wild animals the LORD God had made.
>
> He said to the woman, "Did God really say, 'You must not eat from any tree in the garden'?"
>
> The woman said to the serpent, "We may eat fruit from the trees in the garden, but God did say, 'You must not eat fruit from the tree that is in the middle of the garden, and you must not touch it, or you will die.'"
>
> "You will not certainly die," the serpent said to the woman.
>
> "For God knows that when you eat of it your eyes will be opened, and you will be like God, knowing good and evil." (GENESIS 3:1-5)

With the first question, the serpent evokes within the woman the dynamic of doubt, the first of a series of emotional shifts that occur within Eve. This first incidence of human doubt was just the first link leading to calamity, yet we all have experienced it in one form or another. Doubt includes a left-mode analytic comparison of data, a check for accuracy, and right-versus-wrong thinking (*Did I really say that? Did I measure that correctly? Does God love me?*). Whenever we question reality, we activate our brain's left mode of operation.

But powerfully supporting and fueling our left hemisphere's drive to ensure we are "right" are neural correlates emanating from networks located in our lower brain regions. A surge of emotion emerges from the brain stem as it acts with the amygdala. This energizes the mind's questioning—*What if I'm wrong?*—with an undercurrent of distress in its most basic form: fear.

Fear often does not arrive in grand style. We often barely notice it, especially during moments in which we are less mindful, because it is often unobtrusive. Yet with the first hint of doubt we sense—if we are paying attention—the slight tension in our necks or backs or the minor sensation in our gut. Our heart and breathing rates increase ever so slightly. Our minds reflexively begin to churn through conflicting "facts" in order to know right from wrong. On the surface we believe we are trying to sort out a variety of options in order to be correct. From a brain standpoint we are racing through the mental sifting process in order to reduce our level of distress, eliminate our fear and shame, and bring our physiological states back into equilibrium. Unfortunately, the mental tactics we often use merely reinforce the very fear we are attempting to ameliorate.

In this case I am using the word *fear* to represent the most general, subtlest expression of distress we encounter. The brain stem activates our fight-or-flight response to any form of threat. The strength of its reaction depends on the level of danger. For humans, threat is not limited to physical perils. God's Spirit has, over thousands of millennia, actively breathed the creative process of our minds to the point that we interpret danger not only in terms of our physicality but in terms of our emotions as well. (This is why the childhood phrase "Sticks and stones may break my bones, but words will never hurt me" is horse hooey. We sense words and nonverbal messaging alike to be hurtful or shaming—threatening—through the medium of fear.)

This dynamic of fear expressing itself in the form of doubt is constantly at work within us and between us. We may fear when we doubt our boss's sincerity; our adequacy as a parent; the ability of the school board to do its job; or even that there is a God who knows we are alive, let alone cares, let alone has affection for us.

Fear. This is Eve's introduction to distressing emotion, as it is ours. I find it intriguing that the creature that appears as a vector of evil is a serpent. Not a fox, which is also known as wily. Not an angel, smart, beautiful, and powerful. Unlike the fox or angel, the serpent doesn't correspond with the higher levels of our brain—the limbic circuitry or neocortex. Instead, this first "accuser" (the general meaning of Satan in Scripture) appears in a form that deeply activates our most primitive neural correlates for fear: our brain stem and amygdala.

This being has no intention of being mindful of Eve in any way except one that is dis-integrating and disorganizing. And he, a serpent, introduces himself to Eve by using (and then bypassing) her cortex as a means to activate that part of Eve's mind that is most like him—her reptilian brain. But he does not stop there.

In the opening sentence of Genesis 3, the serpent is described as being "crafty." In other words, he is skillful in the art of trickery. And in order to trick Eve, he first must alter her *memory*.

Notice his initial question to the woman in verse 1: "Did God really say, 'You must not eat from any tree of the garden'?" As many have rightly observed, he is already misrepresenting history.

In Genesis 2 God tells Adam: "You are free to eat from any tree in the garden; but you must not eat from the tree of the knowledge of good and evil, for when you eat of it you will certainly die" (vv. 16-17). No indication of God being stingy. The facts indicate he provided freedom to eat from any tree save one.

Here we see Mr. Crafty facilitating doubt by challenging Eve's *memory*. Of course, God's prohibition was given to Adam before he created and brought the woman to the man (2:22). The man, therefore, may have been responsible for relaying this command to the woman. Presumably, her "memory" is influenced by the limitations of the man's nascent memory. This again is evidence of what neuroscience points to: no brain is truly independent. Our memory is never simply "ours."

As we've seen, memory is not so much about what has happened in the past as what we do in our minds with these recollections in the present to *anticipate the future*. And every time we recall the "past" we change our memory, or our encoding of our experience, whether slightly or dramatically. When I am tricked, it's because I believed that reality was about to unfold in one way (which memory enabled me to anticipate), only to find it unfolding quite differently and in an emotionally distressing way.

In Eve's case, the serpent's slight change in the rendition of the "facts" (what God actually said) begins the unhinging emotional process within her. By the time she responds to the serpent's query, her emotional shift of distress (fear) has begun to shape her memory, or neurally influence those networks that represent her anticipated sense of her connected relationship with God. As a result she gives a different rendition of "history":

> The woman said to the serpent, "We may eat fruit from the trees in the garden, but God did say, 'You must not eat fruit from the tree that is in the middle of the garden, *and you must not touch it*, or you will die.'" (GENESIS 3:2-3, ITALICS MINE)

Eve's anxiety and fear have been activated. As she becomes distressed, her emotional state begins to change the "facts"—her brain stem, limbic circuitry, and right mode of processing begin to override her hippocampal memory circuits, shifting not only these facts but essentially, and primarily *without her paying attention to it*, her experience of her relationship with God.

Already, her mind senses God differently. He now "feels" more restrictive. Not only can she not eat of the tree, she "remembers" that God said she cannot touch it—despite the fact that he said no such thing, according to the text. In remembering, her memory changes.

This is not surprising given the context in which she is being asked to recall what she knows—a setting in which she is not being mentalized in a protective, flexible manner. Instead, the serpent's intent is destructive. This is what fear will begin to do: it changes our perceptions about our relationships, whether with others or with God. We never change the "facts" about people *in our minds* without changing the essence of our relationships with them, whether or not our impressions are consistent with reality.

The serpent's next maneuver is classic. Now that he has effectively activated the woman's fear mechanism while simultaneously inviting her to remember the future differently, this crafty trickster next wields the dynamic of shame.

> "You will not certainly die," the serpent said to the woman. "For God knows that when you eat of it your eyes will be opened, and you will be like God, knowing good and evil." (GENESIS 3:4-5)

Reflect for a moment on the possible tenor of the conversation. Do you think for even a moment the snake is simply providing more accurate data for the woman? If we limit our reading to our left brains, that is what we would likely infer—that the devil is simply giving her a more accurate, logical interpretation of the facts.

But the woman's brain is hearing something more that is painfully wounding her innocence. One can imagine the subtle, calculated disregard with which the snake shames her: "You won't die. But don't trouble yourself. You're probably not interested in finding out more about that anyway. I imagine you're not really sophisticated enough to be concerned with such things."

The array of shame's presentation is vast. The condescension. The disdaining tone. The dismissive glance. His words are the mechanism by which he delivers the nonverbal message: *You believe what? You are that gullible, that naive?* The woman's mind progresses from the primal sensation of fear to the more distinct emotion of shame. At some deep level she begins the descent into the cavern of emotional anguish we use the word *shame* to symbolize. She is immersed in it. Drowning in it.

But her reptilian antagonist comes to her rescue. He distracts her from what she is *feeling* and provides a left-mode, logical, and linear explanation that dis-integrates and disconnects her from her feeling of shame.

In essence he's telling her: "That feeling you're feeling? That sense of being unimportant, dismissed, disregarded, inadequate, inferior? I'll tell you what that's about, Eve. That's God revealing his true regard for you. He's dismissing you. He doesn't want you getting too close to what he has. He doesn't want you to be able to judge right from wrong. You see, Eve, this is about power and who's in charge. And let me tell you right now: you're not. And he aims to keep it that way.

"Listen to me! Eating the fruit would let him know he's not the boss of you! It would tell him that you know about power and are going to rightfully brandish it. And when you have acquired it—when you have the knowledge of good and evil—you'll realize that knowing power is about knowing some *thing*. He would have you believe that knowing is about "relating," about you and him being known—and other such rubbish. But you see where that gets you, this "relating" business. It brings you to where you are right now. Feeling cut out, disenfranchised, dismissed.

"And another thing. See that tree? You can see it; you can touch it—that's what you need. Something solid. Something you can get your hands and mind around. Something with which you can do what you please when you please. On your terms. You need something that is worthy of you, not Someone who makes up silly little rules that seem to suggest in no uncertain terms your unworthiness—your low place on the totem pole. You don't need him. You need something more than him.

"You need something more . . . because you are certainly not enough. . . ."

Ultimately the serpent wants to evoke within the woman the deep sensation of being accused. Shamed that she is *not enough* in her current state of relationship with her God but must seek something else to make up for her inadequacy. Here, she turns to the only friend she has—her left-processing mode. She makes the conscious choice with that part of her mind that is logical and "makes sense" as a way to tolerate her distress.

This is the essence of idolatry, and for us it comes as naturally as breathing. We have an infinite array of coping mechanisms, or idols, at our disposal. They can be constructed out of tangible substances, such as food, alcohol, or golf clubs. Or more likely, out of neurons. We construct them as images, feelings, words, and memories in the neural networks of our minds and put them on display in the world. Judgmentalism. Lust. Gossip. Racism. Ignoring the poor. Wars and rumors of wars.

My liberal license with the story notwithstanding, do you see this playing out in Eve? Shame has a way of saying so very much with as few words as possible. We have all seen the look or heard the tone that has triggered it. In this play, the serpent appears to have very few lines. But he makes the most of them, mobilizing the woman's fear and activating her shame.

And where does shame inevitably lead? Notice how in verses 5 and 6 the center of the conversation shifts to a description of God and from there to the object that would make up for her inadequacy. The snake first invites her into the process of left-mode *analysis*. His first question in the chapter induces doubt; from there he beckons her mind away from relating with God directly to dissecting him from a distance:

> For God knows that when you eat of it your eyes will be opened, and
> you will be like God, knowing good and evil. (GENESIS 3:5)

Here he provides data *about* God. He is coaxing her further away from God in order to get a "better view." He has no intention of moving her closer *to* God. At no point does he say, "I can see you're upset by what I'm telling you. That must feel really uncomfortable and disorienting. Let's go speak with God on the matter. I'm sure he's around here somewhere—and I know he'll want to help." As if.

As we saw in the last chapter, shame is a function of the autonomic nervous system's balance between sympathetic and parasympathetic fibers. Shame is activated when there is too hard an application of the brakes on an engaged accelerator with no subsequent attempt to comfort or buffer the whiplash effect of that transition.

It emerges in the presence of a dis-integrated prefrontal cortex, the part of the brain designed to modulate the two systems (for instance, it helps me modulate my feelings when I am the focus of a practical joke). Yet in Genesis 3, an expectant innocent, one who knows only joy, anticipates only goodness, and is ready to explore and have dominion over both her external and internal worlds—one whose mind is expanding in the rapturous energy of a sympathetic nervous system—slams into the barrier of a parasympathetic system that says "No!" to all she has known, with no recovery help provided in the aftermath. Notice that after verse 5, the serpent quietly exits the stage (so quietly, in fact, that his departure is not even mentioned). He does not hang around to tend to the wounded. At the height of her shame, Eve is left to deal with it alone—exactly where each of us finds ourselves when our shame reaches its peak.

The early part of Genesis 3 is a complete antithesis of Genesis 2. Only one chapter earlier the garden overflowed with a sense of joyful, creative energy. Genesis 2:22 describes not only the relationship between man and woman, but God's creative role:

> Then the LORD God made a woman from the rib he had taken out of the man, and he brought her to the man.

Not only are woman and man made for each other, but God brings them together. He personally reveals them to each other, protectively introducing the woman to the man, actively engaging in their union. And in that protective, mentalizing, secure *community* of relationships, it is no wonder that

> The man and his wife were both naked, and they *felt no shame*.
> (GENESIS 2:25, ITALICS MINE)

And now, one chapter later, the woman is no longer in a state of protective, harmonious community but in a place of shame, the essence of which is fearful isolation.

With the serpent's help, facilitated by her fear and through the dense fog of her shame, she reinterprets God's nature and his posture toward her. Mind you, she does so without checking with God about any of this. Her mental shift is intended in part as a remedy, a left-mode tactic for coping with her fear and shame. Once her attention shifts from what she feels to an "objective," unengaged scrutiny of God, she then can replace him, replace their relationship, with a more controllable *nonrelational* coping mechanism. A piece of fruit.

> When the woman saw that the fruit of the tree was good for food and pleasing to the eye, and also desirable for gaining wisdom, she took some and ate it. She also gave some to her husband, who was with her, and he ate it. (GENESIS 3:6)

Eve never engages in mindful, validating dialogue with someone who can help her make sense out of her story. Not simply cohesive sense—simply lining the facts up accurately—but coherence as well, including a *felt comprehension* of her narrative. She never says, "Hey, Adam, by the way, what *did* God say? What do you think about this idea Mr. Crafty is introducing?" There is no indication either that the man is paying much attention, stepping in to defend her and calm her emotional distress. Nor does Eve come to God with, "Excuse me, but what's up with the snake you put in the jungle? He's cute and all, and very smart. But I've got a bad feeling about this and I need you to help me figure this out." Instead of approaching and relating with God, she analyzes him from a distance. Apparently the rationale provided by her reptilian friend is enough to help Eve cope with her emotional distress of shame.

That's not surprising, since shame exploits our left brain's capacity for analysis. As a means of quickly diminishing the feeling of shame, we often rush to explain why we feel what we feel. This venture into left-mode thinking distracts us—if even only slightly—from the intensity of the sensation of shame itself. This distraction is enough to keep us from wading into the shame in the presence of a safe, flexible, capable, and empowered relationship, the only way for the shame to be truly healed and explained reasonably.

As we can see, Eve does not taste the forbidden fruit on a whim. First, the emotional state of the woman (and presumably the man, who is assumed to be present but silent—go figure) is mobilized to prepare her for this action. God, if he anticipated this tectonic shift in her mental state—and we have no reason to believe he didn't—certainly didn't seem so worried that he created the couple's minds to prevent them from having such shifts. Perhaps he simply hoped that, when such shifts occurred, Adam and Eve would engage each other and him before cutting him out and replacing him with a pear.

This is critical for us to remember: God does not find our emotional states offensive; what he does abhor is our propensity to ignore them and likewise eject him from our minds' landscapes. When we do so, we unwittingly face *death*—the subhuman, withering, devolving existence of comprehensive isolation of our mind(s), within themselves and apart from God and others.

And so, from a neuroscience perspective, the story of the Fall goes something like this (admittedly oversimplified):

- God comes and goes from the couple; his relative disconnection provides them with the opportunity for growth.
- The serpent comes calling at a moment when God's oscillating

movement has taken him away. The crafty creature successfully shifts Eve's attention with his first query.

- He activates her basic fear mechanism—the fight-or-flight circuitry of her brain stem, which is aided by her amygdala. The snake resonates with her reptilian brain.
- In the face of fear, her memory is altered, further changing not only the "facts" but also her relationship with God. The rupture has begun.
- Next her mind recruits additional neural networks, moving her from fear at a very primitive level to the experience of shame.
- Quickly (in brain time, in nano- to microseconds) her cortex is activated, especially those areas of her left brain that accuse, analyze, and judge harshly—not only God, who now seems unsafe—but particularly herself, whom she now sees as inadequate.
- Eve must add something to her life to make up for her deficits. In the process, she separates herself from an awareness of what she feels within herself and follows this dis-integrating spiral as she separates herself from God.
- Eve chooses "knowledge" over life. Object over relationship. She acts out of the state of a dis-integrated mind, her left and right modes vacillating back and forth, each vying for contentious rule of her destiny. At times she is overrun by the lower and right mode's emotion of fear and shame. To cope with this she shuts them off, deferring to her logical, linear left-mode processing that dismisses her emotion in order to keep her from being overwhelmed by it.
- She eats a piece of fruit, supplanting the dynamic, life-breathing experience of being known by God, the one who mentalizes her perfectly and longs to be known by her, with the static, nonrelational, temporal creation of her own mind.
- In rejecting the gift of this perfect relationship with God, she buys the right to acquisition, to forever working to obtain and hoard enough so that she will eventually be enough. Instead of finding abundance and joy in being known, she stakes her claim on disconnection. The rupture is complete.

FALLOUT FROM THE FALL

After the young couple (feeling older by the minute) has feasted on fruit, notice how quickly things unravel.

> Then the eyes of both of them were opened, and they realized they
> were naked; so they sewed fig leaves together and made coverings for
> themselves. (GENESIS 3:7)

We read that their eyes "were opened." By whom? By what? By magic? Not
likely. (This is implied later in verse 11 when God asks, "Who told you that
you were naked?") Perhaps by now they have both become experts in scrutiniz-
ing each other from a distance. Each is perhaps less mindful of the other, less
engaged in being known by making himself or herself vulnerable and open to
the other. Each now quickly recognizes the flaws of the other in response to
his or her own fear and shame.

Perhaps they "realize" they are naked because they begin to point it out to
each other. You can imagine the conversation: "So, Eve, I've noticed you've
put on some weight—in all the wrong places. I mean, it's as plain as day. Not
too surprising given all the fruit you've been eating from *that tree*. You really
should exercise more."

Shocked, she glances just below his waist and responds, "I really think you
should, you know, put *that* away. It's not very attractive. Rather embarrassing,
in fact." No wonder they need fig leaves. After giving up on being known, they
begin the practice of *hiding*. No more intimacy. No more direct engagement.
No more vulnerability. No more safety. Just fig leaves and shame.

From hiding from each other they quickly move to the next inevitable
step: they hide from God.

> Then the man and his wife heard the sound of the LORD God as he
> was walking in the garden in the cool of the day, and they hid from
> the LORD God among the trees of the garden. But the LORD God
> called to the man, "Where are you?"
>
> He answered, "I heard you in the garden, and I was afraid because
> I was naked; so I hid." (3:8-10)

One of the first things we notice here is the sound of the Lord God walking in the cool of the day. He is walking. He is *moving*. God's movement is
independent of, but not mindless of, the couple. The contemplative tradition
of Christian spirituality rightly emphasizes that we are never apart from God.
In fact, if God were to leave us, given our utter dependence on his Spirit for
our very physical integrity, we would cease to exist. His movement toward

and away from people provides an opportunity for our growth in emotional resilience.

We are never away from his mind or beyond the reach of his arm of mercy and justice. Yet with this image of God walking in the cool of the day, we get the impression that he has been out of the picture to some degree, *at least in the minds of the man and the woman.*

God's apparent silence in the opening scene of Genesis 3 affords Eve and Adam the opportunity to feel distress, to ask questions, to admit confusion or fear, and to draw nearer to God and each other. God's attentive restraint opens the path for Adam and Eve to take initiative with him, to seek him out, to ask questions, all along weaving more and more fibers of connection, strengthening the fabric of their relationships.

But they don't. The only threads they eventually weave are used to create fabric out of fig leaves. No longer are they naked and unashamed. They are hiding. Hiding is the first fundamental behavioral outcome of sin. I hide parts of myself from other parts of me. I hide from other people. And I hide from God.

In the larger world, we also hide from each other as ethnic communities, within churches, and between nations. Hiding is so natural, in fact, that we assume it to be a necessary part of maintaining a civilized society. What would we do without clandestine operations, be they the use of our radar detectors, safely preventing a speeding ticket; conversations in which we "objectively assess" the flaws of other friends or family members or the theological shortcomings of our congregations; or negotiating secret arms deals with "our man" in another country's capital? Hiding requires us to put energy into keeping things about ourselves away from our own and others' conscious awareness.

In hiding from God, the man and woman augment their sense of being alone. They move against the relational gravity of creation that led God to declare that it was not good for the man to be alone (Genesis 2:18). But God is not willing to leave them in their isolation. He comes calling. And he does not come calling with accusation, preemptively putting the couple in a box. He does not declare, "I know what you've done, so there's no use hiding." No, he comes *inquiring*: "Where are you?" (3:9).

This is not a question about their physical location as much as it is a question about the states of their minds. He comes seeking to know them. He comes longing to provide them with the opportunity to reveal themselves and in the process *feel God feeling them.* As we explored in chapter 9, interrogative questions that invite true revelation and engagement, that facilitate being known, begin with asking *who, what, where, when,* and *how* in an emotional context of safety.

God is initiating the possibility of repair with his query. Although he is not the responsible party in this serious rupture, he is the majority shareholder of the power gradient. He makes the first move toward reconciliation in a relationship in which the other party still seems to be moving further away. He is not playing a game of smoke and mirrors, simply asking a question he already knows the answer to, in a maneuver to rub the couple's noses in their shame.

He is being who he is, pursuing them relentlessly, but mindful and mental-izing all the while. But you have to wonder, what is God *feeling* at this point? It is easy for us to assume that this whole debacle is taking place in the pres-ence of a Creator who is an emotionally inert bystander, simply watching the play from the audience. We become so consumed with what is happening with Adam and Eve that we simply do not consider God's feelings in the matter.

We know he feels emotion. Scripture provides a robust account of this. God certainly has a "right brain." As I have said previously, we often do not take ourselves nearly as seriously as God does. We either are not aware of or do not believe in our capacity to hurt God. And imagine the intensity of the emotion when God feels sad, hurt, or ignored. Not that he is overwhelmed by that intensity, for he is, as a communal God—Father, Son, and Spirit—able to experience constant mentalization, empathy, and affirmation within his own heart.

He does not shame the man and woman but seeks them out, offering the way home, back on the high road, away from the low road of fear and shame.

Adam responds: "I heard you . . . and I was afraid because I was naked; so I hid" (3:10). Adam and Eve's shame has doubled back on itself. Eve's fear led to shame, which led to hiding (fig leaves)—which led to fear, which led to shame and hiding (behind the trees). This is the basic pattern of sin. It begins with not paying attention—to the voice of the one who tells us we are loved beyond comprehension and who repeatedly asks us where we are—and fol-lows the low road of fear, shame, and concealment. This is what the presence of another who is relentlessly in pursuit of connection and passionately desires the experience of being known will do to us. It will bring us out from behind the trees but force us to address the fear, shame, and strategies we employ to cover ourselves.

God again takes them seriously, further inquiring about their behavior:

And he said, "Who told you that you were naked? Have you eaten
from the tree that I commanded you not to eat from?" (3:11)

Consider the curious progression occuring in God's queries. His first question in verse 11 is not about eating the forbidden fruit. It is not about a broken
rule. It is not about right versus wrong behavior. It is not dominated by a left
mode of operation. It is about shame. "Who told you that you were naked?"

While he probes behavior, it is not from the perspective of "Did you do
the thing I told you not to do?" Instead he approaches their action from the
perspective of "What have you been doing that creates fear, shame, disintegration, and separation?" He includes emotion as an implicitly understood
element that undergirds their behavior. He wants to know as much about
their emotional state as he does about their actual behavior. Again, this is God
perfectly mentalizing his creatures.

This question points back to verse 7, where we learn that Adam and Eve
"realized they were naked." God invites them first to address the underlying
emotional state that fueled this revelation. Shame is reflected, not only in what
we believe or feel within ourselves, but in the ways we allow it to drive what
we do to one another.

The fact that God asks back-to-back questions without giving the couple
the chance to reply also indicates a certain urgency on God's part, as if he
is now feeling the full "emotional" force of his creatures' actions, which are
reflected in their vegetative clothing and avoidant behavior. Am I suggesting
that there are things God does not "know" in advance? We must remember
that this story reveals Adam and Eve's experience of a God before whom
they were *known* and a God who has the experience of *being known* by his
creatures. This experience must take place in the eternal "now," a place of
never-ending discovery, surprise, and joy, a place in which God takes as much
pleasure in being discovered by us as we do in being discovered by him. We
are not static beings who are known by God only in terms of his explicit
memory of the facts of events as they have occurred in the past and will occur
in the future. We are ever-changing and always providing God the potential
for a dynamic, oscillating, joy-filled relationship. We are, in effect, reflecting in our minds the very way he relates with us. For truly, we were created
in his image.

But living in the moment, in the eternal here and now, is something the
couple cannot muster.

The man said, "The woman you put here with me—she gave me some fruit from the tree, and I ate it."

Then the LORD God said to the woman, "What is this you have done?"

The woman said, "The serpent deceived me, and I ate." (3:12-13)

The man's shame is too piercing, his fear too pervasive, his prefrontal cortex too dis-integrated. Instead of paying attention to his emotional state and telling God exactly what is going on inside his head, he impulsively, *mindlessly* turns on Eve as a means of protecting himself. In his shame, he shames her. It appears that turning to reflect on the entirety of his story (his silence, complicity, and passivity in Eve's conflict with the serpent) would require access to memory that at the moment he wants to deny. His implicit memory of fear and shame is being evoked, undermining his prefrontal cortex's capacity to reflect on those parts of his emotional state he finds most painful. His brain stem's fight-or-flight circuitry and limbic system's dysregulation are at full throttle, the specter of spiritual death hovering in the shadows cast by the grove of trees in which he has been hiding.

Exposed, humiliated, and left undefended, Eve follows suit, deflecting responsibility for her behavior at the feet (or the belly, as it were) of the serpent. Notice that God asks uncomplicated questions that could be answered directly. Of Adam, "Have you eaten from the tree?" and of Eve, "What is this you have done?" From Adam, a simple yes or no would suffice. From Eve, a response of "I ate some and gave it to him" would do.

However, each includes data in his or her answer that God didn't ask for. He begins with simple questions, not in order to accuse (as the serpent had done), but rather to truly engage the couple, looking for *someone* to give him a straight answer. They will have none of that.

Nor often will we. Fueled by our fear and shame, we often avoid plumbing our emotional depths, explaining with left-mode alacrity and desperation why it's not our fault but rather someone else's that our marriage is in trouble. That we are immersed in conflict with our pastor. That there is racism at our school or church. Shame, ignited by fear, leads to sin—to the dis-integration of our minds, beginning with the prefrontal cortex and spreading to our individual relationships, communities, and nations.

Chapter 12

THE REPAIR OF
RESURRECTION

The gospel message of the New Testament is this: God, in his relentless, dangerous, and immeasurably joyful love for his creation, has made Jesus King and Lord of the universe. In Jesus' death and resurrection he extinguished the power of fear and shame—death—and ushered in a newly created order of justice and mercy. This new Kingdom will reach its culmination for all creation with the bodily appearance of Jesus when he creates, reveals, and draws together the new heaven and new earth. In the meantime we are to be about the business of living under his rule, practicing who and what we will be when his Kingdom arrives in its fullness.

What would life be like for us if we not only assented to this message but *imagined* this declaration is true? Imagined that the gospel is not primarily about a set of facts, although facts are involved. That it is not all about meeting the "right" behavioral standards. Rather, the gospel is the declaration of the reality of Relationship. A declaration that we are to be known. That the physical world is to be known (the earth can't wait to get there, by the way—recall Romans 8:22). That God is to be known.

To imagine the gospel means to allow space in our minds for an *image* of the Jesus about whom the prophets of the Old Testament foretold, whose life story is revealed in the Gospel narratives, and whose deeper, extended purposes are reflected in the letters of the New Testament. This imagining requires us to access and utilize all the dimensions of our mental lives, including attention, memory, emotion, and awareness of our narratives and attachment patterns. To believe is to "be-living" *as if* the gospel is true. It means living as if Relationship is here and now, ever pressing in to be known and to know. The good news is that Jesus has shown us this new way to be human.

By truly embracing what he heard the Father say—"You are my Son whom I love; with you I am well pleased"—Jesus was able to avoid the pitfall into which Eve and Adam had run headlong. In essence *by paying attention to the mental representations of the memory of hearing his Father's voice and the emotional state that was simultaneously activated,* Jesus effectively reinforced his awareness of God's love for him. Jesus *imagined*—mindfully felt—his Father's love for him and made choices because he believed that love was true. Even when his good friend Peter denounced Jesus' prediction of his own death (Matthew 16:21-23; Mark 8:31-33). Or in Gethsemane, where Jesus' tortured mind was whetted against the cold darkness of his accuser, still trying to convince Jesus that he, like Eve, wasn't enough, and that God was no more interested in being faithful to Jesus than he had been to her.

And when he was heading toward the ultimate rupture—death—Jesus again showed us how God is in the business of repair. In Matthew 27:46 Jesus is being crucified. Most of his friends have abandoned him, and his enemies are mocking him. We hear Jesus plead, "My God, my God, why have you forsaken me?" Curiously, what might appear to be a cry of despair is actually an indication of just how much attention Jesus was paying to his Father at the height of his suffering.

In first-century Palestine, when rabbis were giving instruction about a passage of Scripture, they would speak a phrase or single verse as a means of summoning to mind a larger story or section of Scripture. This would be akin to a teacher saying something like "It was the best of times, it was the worst of times" to bring to his students' minds Dickens's *A Tale of Two Cities.* Jewish writers, such as the Gospel writer Matthew, sometimes used this teaching method also. Given his emphasis on Jesus' role as Messiah, it is quite possible Matthew is doing the same in this passage.

The words Matthew records Jesus saying are the first verse of Psalm 22. It is unlikely that Jesus, who would have known the entire psalm, would remember only a single verse, and one that speaks of abject suffering in the face of God's abandonment at that. Given the entirety of his journey, it seems more likely that he would focus on the beginning of a psalm that, when taken in its entirety, speaks ultimately not of God's abandonment but rather his victory and vindication for the one who trusts in him:

> My God, my God, why have you forsaken me?
>> Why are you so far from saving me,
>> so far from the words of my groaning?
> My God, I cry out by day, but you do not answer,
>> by night, but I find no rest. . . .
> All who see me mock me;
>> they hurl insults, shaking their heads.
> "He trusts in the LORD," they say,
>> "let the LORD rescue him.
> Let him deliver him,
>> since he delights in him." . . .
> I am poured out like water,
>> and all my bones are out of joint.
> My heart has turned to wax;
>> it has melted within me.
> My mouth is dried up like a potsherd,
>> and my tongue sticks to the roof of my mouth;
>> you lay me in the dust of death.
> Dogs surround me,
>> a pack of villains encircles me;
>> they pierce my hands and my feet.
> All my bones are on display;
>> people stare and gloat over me.
> They divide my clothes among them
>> and cast lots for my garment. (PSALM 22:1-2, 7-8, 14-18)

The first half of this psalm reflects a clear picture of one who is suffering, who feels overwhelmed by his circumstances, and who experiences the distress of fear, abandonment, and shame. This is the stuff of rupture. This is the outcome of sin, of dis-integrated minds, families, churches, communities, and nations.

But then comes the second half of the psalm. At verse 19, everything turns:

But you, LORD, do not be far from me.
You are my strength; come quickly to help me.
Deliver me from the sword,
my precious life from the power of the dogs. . . .

I will declare your name to my people;
in the assembly I will praise you.
You who fear the LORD, praise him! . . .
For he has not despised or scorned
the suffering of the afflicted one;
he has not hidden his face from him
but has listened to his cry for help. . . .
All the ends of the earth
will remember and turn to the LORD,
and all the families of the nations
will bow down before him,
for dominion belongs to the LORD
and he rules over the nations. . . .
Posterity will serve him;
future generations will be told about the LORD.
They will proclaim his righteousness,
declaring to a people yet unborn:
He has done it! (PSALM 22:19-20, 22-24, 27-28, 30-31)

These verses communicate a very different sense of the world. These are the words of repair. These are the words of confidence, joy, and vindication *even in the face of suffering*, not in its relief. These are the words of one who is known, who hears the voice of his father while being tortured to death. These verses enable Jesus to pay attention to those parts of his heart that he has been listening to all his life, those deep emotional shifts through which God reminds him of the way the world *is*, not the way it appears to be on the surface.

It may seem somewhat difficult to take this in, given the horror of this rupture, the trauma of crucifixion. But we must remember that this was not the first rupture for Jesus. His family had to flee to Egypt to avoid the brutality of Herod's infanticide. His parents rebuked him at age twelve after they were unable to locate him for three to four days—even though it appears *they* weren't paying attention to his whereabouts—as he "thoughtlessly" became immersed in the joy and vitality of dialoguing with teachers of the Law. There was also his confrontation with the devil following his baptism and forty days of fasting; his family's dismissal and condescension toward him; the scoffing of those who found his healing and offering of forgiveness incredulous—and too threatening for the established economic and political structures. Perhaps most painful were the ruptures he encountered as he approached his death—his followers' abandonment; Judas's betrayal; Peter's expletive-filled denial that he even knew Jesus. And yet throughout this range of experience, Jesus pays attention to his Father's voice.

From the cross he still speaks into the darkness of evil, confident that he is heard by a Father who is mindful and responsive to him despite evidence to the contrary: "Father, forgive them, for they do not know what they are doing" (Luke 23:34). He knows what these men don't. He is mindful and centered, completely integrated at the level of his prefrontal cortex. Those for whom he seeks forgiveness are dis-integrated; disconnected from their emotional states, memories, and narratives; unable to cope with their fear and shame in any other way but through the medium of violence. They have debased themselves to the point of using shame to cope with their shame. At the height of his suffering, at the point at which he would be most likely to lose his mind, Jesus' mind remains clear, mentalizing his executioners and extending to them what they most desperately need: forgiveness.

GOD'S NO AND YES

Through Jesus' death and resurrection, God repairs the rupture of Genesis 3. He takes responsibility for something that only someone as good and as mindful as God could. The horror of what Jesus experienced makes clear that forgiveness is not some cosmic version of letting us off the hook. God does not wink at us and say, "Sin? Oh, no big deal. And that idolatry thing? No worries. The whole murder, lust, greed, contempt, judging, adultery, lying, gluttony, drunkenness, oppression-of-the-powerless-and-poor, racism, ethnic cleansing, and earth-abuse thing? We're cool." There is no forgiveness without measurable action being taken.

Indeed, at the Cross, before God says "Yes!" to new creation, new life, new minds, he says "No!" to evil. At Jesus' death, evil throws everything it has left in its arsenal at God—and is found wanting. With the words "It is finished. . . . Into your hands I commit my spirit," Jesus absorbs the worst that darkness can offer—and extinguishes it. God acknowledges the awfulness of sin and dis-integrated mindlessness, and then crushes its head, as he foretold just after the first rupture: "I will put enmity between you and the woman, and between your offspring and hers; he will crush your head, and you will strike his heel" (Genesis 3:15).

This illustrates that the process of repair requires us to confront the reality of the wound that has taken place. This includes naming the offense (what someone did or failed to do), acknowledging that it has caused pain to the one offended, and pledging to work to never repeat the behavior. In the language of faith we describe this maneuver of repair as confession and repentance—the act of turning around and going in the opposite direction, not merely feeling regret for having done something wrong. In so doing we are saying "No!" to mindlessness and "Yes!" to deeper, richer, more integrated lives intra- and interpersonally. Simple enough on the surface, to confess and repent.

The hard part is confronting our dis-integrated minds, retracing our steps back through our shame and fear so they may be healed and new networks integrated into the larger landscape of our minds. Too often the fear of feeling fear and shame all over again causes us to avoid the discipline of confession and forgo the liberty of forgiveness. Yet it is only when we allow ourselves to be known, when we allow for intimacy, that we permit another person to use all of his or her nonverbal power to activate those parts of our right hemisphere that represent emotional states that are too painful for us to bear in the absence of another brain.

To see how willing God is to know us in this way, we look to John 21, which includes a story about an encounter Jesus has with Peter after the Resurrection. During the hours just before Jesus' crucifixion, Peter, warming himself around a fire (an important detail), denies his friendship with Jesus at least three times. In his shame, Peter cannot tolerate Jesus' looking at him (Luke 22:54-62) and flees the scene.

The events of John 21 occur some days after the Resurrection, and Jesus has prepared breakfast for some of the disciples, Peter included. Jesus initiates a well-known conversation, one of the most remarkable exchanges in the Gospels. He asks his wounded lieutenant, three times in succession, if he loves him.

> When they had finished eating, Jesus said to Simon Peter, "Simon son of John, do you love me more than these?" "Yes, Lord," he said, "you know that I love you." Jesus said, "Feed my lambs."
> Again Jesus said, "Simon son of John, do you love me?" He

answered, "Yes, Lord, you know that I love you." Jesus said, "Take care of my sheep."

The third time he said to him, "Simon son of John, do you love me?"

Peter was hurt because Jesus asked him the third time, "Do you love me?" He said, "Lord, you know all things; you know that I love you."

Jesus said, "Feed my sheep." (JOHN 21:15-17)

Many have noted that Jesus inquires of Peter three times so as to address his triplicate denials. That may be true. But in terms of Jesus offering Peter an opportunity for confession, forgiveness, and a new life direction (or, in the language of neuroscience and attachment, integration of the prefrontal cortex and a more coherent narrative leading to secure attachment), something much more important is going on here.

With each exchange, Jesus gives Peter something to do. "Feed my lambs." "Take care of my sheep." "Feed my sheep." Jesus knows Peter's shame and is relentless in the process of healing it. It would be one thing for Jesus to say to Peter, privately, "You know those denial episodes? Don't worry about them. We're fine." But Jesus knows that Peter's shame runs deep. Peter knows that other disciples, of whom he has supposedly been the leader, know of his denials as well. This is the disciple who claimed that Jesus was the Messiah and that he would go to the wall for him, even if it meant he would die.

Consider what Jesus is doing. Recall that Peter's denials came while warming himself around a fire—not unlike the one Jesus has made on the beach to cook breakfast for his disciples. Charcoal smoke. Flame. Plenty of stimuli to evoke Peter's implicit memory networks through olfactory, visual, heat, and auditory senses that would activate his shame matrix. Jesus is not satisfied with Peter simply confronting his acts of denial. He knows that will not be enough. Jesus takes Peter back through his memory so he can be present with Peter in his shame and his fear—in order to heal them.

Toward the conclusion of the conversation we read that Peter "was hurt because Jesus asked him the third time, 'Do you love me?'" His hurt is not so much *created* by Jesus' query as it is *revealed* by it. Peter is deeply aware of the shame that comes from his clear inability (despite, perhaps, his desire) to love Jesus—he merely need bring to mind his denials (as Jesus is facilitating). And Jesus is leaving no memory unchanged and no emotion left unintegrated at the level of Peter's prefrontal cortex.

He does this by shifting Peter's attention. You can imagine (there is that word again) Jesus' facial expression, his tone of voice, his body language as he firmly grasps Peter's arm or puts his arm around Peter's shoulder and says, looking him in the eye, "Do *this*! Feed and take care of my lambs and my sheep. *Be* the leader you are. You are forgiven. Now live as if it's true. Pay attention to *me* and what you are experiencing right now rather than to your *shame. Remember this moment. All of it.*"

Notice that this confirms that forgiveness always involves *a measurable change in behavior.* It is never simply something we do in our heads, such as letting someone off the hook in our minds. No, it requires some form of action, even if limited to praying about what we feel about the one who has hurt us or praying for him or her. Though we cannot explore the process of forgiveness fully here, it requires a wide-ranging shift in attention, which leads to further alterations in emotion and memory. This enables the victim to finally make sense of his or her own narrative as he or she adjusts to the circumstances surrounding the offense. (For more on what it means to forgive, see the work of Everett Worthington, L. Gregory Jones, Miroslav Volf, and Desmond Tutu, who examine forgiveness and justice from different perspectives but all with great wisdom.)

In this story, then, we see the recapitulation of the Genesis narrative, albeit with a different outcome. In his fear and shame on the night before Jesus' crucifixion, Peter copes by replacing relationship with Jesus with the immediate "safety" of denial, just as Eve and Adam did. Here we sense how the power of the Resurrection reaches back to the beginning, to the trauma in the Garden. In his conversation with Peter, Jesus is also speaking back beyond the *behavior* of eating the fruit and meeting Eve, Adam, and all of us who followed at our most primitive level of neurological awareness—shame and fear.

He is present with all of us in the mess of our dis-integrated prefrontal cortices, mindfully bringing our attention to his compassionate presence and bringing us forward through his death and resurrection.

THE POWER OF CONFESSION

Christian orthodoxy views confession not simply as a listing of wrong behaviors. It is also an ongoing acknowledgment of our human nature. From a neuroscientific standpoint, when we admit our penchant to ignore emotion, to be inattentive to memory, to dis-integrate our minds, and to reap the behavioral consequences—in other words, our penchant to sin—we acknowledge the presence of neural networks that have been, following Hebb's axiom, repeatedly fired to wire in a way that represents our "old self with its practices" (Colossians 3:9).

This "old brain" represents the neural substrates (left-right, higher-lower) out of which emerge the vast array of human suffering. These networks are well established and virtually impossible to disassemble. We will be able to access them until we die. Crucifixion, therefore, is an apt metaphor for Paul to use when he describes what we are to do with this old, sinful self (see Romans 6:6). It takes a long time to die by crucifixion. The killing off of our old neural pathways, much like a Roman execution, seems to take forever.

Confession, however, turns our attention to these old pathways. We become more consistently mindful of them when they are activated, much as Jesus became intimately aware of his potential for taking the low road when he was tempted by Satan in the desert. In this way, confession makes us aware of our old brain/old self, giving us the opportunity to "put on the new self, which is being renewed in knowledge in the image of its Creator" (Colossians 3:10).

Putting on the new self means paying attention to representations within the mind (mental models, attentive shifts to emotion and memory, etc.) that reflect God's relentless, loving pursuit of women and men, and by extension, the rest of the universe. Confession leads to joy, hope, and freedom.

One wonders how the story would have unfolded differently in the Garden had Eve and Adam, instead of hiding, been more attentive to their fear, more willing to turn toward their own shame. What if, when God sought him out, Adam had said, "Here I am, over here! And I'm in quite a state. I feel really bad about this . . . and in fact it terrifies me to tell you what I'm about to say, and I'm really, really embarrassed. As you can see, wearing these rather odd, um . . . clothes, I believe?"

"Yes, I see. Go on," God might have replied.

"Well, the tree you said I couldn't eat from, well, Eve, well . . . that's not important. I mean, I know you probably have to talk with her about her part in this, but let me just say . . . I ate from the tree. Okay, there. I said it. I blew it. I hate that snake, but it's my fault. I'm really sorry.

"I know Eve may be in big trouble too, but really, don't take it out on her. Just do with me what you will. . . ."

Who's to say God's response would not have been, "Well done. I know it's been painful for you to take responsibility for your *and* her behavior. But well, well done. Now there is more for you to learn. . . ."

Although this is an imagined outcome, it reflects how we are encouraged to embrace confession. Epistle writers of the New Testament go further. In his first letter, the apostle John writes,

> If we confess our sins, he is faithful and just and will forgive us our sins and purify us from all unrighteousness. (1 JOHN 1:9)

John does *not* write, "If you confess your sins *and then ask God to forgive you*, he will." There is no middle step. It is as if forgiveness fills the room, waiting for us, and confession merely opens our hearts to receive its flood of relief, joy, and freedom. God is not waiting for us to grovel. He's not into groveling. He does not need or want us to remain in the shame of our sin (though some of us live as if this were the case). Shame merely gets our attention—if we are alert. However, God does wait for us to be real about our shame so he can meet us in it and then rewrite our narratives.

Given that God is the author of forgiveness, can we assume that confession should be made to God alone? John neither says that nor, I think, does he imply it. There is a reason for this. It is in the *physical, bodily sensations of being mindfully mentalized* that we sense, experience, and truly internalize forgiveness. It is not enough simply to hear the words or take in the fact that we are forgiven. That would limit forgiveness to a left-mode operation and would only reinforce our dis-integrated, unforgiven state.

The epistle of James gives us another supporting reason for this form of confession.

> Is anyone among you sick? Let them call the elders of the church to pray over them and anoint them with oil in the name of the Lord.
>
> And the prayer offered in faith will make them well; the Lord will raise them up. If they have sinned, they will be forgiven.
>
> Therefore confess your sins to each other and pray for each other so that you may be healed. The prayer of a righteous person is powerful and effective. (JAMES 5:14-16)

James points to confession as an avenue of healing. Healing of any infirmity begins with the healing of sin. And sin itself begins with our not attending to our emotional states that ultimately leads to the dis-integration of everything. When confession is done in the presence of a mindful recipient, forgiveness fills the room and healing abounds. Rupture is repaired, and we

Group Confession

I encourage you to try the following exercise to make what we have been talk-ing about more real. Prayerfully choose two or three people whom you trust and, ideally, with whom you have frequent interaction. They may be neighbors or members of a Bible study or other small group. These are people who have a real—though not necessarily intended—likelihood of eventually hurting you simply because of the amount of time you spend together. They may not initially be close friends, and you may not trust them absolutely—yet.

As a group, commit to do the following. Anytime a member of the group commits an action—*any action*—of thought, word, or deed against another member of the group, he or she is to confess this, without exception and no matter how "large" or "small" the offense is interpreted by the offender to be, to the offended party as soon as reasonably possible. The offended party is to, without exception, offer forgiveness—with all of its properly attended nonverbal reinforcement. No lip service.

Do this in the prayerful spirit and wisdom of the scriptural passages we have explored (especially those of 1 John, James, and Hebrews), informed by what you have learned about neuroscience and attachment. Commit to doing this for at least six weeks, and then review the process. Reflect on how your relation-ship has changed or stayed the same. How are they closer? How are they farther apart? Has this exercise changed any of your relationships outside this commit-ted group, and if so, how?

There will be varied reactions to this invitation. "You mean I have to tell her *everything*?" Yes, you do. "But what if he doesn't forgive me?" That *can* be scary. Although the person has committed to do this, that doesn't guarantee that he will. But he is more likely to do so as he is mindful that forgiveness is also wait-ing for him when he commits an offense.

"But it would be very difficult to get past all the discomfort—the fear and the shame—to tell her what I thought." Yes, it would—initially. But with the guaran-tee of forgiveness for *everyone*, no one is left alone in his or her fear and shame.

You may ask, "Isn't this going to take a lot of time?" It may seem that way at first. But eventually it will become as seamless and spontaneous as breathing.

"Won't I just hurt the other person's feelings when I tell him or her what I have been saying or thinking about them?" Well, yes, if your intention is to let the person know what you think about him or her. But confession is about admit-ting where *you* have lost your mind, not where the other person has. When you emphasize that it is *your* mindlessness, *your* shame, *your* fear that you are bringing to the table, you will be surprised at the reaction you receive. Few people become defensive when we tell them what a schmo we've been.

In offering forgiveness, we may have other reactions. "What if I don't feel like it? Won't that be disingenuous?" Forgiveness is not letting someone off the hook. Nor is it something about which we have a choice. We have been commanded to do it (though we North Americans aren't that comfortable with commands). I choose either to be a living, breathing embodiment of forgiveness or I die. Slowly, perhaps, but die nonetheless. But even when you do not feel like forgiving, you can always take small incremental steps, such as first electing not to spit on the offender or react with some other retaliatory behavior. Or you might tell God you don't feel like forgiving, but since you've signed on to this agreement you would like his help to change your outlook. If you don't, your unforgiveness will soon lead to resentment, which you will soon have to confess to the offending party.

"But some of this seems so trivial. Why does he have to confess every little thing?" The other person's confession is not just for your sake so that you can feel better about his admitting that he has done you wrong. It is for his sake that no stone is left unturned, so that there is no part of his mind that remains in the clutches of fear or shame.

There could be more objections. But consider how much emotional burden we can carry around with us in all of our unconfessed sin. Consider further how much more we bear given our unresolved hurt, much of which we hardly notice anymore. Imagine what our lives would be like if all that weight were to fall away. Imagine the creativity that might be unleashed if there is no fear of making mistakes, since when you do, confession and forgiveness are the rule.

In the end, you will find that confession and forgiveness are the soil from which grows the fruit of the Spirit. This way of being supports the environment in which love, joy, peace, patience, kindness, goodness, faithfulness, gentleness, and self-control inevitably emerge. This, my friends, is the Kingdom of God on display.

This exercise takes a great deal of courage. Like God, it leads you to say "No!" to the evil of dis-integration and "Yes!" to the mercy, justice, and joy of relationship. I invite you to try it. I believe you will find that it changes your life forever.

are reminded that God, through Jesus, has begun a new work that he will continue through the power of the Holy Spirit (Philippians 1:6).

This is another reason Jesus needed to question Peter three times. It takes Peter's mind some time to formulate a new mental model, a new way of seeing his life unfolding. Peter requires repeated firing of this new neural network sequence in order for it to be wired in such a way that his experience of feeling felt and liberated by Jesus on the beach becomes a more permanent, more easily accessible part of his emotional memory. This requires Peter's encounter with Jesus' nonverbal as well as verbal communication. The story of Jesus and Peter creates hope for a world of relationships in which repair is the standard response to rupture. Confession and forgiveness may be the way to create more flexible, adaptive, coherent, energized, and stable (FACES) individual minds, and by extension, communities that reflect the same qualities.

The writer of the letter to the Hebrews gives us a glimpse of what Jesus did with shame and what we are invited to do as a result:

> [Fix] our eyes on Jesus, the pioneer and perfecter of faith. For the joy set before him he endured the cross, *scorning its shame*, and sat down at the right hand of the throne of God. (HEBREWS 12:2, ITALICS MINE)

Jesus does nothing less than scorn (despise, or ignore, as another translation puts it) shame. He chooses to acknowledge, then disregard it, paying no attention to it so he may pay attention to something else—the joy of sitting next to his Father. We too are called to identify (confess) shame so as to be aware of its presence and then ignore it, turning our attention to the joy of being with the Father, the One who tells us that we are his sons and daughters and that he is deeply pleased that we are on the earth.

That is why we must pay attention to the things we have been learning about in this book. As we attend to memory, emotion, and our narratives, we will be much more aware of shame when it rears its ugly head. This will prevent us from automatically turning to destructive coping mechanisms, as Eve did. We will instead be attentive to how our bodies with their nonverbal cues and mental imagery tempt us to travel down the low road. By turning our attention to alternative images and thoughts, we "repent"—that is, we turn around and go in a different direction.

And the healing we experience is to be extended to the ends of the earth. It will be a hallmark of God's new heaven and earth reaching their zenith at the Second Coming. In Revelation, John foretells of this healing:

Then the angel showed me the river of the water of life, as clear as crystal, flowing from the throne of God and of the Lamb down the middle of the great street of the city. On each side of the river stood the tree of life, bearing twelve crops of fruit, yielding its fruit every month. And the leaves of the tree are for the healing of the nations. (REVELATION 22:1-2)

Healing is not just for us as individuals. Just as mindlessness and disintegration began with the first humans, the risen Jesus, the new Adam, inaugurates the creation of new minds. And just as the mindlessness of the first humans infected all nations—and even the earth—so the healing that comes from confession and forgiveness will be extended to the nations and to the earth itself.

Chapter 13

THE MIND
AND COMMUNITY:
THE BRAIN ON LOVE,
MERCY, AND JUSTICE

The middle-aged man leans back in his seat and sighs. Picking up the letter he just finished with the help of his secretary, he reads his postscript one more time. A church planter and missionary, the man loves bringing the good news of Jesus to people who have never heard it. The downside of being a traveling evangelist, however, is that he rarely stays more than a few years in any one community. Once he has identified and trained leaders, he is off to a new city.

Though the missionary doesn't stay long in one place, he keeps tabs on the churches he has planted. Each congregation is precious to him, and he treasures the updates he receives from his friends all over the region.

Over the past few months, though, he has become increasingly concerned about one church plant. Set in a cosmopolitan city that is a frequent destination of business travelers and pleasure seekers, the church is in a strategic location. While the mix of cultures and ethnicities makes the city an energizing and exciting place to be, this environment also makes it more difficult for church members to understand and appreciate one another.

For months the missionary has been hearing about internal squabbles that seem ready to divide the congregation. Some members are even threatening legal action against other members. In the face of all this division, though, the congregation is turning a blind eye to a fellow member who is cheating on his wife—and doesn't seem to care who knows it. Finally, the missionary

235

is concerned about the church's services, which sound more like free-for-all shouting matches than worship.

The missionary knows he won't be returning to this church anytime soon, so he has decided that writing them is the next-best step. As it turns out, drafting this letter has been one of the most difficult things he has ever done. After all, he has little to commend them for and much to correct.

As you may have suspected, this is not the saga of a twenty-first century church planter but of the apostle Paul. Motivated by his loving concern for the church in Corinth, he prayerfully wrote the letter we know as 1 Corinthians.

Throughout this book we've talked a lot about the dis-integrated, mindless behavior in individuals or families. All along, however, we've gotten glimpses of how this behavior ultimately affects entire communities of people. That certainly was true in the neophyte Corinthian church.

A bit later in this chapter, we will see that Paul's portrayal of the body of Christ seems to be a mirror of the mind when it is functioning in a fully integrated fashion. It's an image he'd like to see the Corinthian church reflect. But before taking a closer look at his letter to the Corinthians, let's consider some recent discoveries of neuroscience and relationships that have particular significance for communities like this church (and ours).

COMPLEX SYSTEMS

In every interaction, even those with God, we are involved in a great dance in which we shift from wanting closeness to needing our space. This dynamic occurs between parents and their children as well as between couples and friends. Different people have varying degrees of need for either closeness or separation. Too much of either one begins to create distress. When we are too close for too long, we may begin to feel "suffocated" or perhaps bored, unimaginative, or uninspired; when we are separated for too long, we begin to feel isolated, lonely, or sad.

This dynamic extends to larger settings. Groups also require times of deep connection interspersed with times of autonomy in order to accomplish their goals. In a healthy business, for instance, it is vital that different departments have enough space to develop their particular special service while sometimes working with other divisions so that the common vision of the business can be realized. This dynamic seems so natural that we may never stop to consider why this oscillation is necessary.

In chapter 8 of *Parenting from the Inside Out*, Dan Siegel introduces the reader to the meaning and importance of complex systems, which help explain why our minds (individually and in community) work most effectively when they experience a healthy balance between connection and independence.

Consider this example from nature: We know that the "rings" around Saturn aren't really solid rings at all but rather collections of large rocks and ice particles that remain in the planet's orbit. While each rock orbits the planet on a path that is virtually impossible to predict over longer periods, it is much easier to predict the behavior of the larger rings as a whole. The rings have "emerged" as more stable, predictable phenomena. They are made up of, but are behaviorally separate from, the individual rocks, whose trajectories cannot be easily anticipated. Both the rings and the rocks influence each other. The paths of the rocks, though individually small by comparison to the size of the rings, have ultimately led to the formation of the much larger rings. The paths of the individual rocks tend to reinforce the ongoing formation of the larger rings, and at many levels the rings are evolving, if ever so slightly.

One of the great mysteries, of course, is how the rings remain as balanced as they are. Why aren't they overcome by the centrifugal forces of the rocks or by gravity so that they disintegrate or implode into the planet's hydrogen atmosphere? The key lies in the equilibrium struck between the tendency toward order (the more predictable rings) and disarray. Scientists posit that those systems that are the most stable, flexible, and adaptive are moving toward this balance or complexity.

Perhaps this tension between independence and connection sounds familiar. After all, it reflects what we have described in terms of our rhythmic hunger and thirst for intimacy on one hand and solitude on the other. We long to live relationally like the rings of Saturn. We want our relationships to reflect stability, flexibility, and the capacity for adaptation.

In fact, the brain/mind matrix is considered by some researchers to be a primary example of complex systems among living things. Like every complex system,

- small interconnected parts (neurons) interact to form larger parts (neural networks), which are completely different from the neurons themselves;
- the system's boundaries are difficult to determine and measure;
- it is an open system that can be influenced from within and without;
- it emerges within and between brains in both embodied and relational ways;
- one cannot predict easily where all the parts within the mind will "go,"

but we can predict with some confidence where the larger system will be a day or two—or five or ten minutes—from now;

- small changes—a glance, a feeling of shame, or physical pain—can lead to larger-than-expected emotional shifts—a raised voice may lead to name calling, which may lead to physical violence;

- attentiveness to the fluctuations between the various functions of the mind, highlighted by the activity of the prefrontal cortex, can lead to greater awareness of the movement between closeness and autonomy.

The world of complex systems is but another way that science—study of God's good creation—points us in the direction God desires for us to go. As humans, we need both deep connection and autonomy. Each is reinforced and energized by the other; harmony between the two leads to lives that are more stable, flexible, and adaptive. This applies not only to us as individuals, but to the communities to which we belong as well.

In fact, this concept leads us to the pinnacle theme of this book: when our brains operate in a flexible, adaptive, coherent, energized, and stable fashion, we are able to live in *community* in a way that encourages those around us to develop these same qualities. For people of faith, it makes sense that God created systems that reflect his heart's desire that the world be populated with individuals exuding joy, peace, patience, kindness, goodness, faithfulness, gentleness, and self-control. When practiced in community, these virtues inexorably emerge as justice and mercy, the two biblical pillars of politics and economics.

Mercy, as we have hinted when speaking about forgiveness, is not simply letting someone off the hook or turning a blind eye to wrongs done. Likewise, justice is not merely or even primarily about punishing someone for a wrong committed. The Hebrew sense of mercy and justice is the notion that God, and we by extension, is in the business of putting all things to right. Together we reflect the attributes of the Spirit listed above.

To live out this biblical calling takes a great deal of hard work and prayerful interchange with others. Confession and forgiveness are not a bad place to start. But the apostle Paul offers us additional help in his first letter to the church at Corinth, which includes a beautiful description of what it means to live as a community of people whose highest callings are to love and be known as well as to know.

FIRST CORINTHIANS 12 AND 13:
INTEGRATION AND DIFFERENTIATION

Paul wrote his letter to the new community of Christians gathered in the city of Corinth, a thriving Greek metropolis, in about AD 57. The group of believers there had become factious, displaying behavior that was counter to what it means to be followers of Jesus. Some members were abusing the disenfranchised; the less powerful were undermining those attempting to lead in good faith. Lines were drawn between socioeconomic classes and races. They were even fighting over who ate what food served at meals. (Imagine that—being emotionally distressed over food.)

All of this dissension occurred in an assembly of folks who were relatively wealthy, educated, talented, and diverse. One would think such an advantaged group would be able to effortlessly demonstrate what the Kingdom of God should look like. Unfortunately, they were in many respects behaving more like the first Adam rather than the second. Too often we, almost two thousand years later, don't look much different.

Mutual appreciation

Paul got wind of this outbreak of dis-integrated, mindless behavior and zipped off the missive that has come to be known as 1 Corinthians. One of the most moving portions of that text is chapters 12 and 13. This passage expands our vision of what it means to move from developing mindful brains to creating communities that love deeply and perceptively. In chapter 12, Paul explains that different people have different gifts, different capacities, and different purposes within the community.

> Now about the gifts of the Spirit, brothers and sisters, I do not want you to be uninformed. . . .
>
> There are different kinds of gifts, but the same Spirit distributes them. There are different kinds of service, but the same Lord. There are different kinds of working, but in all of them and in everyone it is the same God at work.
>
> Now to each one the manifestation of the Spirit is given for the common good. To one there is given through the Spirit a message of wisdom, to another a message of knowledge by means of the same Spirit, to another faith by the same Spirit, to another gifts of healing by that one Spirit, to another miraculous powers, to another prophecy,

to another distinguishing between spirits, to another speaking in different kinds of tongues, and to still another the interpretation of tongues. All these are the work of one and the same Spirit, and he distributes them to each one, just as he determines. (vv. 1, 4-11)

Paul emphasizes that each person's contribution has value and serves the common good. In God's economy, no one is unimportant. (I write that last sentence with considered pause. If you regularly live and work in a setting that keeps you waist deep in the squalor of human suffering and debris that often spawns conduct more becoming of subhuman, rabid animals than of people, this may be harder at times to accept, and I understand.) Note that, for Paul, a person's inherent value is not to be understood merely in terms of his or her individual existence. This emphasis on the individual is a relatively recent perspective, propagated mostly in the West over the last four hundred years. Paul, like any Jew of his day, would not consider the value of an individual apart from that person's place in a larger community. It would not even occur to him to do so. In our day, that would be like considering the inherent value of a particular carburetor apart from the engine in which it is housed.

Just as a body, though one, has many parts, but all its many parts form one body, so it is with Christ. For we were all baptized by one Spirit so as to form one body—whether Jews or Gentiles, slave or free—and we were all given the one Spirit to drink. Even so the body is not made up of one part but of many. (vv. 12-14)

Perhaps you already see connections between Paul's observations of the body of Christ and the nature of the mind. The brain, as we saw in chapter 3, is composed of many parts, all of which together form one organ that operates most efficiently when its separate but correlating functions are given opportunity to be part of the grand symphony. At times the strings are the focus of attention; at others, the brass or woodwinds. Whoever is not carrying the main theme must listen to and support the section that is. No area or correlating utility is unimportant to the function of the mind, and we have seen what happens when we ignore such things as our attention, memory, or emotion in ourselves or in our children. Paul suggests here that this is true for communities of Christians as well.

Paul next tackles the thorny issue of shame.

Now if the foot should say, "Because I am not a hand, I do not belong to the body," it would not for that reason cease to be part of the body. And if the ear should say, "Because I am not an eye, I do not belong to the body," it would not for that reason cease to be part of the body. If the whole body were an eye, where would the sense of hearing be? If the whole body were an ear, where would the sense of smell be? But in fact God has placed the parts in the body, every one of them, just as he wanted them to be. If they were all one part, where would the body be? As it is, there are many parts, but one body. (vv. 15-20)

Here the foot and the ear simply don't think they're enough. Consider the parts of our minds—thoughts, images, feelings, memories—that we see as shameful. Paul is speaking to those in the fellowship at Corinth who do not feel as if they are enough. Sound familiar? Eve sensed her inadequacy and cut herself off from God. Adam did the same. Likewise, a deeply embedded implicit memory may emerge as an unspecific feeling of shame—and if we are not mindful, we too will amputate ourselves from the community, ashamed that we are neither a hand nor an eye.

The reverse is also possible. In our shame we sometimes shame others. We do this subtly, if not blatantly. We sense our intelligence, our economic clout, our relevance, our superiority, our indispensability. Our arrogance, the offspring of shame, flowers and goes to seed. Pride and shame are in fact two sides of the same coin. We do the same within our minds. We cut ourselves off from important phases of brain function when we are unable to cope with particular emotional states or memories. We become dismissive about our need for attachment; we ignore our emotion; we drive sadness, hurt, and in some cases even joy underground, unable to integrate them into the larger context of our minds because of the distress they cause. As we dismiss those weaker parts of our own minds, we eventually do the same in our communities. We become arrogant enough to proclaim (if only to ourselves) that we do not need our weaker, less sophisticated, more needy, more truculent brother or sister.

But Paul would have none of that:

The eye cannot say to the hand, "I don't need you!" And the head cannot say to the feet, "I don't need you!" On the contrary, those parts of the body that seem to be weaker are indispensable, and the parts that we think are less honorable we treat with special honor. And the parts that are unpresentable are treated with special modesty, while our presentable parts need no special treatment. But God has put the body together, giving greater honor to the parts that lacked it, so that there should be no division in the body, but that its parts should have equal concern for each other. If one part suffers, every part suffers with it; if one part is honored, every part rejoices with it. (vv. 21-26)

Paul puts his foot on the throat of toxic shame, of that harsh, judging, dis-integrated prefrontal cortical mindlessness, and crushes it. All parts of the body, he declares, are connected and necessary for the health of the whole. He suggests that you cannot talk about the body of Jesus without including every part. In fact, some who are stronger will be recruited to protect those who are weaker. Some members will be treated more modestly; those who are more resilient will be given tasks that others could never weather. When the least significant is honored, the entire body rejoices. And when there is pain for one, the rest of the body empathically suffers. We are to become embodied mirror neuron systems within our community, taking on the suffering of others as a means for bringing healing to all.

The brain reflects this creative directive as well. Twenty-five years ago neuroscientists believed that if the brain sustained damage or injury there was little that could be done to ameliorate the loss. But recent research with stroke patients and experimental studies in neural plasticity is countering this long-held assumption. Studies that examine the brain's capacity to reallocate particular tasks, such as auditory or tactile perception, to areas of the cortex usually dedicated to another role, such as vision, suggest that the brain can recruit more vital regions to support and carry on the function of weaker or injured areas. This is very hopeful news, for it demonstrates how the function of the weaker parts is protected by the stronger. This is reflected in Paul's imagery. His vision for the body, especially in one so fractured and injured as the one in Corinth, is a vision of hope. For this is a vision of a world—God's Kingdom—without shame. This is a world that lives with hopeful expectation in the context of confession and forgiveness.

Different domains

After stressing the body's integration, Paul next emphasizes that the body is also *differentiated*. Each part has particular roles it must play. Furthermore, there is a certain *functional hierarchy* to the body.

Now you are the body of Christ, and each one of you is a part of it. And God has placed in the church first of all apostles, second prophets, third teachers, then miracles, then gifts of healing, of helping, of guidance, and of different kinds of tongues. Are all apostles? Are all prophets? Are all teachers? Do all work miracles? Do all have gifts of healing? Do all speak in tongues? Do all interpret? Now eagerly desire the greater gifts. (vv. 27-31)

Some will be leaders. Some will be followers. But each has authority—the power to *author* or *create*—in his or her respective domain. This is not unlike the mind that is composed of what we would describe as "higher" and "lower" brain functions. We know that without the advanced functioning of the prefrontal cortex, we would be more like cats or dogs. And without the limbic circuitry, we would be more like alligators. But just as most of human life is managed by the parts of our brains that are more like the brains of reptiles and lower mammals, so too the bulk of the work of the body of Christ is done by people with gifts that are often taken for granted.

In our culture we tend to seek and honor those vocational callings that are more visible, more powerful, more desirable. We are less attracted to roles that go unnoticed. We confuse visibility with significance, and position with authority. This attitude models our tendency to be unaware of certain functions within our minds—whether emotional states, memories, or input from the extended brain—that call for our attention now. We shift our awareness when those functions are too distressing, only to find ourselves disconnected within our own minds—and ultimately even more distressed with our anxiety, depression, substance abuse, workaholism, and fractured relationships.

Paul pulls no punches in affirming that there is indeed differentiation, or specialization, within the body of Christ. Similarly, the brain has two hemispheres that are responsible for very different functions, and different areas within each hemisphere serve different purposes. The parts that control breathing do not write symphonies. And the part that enables me to think about what I'm writing does not control my fingers as I type. The brain—differentiated, but integrated—reflects Paul's imagery of the body.

The right and left hemispheres of the brain also differ in their focus. The right is deeply aware of the present moment and the individual's connection to all things—the state of "we." The left, on the other hand, is concerned not with the present moment but with the past and the future. It keeps track of what has come before in order to protect the individual from future danger.

The left hemisphere sets me apart as "me," someone who is separate and individuated. Again, we hear the echo of a complex system, with the whole and the antecedent parts living in a deep, mysterious tension of connection and individuation.

Paul speaks of believers as Jesus' body. As we engage this role, we come to a place of deep integration of the "we" and "I." This is what it means to be the body of Christ, but in order for this to happen, our individual minds and our corporate community must step into the path that Paul so eloquently describes next.

The most excellent way

First Corinthians 13 is one of the best-known passages of Scripture. It is introduced by the last verse of chapter 12:

> And yet I will show you the most excellent way. (v. 31)

Paul describes love as a "way." Not something objective or static, but dynamic and moving. Not something limited to a logical, linear, literal left mode. Not something ill-defined, amorphous, and awash only in right-mode, primary emotional states with no sense of direction. But rather a *way*—a path characterized by mobility along a structured course; the mindful integration of living in the awareness of the present moment. As we are soon to see, love does not exist apart from action. From a brain standpoint, there is no such thing as "love" per se as an independent abstract reality. Love emerges only in the context of loving thoughts, words, or deeds.

In modern translations of the Bible, 1 Corinthians 13 is presented as prose. Originally, however, it was formatted as a hymn, a poetic dance of imagery and language, emotion and linear instruction. It is a synthesis of right- and left-mode operations that begins in the foothills of love, taking readers on a climb that leads from differentiating love from its counterfeits to understanding love as a dynamic that is fully revealed only within the context of relationship. The ascent reaches its peak in the experience of being known by the One who is complete.

Paul opens this section of the text critiquing the value of particular abilities and skills uncoupled from the way of love.

> If I speak in human or angelic tongues, but do not have love, I am
> only a resounding gong or a clanging cymbal.

If I have the gift of prophecy and can fathom all mysteries and all knowledge, and if I have a faith that can move mountains, but do not have love, I am nothing.

If I give all I possess to the poor and give over my body to hardship that I may boast, but do not have love, I gain nothing. (vv. 1-3)

Who would make it on the list of the world's most admired people? The self-sacrificing parents who give up everything for their children? The pastors who work tirelessly for the benefit of their congregations? The researchers who spend endless hours in the lab to find the cure for MDR tuberculosis? Such people may in fact be engaged in meaningful callings because of their desire to bring goodness and healing to a broken world.

However, sometimes the most seemingly admirable people (as well as the rest of us) hide their own emotional brokenness behind a wall of altruism. Paul doesn't need to point out that scurrilous conduct is void of loving intention. That is self-evident. What stands out is how laudable gifts and actions can be just as disconnected from love. Many behaviors that appear admirable, if done apart from love, are actually lifeless and decaying.

In the same way, certain ways of coping with distressing situations and disorienting memories may look admirable from the outside. Paul bluntly says, however, that good deeds done by a soul empty of love are actually worth nothing. Love is emblematic of an integrated brain, one that is mindful of the mind of God and others. And what does that look like? Paul details it this way:

Love is patient, love is kind. It does not envy, it does not boast, it is not proud.

It does not dishonor others, it is not self-seeking, it is not easily angered, it keeps no record of wrongs.

Love does not delight in evil but rejoices with the truth.

It always protects, always trusts, always hopes, always perseveres. (vv. 4-7)

Notice again that so much of what Paul describes is something that love does or does not *do*. Love behaves patiently. Love leaves wrongs appropriately behind. These are the actions that begin in the mind of one whose prefrontal cortex is integrated, drawing together the parts of the brain's function, connecting areas of neural networks and subjective narrative experience in a way that is demonstrative of the FACES characteristics.

Paul then begins to scale the last steeply ascending face of the subject of this chapter:

> Love never fails. But where there are prophecies, they will cease; where there are tongues, they will be stilled; where there is knowledge, it will pass away.
>
> For we know in part and we prophesy in part, but when completeness comes, what is in part disappears. (13:8-10)

Here Paul suggests that history anticipates a future. Not any random future, but rather one in which those things that endure—the new earth/new heaven realm with our new bodies and our new work to do—will be defined by the spirit of love. The coping strategies we try to substitute for relationship eventually will falter and die. They will pass away. All of our private and public acts of goodness, as well as those old neural networks that lead us down the low road of shame and fear will "pass away."

In fact, even the person with a truly integrated brain currently functions "in part." Whenever we prophesy or know or think or feel or remember—or do anything else that the mind initiates—we do it incompletely. We attend to things imperfectly. We are not fully aware of all our memory and its impact on our lives. We have not yet fully integrated our prefrontal cortices. We may still at times allow our reptilian and limbic circuitry to lead the charge over the cliff, bypassing the neocortex in the process.

But when *completeness* comes, what is incomplete, dis-integrated and living apart from the present moment; what is judging, shaming, and fearful, will disappear. And what is this completeness? For Paul it is the appearance of Jesus and the culmination of the new heaven/new earth re-creation that God began when he raised Jesus from the dead. It is not unreasonable to suggest that it is this completeness to which research in attachment and neuroscience point. As I mentioned in the introduction, this observation does not *prove* the Kingdom of God—a limited left-mode operational maneuver—but rather reflects it and invites us to trust that Jesus is the Lord of the universe and therefore we have nothing to fear.

This completeness suggests what it means to be in the presence of Wholeness. Not wholeness as some disembodied idea or abstract sense of oneness with nature and other people. This is not pantheism or panentheism. Instead, it is the wholeness that comes from being in the presence of Jesus, the one perfectly whole person. We who are followers of Jesus believe that he took the ultimate initiative to be mindful of *us*, coming to us as Immanuel, God *with* us. Jesus is with you, not only the way the book you are reading is with you in your lap, but in such a way that you are wholly known, completely and perfectly mentalized by him.

Imagine what it will be like for us not only to be in a physical world that is whole, perfect, and complete but to be able to interact with the One who is perfectly, completely, and wholly able to mentalize us in a way that enables us to do the same with him and others. We will, in fact, be transformed in the presence of Jesus, whose mind will pierce ours with precision and gentleness, making possible the "integration" for which our current work on earth is preparing us. Our newly embodied minds will be ushered into a place of not just secure, but complete, perfect, and whole attachment.

Paul compares this transformation from the present to the anticipated future of God's Kingdom to the experiences of maturing from childhood to adulthood.

> When I was a child, I talked like a child, I thought like a child,
> I reasoned like a child. When I became a man, I put the ways of
> childhood behind me. (13:11)

Paul then brings this poetic passage to its climax.

> For now we see only a reflection as in a mirror; then we shall see face
> to face. Now I know in part; then I shall know fully, *even as I am fully
> known.*
>
> And now these three remain: faith, hope and love. But the greatest
> of these is love. (vv. 12-13, ITALICS MINE)

In ancient Corinth, mirrors were made of polished metal and were much more imperfectly reflective than those we use today. Naturally images were somewhat distorted. These distortions are comparable to what it means for us to be limited not only in how and what we know but also the degree to which we experience *being known.* When I instead see others face-to-face, I not only see them clearly; I also *clearly see them seeing me*—perfectly, just as a child sees a parent seeing her, taking in all the nonverbal cues that lead, in secure attachments, to a fully functioning prefrontal cortex.

I suggest that we will fully experience love only when we are in the position of clearly being seen by One into whose face we are directly looking. Paul reiterates this when he emphasizes that we shall eventually know even as we are fully known. To "know" in this sense is not limited to factual information or logical understanding of how the mysterious interlockings of God's purposes fit together. We will also become fully mindful in the way that God is fully mindful of us.

In that day, when we are able to mentalize, sense, and discern in the way that Jesus does, our desire to understand mysteries and figure out the answers to all our *why* questions will likely fade in the light of being known. Why did God allow my father to sexually abuse me? Why did my child die? Why did I lose my job? Why did my marriage fail? People (perhaps even you) have asked such questions down through the ages.

But remember that *why* is something we often ask when the emotional pain we are experiencing is too great to engage. And we are often overwhelmed precisely because of our limited awareness of a Presence who is mindfully loving us. In that day, however, perfect mindfulness embodied in Jesus will swallow that pain in the joy and beauty of the present moment of the new earth and heaven.

Paul concludes this hymn of love by reminding us that all of life stands on three basic but unequal expressions: faith, hope, and love. This is consistent with what neuroscience and attachment tell us. All relationships, even at the most primitive level, must begin with faith—with trust, a basic building block for all secure attachments. When we trust, we risk the possibility of rupture for the payoff of repair and more deeply joyful integration within and between our minds.

Faith, however, is never blind. In our minds it never acts without first anticipating a particular outcome that we desire. As the writer of the New Testament letter to the Hebrews suggests, faith is "being sure of what we hope for" (11:1), not of what we know or already have. Hope energizes and draws trust into motion and into the future. We anticipate becoming more than we are. If our appetite for such things was anorectic, we would have no impetus for trust. Hope is that appetite.

But neither hope nor faith has a pulse in the absence of love. Only love perfectly mentalizes. Only love, clothed in the light of its perfectly coherent narrative, approaches another with mindfulness that fears nothing, ignores shame, and repairs the ultimate rupture in Jesus' death and resurrection. Only love can create the context in which faith or hope is born and sustained.

In the new heaven/earth realm, the need for faith or hope is unlikely, for both are dependent on future states. Love is about the present moment. Our brains, through faith energized by hope, are kept alive to the Love that is here and yet still coming in its fullness.

We have been called to embody all the virtues listed in 1 Corinthians 13:4-7, but without love we cannot do so. And I suggest that the path to developing such love includes

- the process of being known;
- the experience of feeling felt;
- the encounter of being validated but never coddled;
- being cared for but not overwhelmed or patronized;
- being fully understood while called into proper risk-taking adventure;
- being healed and awakened to growth, compassion, and responsibility.

Furthermore, this process *requires* us to live in close proximity to one another. Becoming a body that breathes justice and mercy requires the presence of love, which then doubles back, its full development depending on that very community. Ultimately this cycle is empowered by the Holy Spirit, who creates all of this through the process of being known.

This is the community—the body—that Paul describes in 1 Corinthians 12. We are to be people who are as fully known by each other as possible. This is accomplished in the freedom and power of confession and forgiveness. This practice efficaciously repairs ruptures, and in so doing puts bone and flesh on Jesus' words to the apostle Peter to forgive "seventy-seven times."

Paul's vision of community is that of a complex system—though he doesn't, of course, use this term—a system that thrives in the oscillating balance between the rigidity of sameness and the chaos of mental bedlam, both within and between minds. In such a community of intimacy—a community of integrated prefrontal cortices—members are quick to honor and protect those who are most vulnerable. In our world that includes those trapped on the lower end of society's power gradient, including the poor, the elderly, and those of different ethnicity, culture, or sexual orientation. In such a community, members also confidently and kindly set limits on behavior that undermines the group's integration and differentiation.

This ruthless commitment to differentiation and integration in turn liberates us as individuals and as a community to *create*. To do what we were commanded to do in Eden. To have dominion is to care for and to create with. It is to do what God does for us, and so reflect his image.

REAL LOVE, REAL CHANGE

Laura had seen multiple psychiatrists, many of whom had tried to be thoughtful and thorough in their approach; but they had all told her the same thing. She had a form of depression that likely would be with her to some degree for the rest of her life. Twice hospitalized, once as a teenager and once as an adult, she was told the best she could hope for would be to manage her depression through medication and counseling. Certainly, neither seemed to deliver a permanent solution. But then again, regular prayer and Bible study hadn't provided one either.

In the meantime, Laura's marriage languished. Her husband had become much more affectionate with a Jim Beam bottle than he was with her. And she had so little energy for her children that they were left to fend for themselves emotionally. This only added to her shame and guilt.

Fearful of being found out, Laura frequently turned down offers to become part of a prayer group or another small group at church, effectively disconnecting herself from that community. Laura was terrified of being known, ashamed of her own narrative. Her father, a pastor, had engaged in several extramarital affairs before being defrocked; her mother's emotional coldness fueled her father's excuses for his adultery, and her mother had withdrawn even further into her frozen tundra when she learned of her husband's infidelity. Laura knew she herself had made poor choices—before marriage she had been sexually promiscuous and had dabbled in substance abuse. Laura's story is not atypical of many who pass through my office door. But she was willing to begin the hard journey of faith, hope, and love.

Laura began learning about the way of love as she squarely faced the functions of her mind. Over many months, she took a number of steps that prevented her from spiraling down into the depths of depression.

1. She learned that the more she paid attention to what she was paying attention to, the more she noticed feelings that had previously been too dangerous for her to acknowledge.
2. She developed a greater awareness of her body and her responses to the slightest provocation. She learned to quiet her inner demons that had presented themselves as headaches and a rapid heartbeat.
3. She wrote and told her story, initially with great trepidation, but eventually fearlessly. As she did so, her story changed, for she began to tell it to listeners who were mindful of her—first me, and then carefully selected

friends with whom she met to pray about her travails. This community provided a secure place to confess the entire reality of her life and feel felt, not shamed. Her experience of this community let Laura experience being known and awash in God's love.

4. Laura was also willing to consider that the God of her story was not the God of the Bible, but a distorted mental representation she had created to cope with her constant, overwhelming emotions of shame and loneliness. She was willing to begin paying attention to the Voice who had been telling her from the time he first thought of her, "You are my daughter—one I love. I am so very pleased you are on the earth." She also learned to ignore the voice that emerged from the depths of her reptilian and limbic circuitry, donning the emotion of shame and guilt, hijacking her cortex and shrouding itself within the linguistic cloak of "You're not enough. You're alone, and you are nothing." Slowly, she turned her gaze directly to the scenes in her narrative that had been so harrowing.

5. She developed a keen awareness of her implicit memory as it tried to make its way into her conscious life, hauling so much shame and sadness along with it. She recognized how these had shaped her sense of who she was. Then she began to reframe them as neural correlates—firing patterns from old, dis-integrated parts of her brain—that she, through the practice of mental imagery, could crucify daily. She learned to identify her mental and physical representations of toxic shame, and like Jesus before her, began to scorn them. This enabled her to begin writing a different narrative, one that was caught in the vortex of God's story.

6. Spiritual disciplines like meditation, prayer, and fasting led to a deeper awareness of God's presence as it was mediated through her emotional and mental states. She became more energized and emotionally available for her husband and children.

7. She confronted her husband about the reality of their foundering marriage, confessing her role in its deterioration. Although he was slow to trust that her transformation was genuine, he, too, eventually came to address his own story in a more mindful, integrated way.

At first Laura's children simply did not know what to do with her. After so many years of neglect, Laura's growing interest in their lives was disorienting and distressing. Her daughters' journey to a place of more secure attachment with a mother who was more mindful of their emotional states was a bit bumpy. It didn't make it any easier that Laura's transformation began as her children entered early adolescence. But as I told Laura, it was better to engage them now than after their brains had become more like hardened concrete.

And what became of Laura's recurrent depression? In short, over time she came to a place where it no longer plagued her to any degree of serious consequence. As her mind and life became more integrated, Laura's depression became less frequent and less intense. She understood it was a constellation of symptoms that together were a complex outgrowth of the dis-integrated state of her mind/brain/narrative.

That's not to say she never struggles. The vestigal elements of her virtual lifetime of depression remain. She will on occasion, during times of extended or heightened stress, experience traces of her old mood shifts. We continue to discuss what it means to live with a brain that does not forget things we wish it would. She wishes that her old self, with its Hebbian memory networks, would simply vanish. Laura resonates with the words of the apostle Paul in Romans 7, where he admits his exasperation with his own behavior, an outgrowth of his dis-integrated mind. There he confesses that the only thing that will eventually put his mind at ease is Jesus (see Romans 7:24-25).

I remind Laura that the neural pathways that have been fired in particular ways repeatedly during her experience of depressed states will probably never go away, but they will have continually decreasing potency as she connects and strengthens new neural networks developed by the transforming renewal of her mind (Romans 12:2).

Because elements of those old networks and experiences remain, Laura continues to take an antidepressant, though at a reduced dosage. I remind her that this pharmacologic intervention supports the ongoing work she is doing to work out her salvation and become the woman God longs for her to be. I often remind her, as I remind all my patients, that it is never my goal for them to be on or off medication. My goal is for them to be well.

Okay, so what? you may be thinking. *This is a nice story, but what's the point?* What about all my patients who *don't* make changes, who don't pay attention despite my invitation for them to do so? What about the folks who try hard to make changes but simply seem unable to start exercising, develop new relationships, learn to play a new instrument, meditate, pray like a monk (a really good monk), fast, confess the truth of their lives, take their medication faithfully, love their friends or spouses in new and mindful ways, all in the same week? These are good questions. And what about those people who believe they have worked hard for a long time without seeing the changes they long for in their marriages, friendships, parent-child relationships, or church or school communities?

There is nothing magic here. There is nothing contained within these pages that does not boil down to really hard work empowered by the Holy Spirit. (Whatever exactly that means, I admit. I really mean that. I believe that anything good that comes to pass on the earth is of God, energized by his Spirit, no matter the agent. However, trying to capture and delineate *what* constitutes the power of the Holy Spirit as opposed to my own volition, or understanding where I stop and the Spirit starts—or vice versa—is rather like, as folk-rock singer David Wilcox poetically describes it, trying to catch the wind in my fist. Not to mention an exercise that when pursued too intently becomes limited to a disconnecting left-mode pursuit that is isolated from the right mode of operation.)

Without question some individuals have narratives that are complicated beyond the pale of credulity. Others may have neurobiological systems that seem to outflank nonmedical interventions (such as those with schizophrenia, intractable bipolar syndromes, personality disorders, malignant forms of obsessive-compulsive disorder, dementia, and a host of other expressions of mental disintegration). These individuals may require lengthy exposure to many relationships, whether professional, personal, or both, that will patiently, faithfully provide a "communal container" in which they may discover what true integration is all about.

Others believe that they have been working hard to change, but in fact are quite mistaken. They may have been working hard but, unbeknownst to them, working in ways that reinforce the mental and behavioral states in which they are encased. Not until they cross into a painful enough place (and that threshold will vary from person to person) will they be energized enough to want to change.

The prevalence of individual (and might I add generational) wounds means that many communities—churches, schools, neighborhoods, ethnic groups, and nations—face difficult struggles. The process of repairing ruptures through mindful awareness of such reconciliation, confession, and forgiveness which pave the way for repentance has undeniably been demonstrated on the world stage. One of the best examples of repair is the Truth and Reconciliation Commission of South Africa, led by Archbishop Desmond Tutu, whose now-concluded work effectively helped regenerate an entire country torn by the rupture of apartheid.

You may not live in South Africa, but perhaps you live in another war-torn territory—a neighborhood with absent landlords, drug dealers, and guns; an extended family in which some adults don't talk with each other because of something that happened between their children; a church where the pastor left under a cloud, rending the fabric of the congregation; or a county whose board of supervisors sometimes functions like children in need of supervision themselves.

Even in such situations the vision of obtaining God's political agenda of justice and mercy can be realized. In these macro settings, paying attention to the mind leads us ultimately to the way of love that is shared, not only between individuals, but between groups torn asunder as well.

I am acutely aware that to suggest we apply the tenets of this book to the above settings may seem overly simplistic or naive. Certainly, life is so complicated that even getting individuals to work toward repairing ruptures and engaging in healing dialogue feels overwhelming. Imagining these occurring in the context of a community may seem completely out of the question. But remember that although at one level we admit to the presence of large problems in our world, at another level there is no such thing as large problems, merely collections of interchanges between individuals who with every relational interaction choose to become either more or less mindful. More or less known. More or less loved and loving.

Laura's story is no hoax. It is, admittedly, a composite of many people whom I have seen liberated by the things I describe her as doing. And what it points to is this: the essence of God—and our lives—is love. And the fundamental dynamic of love, springing forth necessarily as it does not only from and within *a* mind but also *between* minds, is manifested in terms of being known. Through this process, we are deeply integrated in all of our right and left hemispheric beauty—mentalized, if you will—while simultaneously invited to experience the adventure and joy that come from helping to usher in a new creation.

This is the means by and through which the Holy Spirit both declares and vitalizes the gospel. His love is most powerfully demonstrated in the context of this interdependent individual-community dynamic. And this dynamic is a most powerful means by which God builds his Kingdom. When individuals are committed to this process, the invariable result is a community of believers who demonstrate an integrated balance of differentiation and integration.

This is intended to be a book about hope. My desire is that you have been persuaded that

- there is real hope for change in all the relational areas that count, and that
- hope in God's Kingdom is not merely a theological construct but is being actively co-constructed by God and the rest of us as we are transformed by the renewing of our minds.

In fact, our minds—the energy of our brains/bodies and the information of our experiences—reflect this very way of community and love of which Paul so beautifully writes in 1 Corinthians. When we pay attention to signs within creation—whether our minds, their various elements and functions, or the nature of how our minds, relationships, and narratives most helpfully shape each other—we see they are pointing us to God's narrative as found in the stories of Scripture. His story in turn beautifully illuminates those elements of creation we have been examining, renewing them and providing us with yet another dialect to describe how we can live more creatively, more joyfully, more fearlessly as we do our part to usher in God's Kingdom.

Epilogue

A s you know by now, my work involves helping people pay attention to the elements of their minds—including attachment, memory, emotion, and storytelling—and then integrating these disparate parts so that we can live a life of mercy and justice in every realm and dimension of life together. I believe God's Kingdom advances when this integration occurs in the community as well as in the individual.

I want to conclude this book by challenging you to consider how recent discoveries in neuroscience, when considered in light of Christian texts and traditions, might transform the work you are doing within your own vocation. To show you what I mean, I will consider the implications of such an inquiry on just a few fields that naturally carry a deep responsibility for creating health and healing in our world.

I am not posing as an expert in any of these fields and do not have specific solutions for specific problems. Nor am I suggesting that the principles of interpersonal neurobiology can substitute for the basic endeavors of each particular field. I am simply asking you to consider how these principles can enrich and strengthen the work you are already doing.

As a starting point, you might dig more deeply into the literature listed in the bibliography and begin integrating interpersonal neurobiology into the domain where God has called you to be his steward. It seems to me that as our minds become more like that of Jesus, we will not simply be nicer people, we will be more whole, and as such more complete in the areas in which we are called to work and serve.

Family and Church Life. Out of our families our stories evolve, and out of our encounters with God's story within the church our stories are transformed. It is within home and church that we can be most fully known. Committing to a venue in which you can share your life with others and open yourself to being fully known is a way to begin. It is hard work, but work that has an immeasurable payoff of joy.

How do you invite others to join you in the process of being known? You might begin by speaking with someone you trust, be it a counselor, pastor, or wise family member. For change to occur, at least one person in the group must have enough courage to take the first step. Within a church, it might be the deacon who chooses to stop gossiping about the other deacons who are gossiping about her. Or it might be one couple who want to connect with two or three other couples to create life together in a confessional, regenerating fashion. In the home it might be the father or mother who wants his or her relationships with a spouse or children to be categorically different. Regardless of the setting, such a group seeks a community that is more life-giving; more liberated; more willing to be messy; more willing to make room for mistakes without shame; more willing to pulsate confession and forgiveness in all their interactions; and more willing and able to be the body of Christ because each member strives to live with the mind of Christ.

You can begin, either with one other person or within a small group of six to eight people, simply by meeting together in a place that is physically comfortable and allows for open conversation. Each of you may introduce what you want to accomplish as an outcome of your conversation. For example you might say, "I want to have a better relationship with you." Another member might say, "I don't like the way I have been reacting to you, and I want to change that but I don't know how."

From there you each might reveal anything about your intended conversation that evokes fear within you. "I'm afraid that when I bring this up you will think I'm foolish." "I'm worried you will want nothing to do with me once I share what I'm about to say." Next, you and the other participants can begin to reflect on what you *feel* (what emotions are being elicited within you, not what you "feel" about the other people or what they think or have done). You should resist the temptation to talk about the other people and their behavior or what you are "sure" they are thinking or what they believe, especially about you.

Those who are listening can then, as they are able, validate one another's feelings and ask questions (who, what, where, when, how) to gain a better understanding of the speaker's story. This may ultimately lead to that person reflecting on other parts of his or her narrative's formative features (experiences from the first twenty years of life), sharing them with a friend, family, or group, and coming to a more coherent comprehension of his or her life (see the exercise on writing a personal narrative in chapter 5). Ultimately, the group can begin to pray for and with one another about what each person has brought before them in ways that etch onto each member's heart—and brain—concrete images representing God's voice of mercy and expectation. Obviously this is a conversation that will take place over a long time and extend beyond death. These redemptive dialogues are some of the very stones God is using to build his temple, the cornerstone of which is Jesus, and whose completion and fullness will be realized in the Parousia.

Science. I turn next to this realm because it is one that I live in. Those who are not professional scientists or science philosophers generally assume that this field is strictly limited to logical interpretation of data and that other elements of the mind, such as emotion or memory (especially implicit memory), do not peddle much influence.

Real life tells us otherwise. Just listen in on a water-cooler conversation when someone brings up a cable news segment on the discovery of what looks like water on Mars and what it says about the possibility of life there. Fascination abounds as the imaginations of these coworkers soar.

Or imagine a medical conference in which academicians are debating the meaning and value of particular data that have emerged in someone's experiments about a novel antidepressant. These conversations are filled with emotion, despite all parties supposedly looking at the same data. Occasionally "rational" scientists even fall onto the low road, arguing about who is more right or wrong. Of course, they would claim their commitment to "good science" drives their passion, but they are not expressing their views very scientifically. In fact, Daniel Carlat, a New England psychiatrist, wrote an illuminating article about his internal conflicts and rationalizations during his year moonlighting as a drug rep for a major pharmaceutical company. Though he got off to an auspicious start, his misgivings got the better of him and he stopped making sales pitches after a year. (See "Dr. Drug Rep," *New York Times Magazine*, November 25, 2007.) His reflections on this experience provide an illuminating introduction into the conflicts inherent in scientists' attempts to be objective and rational.

Furthermore, scientists often investigate questions that have little to do with logical, linear interpretation of cold, hard data. Is chronic fatigue syndrome a real disease? Are the pattern and intensity of hurricanes changing and if so, is this due to global warming? Is the latest anti-inflammatory drug safe? An observer to these debates would be hard pressed to differentiate between the logical, linear, "provable" data—which emanate strictly from the left-mode function of the mind—and the emotion and memory (especially implicit) that influence the interpretation of this data. In his helpful book *Proper Confidence: Faith, Doubt and Certainty in Christian Discipleship*, Lesslie Newbigin goes even further, with the assistance of the work of Michael Polanyi, pointing out that there is, in fact, no way of knowing anything without committing oneself in faith to something outside oneself, something that cannot be controlled and therefore is doubtable.

I am aware that this is not new information to novice, let alone seasoned, scientists. Most are well-aware of the Heisenberg principle, which posits that the very act of observing some phenomenon alters that phenomenon in some way. In addition, the scientists I know work hard to remain aware of these synthesizing and (at times) competing elements of the mind in order to practice their trade with integrity.

Still, I believe it would be helpful for science communities to explore together how they are living out their vocation and how alternative parts of their minds shape the way they process and interpret data.

The Arts. Just as our world benefits from the proper place and integration of science, so also it hungers and thirsts for beauty. And so much of beauty is created and discovered in the aesthetic. Nowhere does the power and grace of interpersonal neurobiology speak more eloquently than in and through the arts. For it is drama, painting, music, sculpture, poetry, and dance (to name but a few) that activate the resonance circuits of the right hemisphere and weave a deeply felt sense of meaning into the more logical tapestry of the left brain. As such, the arts have the potential to facilitate the integration of our minds. Perhaps they do so because they reflect our Creator's beauty, not unlike so many wonders we observe in the natural universe.

Few of us spend enough time paying attention to beauty. When we do—and resist the temptation to exploit it—it will transform us as no left-mode-only experience can. In fact, employing genuinely meaningful aesthetics in our lives will advance the possibility for integration in our minds. This is why the presence of this domain is so essential in our homes, our worship, our education, and the work of our hands, no matter our particular vocation. For example, it is good to incorporate artistic expression as part of *all* of our children's educational endeavors, rather than sequestering it off in "art class." Likewise, intentionally including the visual and movement arts in our worship will draw our whole minds to the place where they are most easily reminded of God's beauty and strength.

My friend Marty is a gifted artist who has focused on abstract painting for the last few years. Recently she completed a work that I requested she paint for my office. (To view it, go to http://martycampolo.com. Look for "What Light May Come" in the "Commissions" section of Marty's Web site.) As I write this, the painting has been on my wall for less than a week, and it is already working its magic. One of the first patients to see it found herself so drawn to it and all of its interlocking themes that she was more interested in "staying with" the painting than talking with me. As she continued to engage it, she spoke of things she was beginning to feel that she had been virtually unaware of before. The painting evoked memories, both joyful and sad, of events she had not reflected on for years—memories and feelings a more lengthy conversation may never have revealed. All of that in less than ten minutes.

This is what thoughtfully crafted art does. It bypasses our carefully designed mental roadblocks, often revealing pain and awakening us to wonder. Anything we can do to make this realm of life more prominent will make us deeper and more playful; in other words, more like Jesus.

Hermeneutics and Theology. An important focus of this book has been how the movement toward integrated minds changes our lives as followers of Jesus. I am not a theologian, but I have been deeply shaped by theology, which is often dominated by a left mode of operation. Certain traditions depend on logical, linear processes as a means to maintain internal integrity. Sometimes, however, they do so at the expense of right-mode processes that would more richly inform the overall endeavor. Often we judge whether someone is a Christian based mostly on what that person "believes"—in other words, logical, linear, literal thought processes about perceived propositional truth. To prove they are Christians, people need only reel off a few sentences reflective of left-mode mental processing. But this is not the same as *being* a Christian, which demands the full integration of right-mode operation along with cognitive, factual expressions of faith. (Remember our conversation in chapter 13 about 1 Corinthians 13.)

Alternatively, other traditions pay homage to functions of the right mode of operation, not giving the left mode a proper opportunity to both interpret what the right mode sends it and inform it and set proper limits on it. This can lead to behavior that is dominated by the emotional surges of the lower brain and right hemisphere and circumvents the integrating function of the prefrontal cortex. In situations in which either the left or right mode is more exclusively dominating the picture, people are bound to get hurt.

Good theologians are often aware that their experience shapes how they think about their work. However, I encourage women and men in this field to be as ruthless as possible in terms of the specific dimensions of what they mean by "experience." From the standpoint of neuroscience, this includes not only the facts of where they grew up or a list of the most influential persons in their lives but also an understanding of how implicit memory shapes how they read Scripture and how they interpret the history behind what is read.

For instance, many theologians are involved in intense deliberation on what has been called "a new perspective on Paul" (essentially an effort to view the apostle Paul's writing in light of first-century Judaism rather than the sixteenth-century Reformers, whose reading of those texts was influenced by the Roman Catholic Church of their day). N. T. Wright, a New Testament scholar and bishop in the Church of England, has written prolifically on his understanding of justification as it has been shaped by this frame of reference. The varying reactions to his arguments—from appreciative assent to hostile opposition—show how intensely theologians debate such weighty matters. From my perspective, the issues will not be resolved simply by looking at the data and deriving a straightforward conclusion based on the facts.

We will always need theologians who, under the invigorating power of the Holy Spirit, rigorously study the Scriptures and traditions of the church not just so we will "know" the truth but so we may live more truly and embody integrated minds, which will inevitably lead to mercy and justice. Good theology is not primarily about being right. It is about being good. The more that memory, emotion, attachment, and narrative are kept in view, the more theology will lead to the emergence of the mind of Christ and the strengthening of his body.

Homiletics and Evangelism. It is fair to say that the first converts in the church did not begin to follow Jesus *primarily* because they were presented with a logical set of posited truths. Likewise, most people today do not step across the threshold of the house of God in response to a presentation restricted to left-mode processing. Yet there is no denying that preaching, as well as evangelism, is one of the primary means, though not the only one, by which people hear the gospel's basic message and then encounter its nuances, expectations, and instructional teaching.

Many would argue that over the last four hundred years, those of us in the

West have read and preached the Gospels through the eyes of Paul rather than the other way around. In other words, rather than understanding Paul's letters through the Gospels, which reflect first-century Palestine, we tend to first be taught the logical, linear theology of Paul and then fit the Gospel stories into it. This way of learning is not inherently wrong or unhelpful. Far from it. However, when we adopt a left-mode mind-set, our encounters with Jesus come through a dominantly left-mode process. Our brains simply do not tend to like it if that is the primary way they encounter him.

Do not misunderstand. Our stories must have logical, linear trajectories that make sense. However, we do not believe stories simply because they make sense. We believe stories because they compel us by moving our right hemispheres in holistic, nonverbal emotional currents. Yes, we need the rudder of the left brain, but without the current of our right brain, our boat goes nowhere. It is important, therefore, that whenever we're involved in preaching or evangelism, we are attentive, first, to the story we are telling and, second, to the ways *our* story is shaping how we tell God's story.

When we do so, we can be sure that we are entering into God's great storytelling epic, a narrative that is mindful of explicit and implicit memory, emotion, attention to our intentions, and the deep connections that all of these inherently maintain. Rob Bell, teaching pastor at Mars Hill Bible Church in Grand Rapids, Michigan, is one who over the last few years has embodied his awareness of this principle in his books, video productions, and now in his touring speaking engagements. I encourage you to explore some of what he is doing to get a better picture of what I'm talking about.

Ministries of Healing. The experience of being known is common in those congregations that have intentionally and faithfully begun ministries of healing prayer, even though most of them don't realize it. This connection is inevitable because of the process by which those who seek healing submit to those who will intercede on their behalf (and reflect James 5:14). They, along with many in the vanguard of the modern-day healing movement, promote the very processes of integration and differentiation that this book explores.

The role of healing in the church has champions and detractors. Yet wherever there are vibrant ministries of healing—spiritual, emotional, physical, generational, and deliverance from demonic phenomena—the family of God is welcoming a flood of new sisters and brothers and growing to new depths of relationship with Jesus and one another. This has been true since the dawn of the early church. I encourage you to become more familiar with how God, through his healing and integrating Spirit, is working in your community, even if it is not in the congregation in which you worship.

Religious Diversity and Peacemaking. I include these subjects together because it is often the way we live out our diversity among one another that most exemplifies our skill at peacemaking, religious or otherwise. Whether we are speaking about denominational separation within the Christian church or larger diverse religious groups (Christianity, Judaism, Islam, Hinduism, Buddhism, and others), being mindful of the elements of interpersonal neurobiology enable us to interact with each other in more productive ways. As a follower of Jesus, I believe that history is traveling in a particular direction and that at its culmination we will all submit to him as Lord of heaven and earth. I believe that the best of all religious experience, explicitly Christian or not, will ultimately lead to Jesus, and salvation in every sense will come through a relationship with him. How God brings this to pass is a mystery, and I have no doubt that some will want no part of the salvation offered.

But in the meantime those of different denominations and different macroreligious backgrounds must be more mindful of our narratives and how they may be enabling or limiting our capacity to create peace where open warfare or clandestine subversion exists. Jesus leaves no doubt that war as a way of life, whether between family members, factions within a congregation, denominations, worldview representatives, nations, or humans and the earth, leads to mindless dis-integration of the environment, individuals, families, and communities. An active commitment to identifying who our enemies are and deliberately seeking to make peace with them using the prayerful principles of interpersonal neurobiology is a way by which God enables us to live out the beatitude: "Blessed are the peacemakers, for they will be called children of God" (Matthew 5:9).

Education. Most public (and many private) educational goals, beginning in elementary school and emphasized even more in middle and high schools, are fundamentally linked with left-brain processing. In my state of Virginia, public school students must meet Standard of Learning requirements before advancing to the next grade. Children take tests that are largely nonintegrating in their design and thus unable to fully assess whether or not a child is becoming a more engaged learner, equipped not only to do math and read but to capture the sense of the purpose of math and reading.

The motto of Rivendell School, where my children spent their formative years, is "to explore God's world and discover their place in it." This goal, I believe, echoes the work of Parker Palmer and Ellen Langer, who advocate a more holistic neurological and spiritual approach to education. This includes more than simply exploring facts to be recalled when taking a standardized test; it also means exploring the nature of relationships.

According to Parker Palmer, it is in the experience of being known that students find the energy and interest to excavate and build, to inquire, to make and correct mistakes and messes. All of this is part of the joy of discovery that enables them to live more freely, more generously, and, I would suggest, in a more integrated fashion. Ellen Langer encourages us to be more willing to be open to possibility, rather than limiting ourselves to a set right answer for every question.

Education, then, is a vocational field in which being open to the integration of the mind provides students the option of being known, which in turn lines them up with the mind of Christ so that they can encounter Jesus in ways that may surprise them.

Business. Even though I operate a small private practice in psychiatry, I do not consider myself an expert in running a business. Still, I have observed that the business of business provides a scaffolding on which so much of life is constructed. Think of how much effort is expended in the process of creating, maintaining, growing, or closing a business.

In essence, the degree to which we become mindful followers of Jesus will in no small way influence how we engage our employees and employers. It eventually and inevitably leads us, again, to issues of mercy and justice, which lead to issues of politics and economics.

Being open to the differentiation and integration of the mind—and therefore its distinct yet connected parts—makes us more open to those disparate yet interrelated parts of the businesses in which we participate. As we focus more of our attention on the elements of our employees' minds or our supervisors' motivations, we invite greater cooperation and integration. The dynamics of even larger communities, including "the union" or "management," would inevitably change shape should the members become more mindful.

From here we could go further into the domains of leadership, politics, economics, ecology, human sexuality, and many others. Each of these and the ones named above deserve their own stage on which they can be explored as followers of Jesus with the assistance of the elements of creation contained within interpersonal neurobiology. I invite you now to take what you have learned, study it further with the assistance of the titles provided in the bibliography, and expand your working knowledge of this material—but not without your expanded experience of being known. For as you are known in the manner in which we have spoken, you will experience the freedom and courage of love—and the liberation and confidence to encounter God and assist him in the construction of his Kingdom.

I wish you every joy along the journey.

Bibliography

I hope you will find this list of books and articles helpful in your ongoing growth in following Jesus, attending to the integration of your mind (and those of others) along the way. Their authors are largely responsible for my education over the last several years on the beauty and mystery that stem from the influence of the mind/brain and relationships on one another.

I have arranged the resources in groups that relate to particular subjects we have explored, including interpersonal neurobiology, spiritual disciplines, and the like. Many of them will help expand your understanding of multiple functions of the mind, and so serve the very purpose of connecting separate but related areas, a goal of this book in general.

Feel free to think broadly and deeply, synthesizing your own understanding of what you read with what you've learned in this book. Be faithful to the research, but not in the absence of what you intuit, feel, or sense. I also encourage you to discuss your conclusions with others with whom you are having the pleasure of being known (and who certainly will be having the pleasure of knowing you!). I hope you will collectively use this material for walking, as C. S. Lewis described, "further up and further in" to the Kingdom of our Lord.

SCIENCE AND THE MIND/RELATIONSHIP MATRIX

Baars, Bernard J. *Cognition, Brain and Consciousness.* Edited by Nicole M. Gage. London: Elsevier, Academic Press, 2007.

Begley, Sharon. *Train Your Mind, Change Your Brain.* New York: Random House, Ballantine, 2007.

Beitman, Bernard D. and George I. Viamontes, eds. "The Neurobiology of Psychotherapy." *Psychiatric Annals* 36, no. 4 (2006): 214–220, 225–293.

Bowlby, John. *Attachment and Loss.* Vol. 1, *Attachment.* New York: Basic Books, 1969.

Bowlby, John. *Attachment and Loss,* Vol. 2, *Separation.* New York: Basic Books, 1973.

Bowlby, John. *Attachment and Loss,* Vol. 3, *Loss.* New York: Basic Books, 1980.

Bowlby, John. *Child Care and the Growth of Love.* London: Penguin Books, 1965.

Damasio, Antonio. *The Feeling of What Happens.* Orlando: Harcourt, 1999.

Doidge, Norman. *The Brain That Changes Itself.* New York: Penguin, 2007.

Fonagy, Peter, Gyorgy Gergely, Elliot Jurist, and Mary Target. *Affect Regulation, Mentalization, and the Development of the Self.* New York: Other Press, 2002.

Gottman, John. *Raising an Emotionally Intelligent Child.* New York: Fireside, 1997.

Lewis, Thomas, Fari Amini, and Richard Lannon. *A General Theory of Love.* New York: Random House, Vintage, 2000.

Lipton, Bruce H. *The Biology of Belief.* Santa Rosa: Mountain of Love/Elite Books, 2005.

Newberg, Andrew, and Mark Robert Waldman. *How God Changes Your Brain.* New York: Random House, Ballantine, 2009.

Newbigin, Lesslie. *Proper Confidence: Faith, Doubt and Certainty in Christian Discipleship.* Grand Rapids: Eerdmans, 1995.

Schacter, Daniel L. *The Seven Sins of Memory.* New York: Houghton Mifflin, 2001.

Seybold, Kevin S. *Explorations in Neuroscience, Psychology and Religion.* Burlington, VT: Ashgate, 2007.

Siegel, Daniel J. *The Developing Mind.* New York: Guilford, 1999.

Siegel, Daniel J. and Mary Hartzell. *Parenting from the Inside Out.* New York: Tarcher/Penguin, 2003.

Stern, Peter and John Travis. "Of Bytes and Brains" in "Modeling the Mind." Special issue, *Science* 314, no. 5796 (2006): 75–94.

Vaillant, George E. *Spiritual Evolution.* New York: Broadway Books, 2008.

Viamontes, George I. and Bernard D. Beitman, eds. "Neurobiology of the Unconscious." *Psychiatric Annals* 37, no. 4 (2007): 222–224, 236–287.

Viamontes, George I. and Bernard Beitman, eds.. "Mechanisms of Action in Psychiatry." *Psychiatric Annals* 38, no. 4 (2008): 220–223, 235–305.

Norton Series on Interpersonal Neurobiology (founding editor Daniel J. Siegel, edited by Allan Schore) contains a number of titles that exhaustively explore the nature of the mind and how our understanding of it from an interpersonal neurobiological perspective can be enhanced. Most of these are written for professional therapists, but they are certainly worth perusing if you are interested. The series includes titles not included in the following list. The books listed below are sources from which the synthesis of this book has been drawn:

Badenoch, Bonnie. *Being a Brain-Wise Therapist.* New York: Norton, 2008.

Bremner, J. Douglas. *Brain Imaging Handbook.* New York: Norton, 2005.

Bremner, J. Douglas. *Does Stress Damage the Brain?* New York: Norton, 2005.

Cozolino, Louis. *The Neuroscience of Psychotherapy.* New York: Norton, 2002.

Cozolino, Louis. *The Neuroscience of Human Relationships.* New York: Norton, 2006.

Fosha, Diana, Daniel J. Siegel, and Marion F. Solomon, eds. *The Healing Power of Emotion*. New York: Norton, 2009.

Ogden, Pat, Kekuni Minton, and Clare Pain. *Trauma and the Body*. New York: Norton, 2006.

Schore, Allan N. *Affect Dysregulation and Disorders of the Self*. New York: Norton, 2003.

Schore, Allan. *Affect Regulation and the Repair of the Self*. New York: Norton, 2003.

Siegel, Daniel J. *The Mindful Brain*. New York: Norton, 2007.

Solomon, Marion F. and Daniel J. Siegel, eds. *Healing Trauma: Attachment, Mind, Body, and Brain*. New York: Norton, 2003.

Stern, Daniel J. *The Present Moment in Psychotherapy and Everyday Life*. New York: Norton, 2004.

THE ARTS AND THE MIND

The following are three selections that either instruct or reveal the helpful role played by writing, drawing, and music.

Edwards, Betty. *Drawing on the Right Side of the Brain*. New York: Tarcher-Penguin, 1979.

Levitin, Daniel J. *This Is Your Brain on Music*. New York: Penguin, Plume, 2006.

Pennebaker, James W. *Writing to Heal*. Oakland: New Harbinger, 2004.

If you would like to engage abstract art (even if you are unfamiliar with it, or suspect you won't "like it") as a way to more deeply awaken and integrate your mind, go to http://www.martycampolo.com. To find the painting she did for my office, click on "Commissions." The title is *What Light May Come*.

Additionally, to catch a glimpse of how the art of film can provide a means to integrate our minds while unveiling how God's story is intersecting with ours, check out the NOOMA DVD series featuring Rob Bell. You can find it at http://www.nooma.com.

SPIRITUAL FORMATION AND THE MIND

The next section encompasses a set of works that provide both thoughtful and concrete approaches to the realm of Christian spiritual formation that are important in the development of the mind.

Chittister, Joan. *Wisdom Distilled from the Daily*. New York: HarperCollins, 1990.

Ford, David F. *The Shape of Living*. Grand Rapids, MI: Baker Books, 1997.

Foster, Richard. *Celebration of Discipline*. New York: Harper & Row, 1978.

Keating, Thomas. *Open Mind, Open Heart*. New York: Continuum, 1986.

Keating, Thomas. *Invitation to Love*. New York: Continuum, 1992.

Kelly, Thomas. *A Testament of Devotion*. New York: Harper & Brothers, 1941.

Lewis, C. S. *Mere Christianity*. New York: Macmillan, 1943.

Lewis, C. S. *The Weight of Glory*. New York: Macmillan, 1949.

Lewis, C. S. The Chronicles of Narnia. 7 books. New York: HarperCollins, 1950–1956.

Nouwen, Henri. *Reaching Out*. New York: Doubleday, Image, 1975.

Pennington, M. Basil. *Centering Prayer*. New York: Doubleday, Image, 1980.

Searcy, Edwin, ed. *Awed to Heaven, Rooted in Earth—Prayers of Walter Brueggemann*. Minneapolis: Augsburg Fortress, 2003.

Shannon, William. *Silence on Fire*. New York: Crossroad, 1999.

Silf, Margaret. *Inner Compass*. Chicago: Loyola Press, 1999.

SCRIPTURE AND THE MIND

The following four selections will help you weave together the narratives of Scripture and the realities of mental life, both from an individual as well as corporate standpoint.

Brueggemann, Walter. *The Covenanted Self*. Minneapolis: Augsburg Fortress, 1999.

Brueggemann, Walter. *Texts That Linger, Words That Explode*. Minneapolis: Augsburg Fortress, 2000.

Brueggemann, Walter. *Deep Memory, Exuberant Hope*. Minneapolis: Augsburg Fortress, 2000.

Elliott, Matthew A. *Faithful Feelings*. Grand Rapids, MI: Kregel, 2006.

Two texts by N. T. Wright and one by Peter Gomes shed helpful light on the place and power of Scripture and how a biblical understanding of the Resurrection energizes, among other things, the renewal of our minds on the way to the new heaven and new earth.

Gomes, Peter S. *The Good Book*. New York: HarperCollins, 1996.

Wright, N. T. *The Last Word*. New York: HarperCollins, HarperSanFrancisco, 2005.

Wright, N. T. *Surprised by Hope*. New York: HarperCollins, HarperOne, 2008.

EDUCATION AND INTERPERSONAL NEUROBIOLOGY

I mention in the epilogue a limited number of creation areas for which greater integration work with interpersonal neurobiology could be helpful. One of those areas is education. The following three selections provide further grounding in this integration process.

Langer, Ellen J. *Mindfulness*. Cambridge: Da Capo Press, 1989.

Langer, Ellen J. *The Power of Mindful Learning*. Cambridge: Da Capo Press, 1997.

Palmer, Parker J. *To Know as We Are Known*. San Francisco: Harper & Row, 1983.

GOD AND THE MIND

Last, I suggest the following as examples of works that demonstrate in practical terms what God is up to as he renews minds and heals in the process.

Bell, Rob. *Drops Like Stars*. Grand Rapids, MI: Zondervan, 2009.

Bell, Rob. *Sex God*. Grand Rapids, MI: Zondervan, 2007.

Bradshaw, John. *Healing the Shame that Binds You*. Deerfield Beach, FL: Health Communications, 1988.

Jones, L. Gregory. *Embodying Forgiveness*. Grand Rapids, MI: Eerdmans, 1995.

MacNutt, Francis. *Healing*. Notre Dame: Ave Maria Press, 1974.

Marin, Andrew. *Love Is an Orientation*. Downers Grove, IL: InterVarsity Press, 2009.

Miller, Donald. *Blue Like Jazz*. Nashville: Thomas Nelson, 2003.

Tutu, Desmond. *No Future Without Forgiveness*. New York: Doubleday, Image, 1999.

Volf, Miroslav. *Exclusion & Embrace*. Nashville: Abingdon Press, 1996.

Worthington, Everett L. *Forgiving and Reconciling*. Downers Grove, IL: InterVarsity Press, 2003.

Wright, N. T. *Evil and the Justice of God*. Downers Grove, IL: InterVarsity Press, 2006.

Reflection
Questions

Chapter 1—Neuroscience: A Window into the Mind

1. Describe a time when you, like Cara, wondered why disciplines like prayer and Scripture reading seemed so ineffectual in making you the person you long to become.

2. In what ways have you considered how your mind is working and the effects of your feelings and thoughts—either positive or negative—on your life?

3. What do you think of the author's invitation to, as you read this book, trust in the impressions, feelings, and sensations that your mind is communicating to you?

Chapter 2—As We Are Known

1. Take some time to reflect on how much you depend on knowing things. Now compare this to your experience of being known. Can you identify anyone with whom you have had this experience? To what degree would you say that, as you were growing up, you had the experience of being known by your parents? Explain.

2. Consider sharing your thoughts about question 1 with a trusted friend and then asking him or her to do the same with you. Sharing your stories is a way in and of itself of being known. When you're finished, notice what you begin to feel and think that is perhaps different from how you were feeling before you shared your story with your friend. How would you describe the differences?

Chapter 3—Love the Lord Your God with All Your . . . Mind

1. Which of the elements of the mind that we have just explored were novel to you? What insights surprised you?

2. What attributes of the mind would you say represent your strengths (such as awareness of nonverbal cues, logical thinking, etc.)? Which ones do you find more challenging to be aware of or to employ?

3. In what ways are your relationships either helped or hindered by the relative strengths or weaknesses of the various aspects of your mind/brain matrix?

Chapter 4—Are You Paying Attention?

1. How well do you pay attention to what you are paying attention to? Dan Siegel has suggested that it is important to pay attention to our *intention*, or what we are intending to do. How well do you do that?

2. For one day, keep a pencil and pad of paper handy and monitor what you are paying attention to. Every hour or so, simply jot down what you have been paying attention to over the last hour. At the end of the day, review the course your mind has taken. Have you been paying attention to those things that promote within you, and between you and others, the qualities you long to emerge in your life? Has your attention been more or less likely to facilitate the growth of love, joy, peace, courage, kindness, and gentleness?

Chapter 5—Remembering the Future

Now that you have considered the importance of memory in your life, you may have many questions:

> How can I become more aware of my implicit memory, especially if it is mostly unconscious?
> Is there any way I can begin to remember more of my childhood?
> How can I begin to have a different remembrance of God if my memories keep getting in the way?
> If I know I have helped create some hurtful memories for my children, is there any way to change them?
> How can I tell my story in a way that changes my memory?

These may be only a smattering of the questions you may be asking. To help you answer them, reflect on some of the following questions.

1. How well do you remember the story of your life?

2. Are there stages of your life that you do not recall as easily as others do?

3. To whom do you regularly tell the story of your life, not just the facts, but also what you felt during those events and what you think they mean?

4. How easily do you sense (that is, *experience*, not merely as a fact, but as a *felt reality*) that God remembers you? Can you describe that sensation to someone?

5. In what ways do you, like Elijah, experience moments in which your implicit memory tends to overtake your explicit memory?

If you haven't completed the exercise "Writing Your Autobiography" on pages 79–80, now might be a good time to consider doing so.

Chapter 6—Emotion: The Experience of God

1. What emotion is evoked in you when you are with someone you are close to? This question is not seeking what you think, or what your analysis is, but rather your emotion, so consider words such as *delighted, peaceful, anxious, distressed, nervous, irritable, happy, sad*, etc.

2. What is your level of awareness of what you sense in your body when you experience emotion?

3. On a regular basis, what do you feel God feeling?

4. Do you easily have the experience of "feeling felt"?

5. What is your level of awareness of the "contingency" of your emotional states upon others?

6. How does telling your story begin to change the way you experience the emotion of it?

Chapter 7—Attachment: The Connections of Life

Here we return to the handwritten autobiography that we explored in chapter 5. It can also serve as a vehicle for better understanding your attachment. After reviewing it, consider the following questions.

1. What was it like growing up in your family? Who was present in your home?

2. What was your relationship like with each of your primary caregivers? How was your relationship with each of them similar or different? Do you have a general idea of what your attachment pattern may be in respect to each of them?

3. How did people in your family or home approach emotion? Did you talk about what you felt, not just what you "thought"? Did either or both of your parents seem genuinely interested in your emotional states?

4. If you had siblings, did you ever sense that either of your parents behaved differently toward them than they did toward you?

5. In what manner did your parents apply discipline in your home? When there was conflict, did family members talk directly about it, or did they find ways to avoid it?

6. How is the way you remember (or what you remember) and how you experience emotion connected to your particular pattern of attachment?

7. If you do not recall much of your early history, is there someone who would have known you well enough to inform you of your early years? Consider asking that person to tell you what he or she remembers of your life.

8. Is it difficult to make sense of what you have written? Do you gather a deep sense of well-being or increased discomfort when you recount what your narrative reveals?

9. Was there anyone else in your life, such as a teacher, coach, youth group leader, or friend's parent, who created within you the sense that you were cared for and important?

10. How is your attachment pattern reflected in how you relate to God? Or, how does the way you relate to God and the stories of Scripture reveal something to you about your attachment?

11. How do you mentalize God, and how do you imagine him mentalizing you?

Chapter 8—Earned Secure Attachment: Pointing to the New Creation

1. Can you recall a time when someone listened to your story with such interest and compassion that you were able to see your experience in a different light? Explain.

2. How does Romans 12:2 (see page 138) speak to the issue of earned secure attachment?

3. Describe your reaction to the author's suggestion that the way we approach and react to God's story as told in the Bible is itself affected by our own stories.

4. What clues do we find in David's psalms that suggest he felt known by God?

Chapter 9—The Prefrontal Cortex and the Mind of Christ

1. Reflect on the features of an integrated life (FACES): flexible, adaptive, coherent, energized, and stable. Consider the ways you might do what is necessary to deepen the presence of these characteristics in your life. Take some time to reflect on how your early relationships and attachment posture have enhanced or limited the development of these qualities in your life. How do your present relationships do the same?

2. Identify a recent time in which you found yourself on the low road. Reflect on the trigger(s), the transition, the level of immersion in which you found yourself, and the recovery from that episode.

3. How was this journey onto the low road a response to implicit memory and primary emotion, not simply a response to the circumstances of the present moment?

4. Consider the effect that meditating on the words found in Luke 3:22 ("You are my Son, whom I love; with you I am well pleased") could have on this kind of event.

5. Review the nine functions of the middle prefrontal cortex on pages 161–162. Which of these do you consciously engage well? Which are challenges for you?

6. Reflect on how often you ask questions, and how you ask them. Where might you ask *who, what, where, when,* and *how,* instead of *why*?

7. Which of the spiritual disciplines might you be willing to undertake, even in a small way, to facilitate the emergence of the mind of Christ within you? Consider doing this also with a group of people who can support each other's efforts.

Chapter 10—Neuroscience: Sin and Redemption

1. Reflect for a moment on how ruptures occurred in your family growing up. What usually triggered them? Did your parents demonstrate the ability to repair them? If so, how? If not, what did you do to cope with an unrepaired rupture?

2. How quickly do you become aware of ruptures when they occur? What are the internal or external signals that alert you to a rupture?

3. What is your general response to ruptures in their various forms (oscillating disengagement; benign ruptures; limit setting; toxic ruptures)? What emotions emerge in you? What do you notice physically? What thoughts go through your mind?

4. How do your responses to ruptures affect your intimate relationships?

5. To what degree are you aware of the role that shame plays in your life? What triggers activate shame in your mind/body matrix? What do you typically do to address the problem of shame?

6. What aspects of repair do you find to be challenging?

7. If you have children, in what ways do ruptures most often occur in your relationships? How do you engage in the process of repair with them?

Chapter 11—The Rupture of Sin

1. Describe a time when you viewed God from a distorted perspective and either (a) created God in your own image through the lens of your attachment pattern; (b) formed your own god out of a coping mechanism; or (c) went ahead and did what you pleased.

2. In what ways do doubt and fear play a role in your story?

3. Think of a time when you were overcome with distress, anxiety, and fear. How did that affect your emotional state? How did these feelings affect your perception of God and your memory of his past dealings with you?

4. In what area of life might God be asking you, "Where are you?"

Chapter 12—The Repair of Resurrection

1. In what ways did Jesus experience rupture? What does his response to these breaches have to teach us?

2. How did Jesus mend the rupture between himself and Peter?

3. Explain the connection between Hebb's axiom (neurons that fire together wire together) and confession.

4. Why is it important to confess, not only to God, but to other people?

Chapter 13—The Mind and Community: The Brain on Love, Mercy, and Justice

1. Think of one of your most important relationships. How do the characteristics of a complex system (see list on pages 237–238) apply to that relationship?

2. How does your church body (or the Christian church as a whole) act in ways that seem mindful? mindless?

3. Explain why a mind that is flexible, adaptive, coherent, energized, and stable seeks to advance mercy and justice.

4. As you conclude this book, what discoveries from neuroscience and attachment research would you say have impacted your reading of Scripture?

5. If you are discussing this book in a group setting, how might you continue to encourage one another in your pursuit of living in a mindful, integrated way?

Acknowledgments

There is no question that this book does not belong to me. I feel more like a conduit through which so much from so many has been lovingly, thoughtfully offered. It was veritably willed into existence with unending patience and encouragement by my agent, Leslie Nunn Reed, without whose curiosities and promptings over many years I would never have considered this project. Thank you so much, Leslie, for your perseverance.

Thank you to Dennis Hollinger, pastor, scholar, and friend, whose timely word filled me with the needed confidence to pursue putting what was initially a Sunday school series into print.

I cannot speak enough of Jeannie Herbert and her band of allies, who enthusiastically read portions of the text, asked probing and shaping questions, offered constructive criticism, and generally helped me become more comfortable with the necessary gates one must go through in the process of writing. These folks, along with my covenant group at Washington Community Fellowship, have been a constant source of affirmation, especially when it was uncertain that this work would be published.

For the last twelve years the Reverend David Harper has been my spiritual director, fathering me to the place I find myself now. Thank you, David, for keeping me on the rails and reflecting the glory.

I am eternally grateful to my patients, whose lives have been the soil out of which stories of hope and healing have emerged, mostly due to their unending courage to reveal their narratives with trusting vulnerability. Noteworthy among them is Steve Hayes, a gifted writer and inspired title-bearer. During one session, we were talking about the book and I mentioned that I still hadn't decided on a title. Steve seamlessly mused, "You should call it

Anatomy of the Soul." And just like that, the work was named. Thank you to Steve and the rest of my patients for listening and reflecting, providing the opportunity as much for my growth as for their own.

I am daily wrapped in the prayer and professionalism of my colleagues in my practice. They have been deeply inquisitive learners and now are teachers of the integration of interpersonal neurobiology and Christian spirituality. This collaborative effort of caring for our patients and each other shaped the content of the book in a way that has hopefully helped it make sense. Thanks to all of you in our little office for being the bone and blood of regeneration for so many who come through our doors.

As I mentioned in the book, without Dan Siegel's work, this project would not have been possible. I am so very grateful for his kindness, his wisdom, and his wit. His commendation for the book proposal was a generous offering from a gifted clinician whose faithful support has been of immeasurable value. Many thanks to you, Dan, and to my colleagues at GAINS (the Global Association for Interpersonal Neurobiology Studies) whose work and energy have created the opportunity for the most significant professional growth for me since I was a resident.

I am so grateful for the people at Tyndale who have taken the chance on a first-time author. Thanks to Jan Long Harris, who has championed the book from the beginning and tolerated my verbosity with the patience of Job. To Sarah Atkinson and the design team, I am thankful for your calm willingness to explore the world of neural networks as they might appear on a book cover. And thank you, Nancy Clausen and Yolanda Sidney, for gently ushering me together into the world of marketing this project.

If writing a book is like giving birth (as I am told it is), then my editor, Kim Miller, was the perfect midwife. She fearlessly led me through the difficult task of pruning and expanding the text (while taking a crash course in neuroscience and attachment), and buoyed my spirits when I was certain that perhaps either what I wrote or the way I wrote it seemed flat, dull, or at the very worst, simply unhelpful and a waste of the reader's time. For certainly, there were times when I thought any or all of those things about particular sections of the book. Kim, you are the best!

And finally, to my family, who over the last three years has labored with me, hoped with me, and pushed me when needed—my gratitude is ever yours. I will not forget your kindnesses and ever-present encouragement as I went off to the "war room" to write. No one has worked harder than you in helping me complete this book. Hats off to three of my favorite people in the world.